"ESPECIALLY ILLUMINATING ON THE CLOSE RELATIONSHIP OF RELIGION AND WHAT THE WEST WOULD CONSIDER SECULAR POLITICS IN THE MUSLIM WORLD."

—*Library Journal*

There are over one billion people who follow the Islamic faith. Muslims include those of virtually every race and nation, from Senegal to China, from Nigeria to the former Soviet Union, from Egypt to America. They may be rich or poor, conservative or radical, warlike or peaceful, primitive or sophisticated, but the lives and actions of all of them are profoundly affected by the teachings of Muhammad and by Muslim traditions that have developed over the past thirteen hundred years.

Now, this completely updated and expanded study of the Muslim world, from its earliest roots to today's global power politics, makes Islam's far-reaching influence comprehensible to western readers.

"HIS HANDLING OF MODERN ISSUES IS CLEAR AND THOUGHT-PROVOKING, PROVIDING BOTH NEW INFORMATION AND NEW INSIGHTS." —*The Middle East Journal*

THOMAS W. LIPPMAN served in Cairo as *Washington Post* bureau chief for the Middle East for over three years, gaining sharp insight into the complex realities of that turbulent region. He has also been a correspondent in Indochina and has traveled throughout the Islamic world. He currently reports on foreign policy issues for the *Washington Post,* and he is the author of *Egypt After Nasser*.

UNDERSTANDING ISLAM

AN INTRODUCTION TO THE MUSLIM WORLD

THOMAS W. LIPPMAN

Second Revised Edition

A MERIDIAN BOOK

MERIDIAN
Published by the Penguin Group
Penguin Books USA Inc., 375 Hudson Street,
New York, New York 10014, U.S.A.
Penguin Books Ltd, 27 Wrights Lane,
London W8 5TZ, England
Penguin Books Australia Ltd, Ringwood,
Victoria, Australia
Penguin Books Canada Ltd, 10 Alcorn Avenue,
Toronto, Ontario, Canada M4V 3B2
Penguin Books (N.Z.) Ltd, 182–190 Wairau Road,
Auckland 10, New Zealand

Penguin Books Ltd, Registered Offices:
Harmondsworth, Middlesex, England

Published by Meridian, an imprint of Dutton Signet,
a division of Penguin Books USA Inc. Previously published
in a Mentor edition.

First Meridian Printing (Second Revised Edition), September, 1995
10 9 8 7 6

LIBRARY OF CONGRESS CATALOGING-IN-PUBLICATION DATA:

Lippman, Thomas W.
Understanding Islam : an introduction to the Muslim world / by Thomas W. Lippman. — 2nd rev. ed.
p. cm.
ISBN 0-452-01160-4
1. Islam. I. Title.
BP161.2.L56 1995
297—dc20
95-24015
CIP

Printed in the United States of America

Contents

AUTHOR'S NOTE vi

INTRODUCTION vii

Chapter One
Basic Beliefs and Practices 1

Chapter Two
The Prophet Muhammad 33

Chapter Three
The Koran 56

Chapter Four
Law and Government in Islam 70

Chapter Five
The Advance of Islam 106

Chapter Six
Schism and Mysticism 136

Chapter Seven
The Islamic Community Today 166

GLOSSARY 182

BIBLIOGRAPHY 186

INDEX 189

Author's Note

Unless otherwise indicated, all quotations from the Holy Koran used here are from the translation by N. J. Dawood in the Penguin Classics, Fourth Revised Edition, 1974. Dawood's is an extremely free translation, which makes little attempt to reproduce the style of the original, but it is probably the easiest for the nonspecialist to read. Each citation is followed by a notation giving the chapter and verse of the Arabic original to which it corresponds. I am grateful to Penguin Books Ltd. for permission to use the material.

I am also grateful to Laraine Carter, who generously read the manuscript and gave me the benefit of her encyclopedic knowledge; to the staff of the Middle East Institute in Washington and the Council on Foreign Relations in New York, who were unfailingly helpful; to the editors of *The Washington Post,* who gave me the opportunity to work in the Islamic countries; and to my wife, whose patience held us together.

The transliterations of Arabic words and names are in the simplified form commonly used in newspapers in the United States. No attempt has been made to reproduce the diacritical marks, glottal stops, long vowelings, and unique consonants of the original, except where they are part of the standard transliteration. In quotations of works by other authors, however, their transliterations and alternate spellings have been retained; therefore Koran sometimes appears as Qur'an.

Introduction

A casual reader of the daily newspapers could be forgiven for thinking that the word "Muslim" is an adjective used to explain violent events in remote parts of the world that are otherwise incomprehensible.

"Muslim militants" rebel in Algeria, "Muslim guerrillas" battle each other in Afghanistan, "Muslim extremists" attack airliners in the Philippines, a British novelist lives in the shadow of a death sentence proclaimed by a "Muslim cleric," "Muslim extremists" attack tourists in Egypt and seize power in Sudan.

It fosters the impression that Muslims—that is, those who practice the religion of Islam—are generally troublemaking fanatics whose penchant for working out religious conflict through violence is a menace to the rest of the world. It oversimplifies complex events in which religion is only one element. It validates the belief that Islam promotes violence, which is at best a half-truth. And it belittles Africans, Arabs, and Asians by imputing to them primitive or irrational motivations that we may not ascribe to the participants in violent upheavals in non-Muslim countries. Press accounts of the turmoil in El Salvador did not, for example, describe the rightwing hard-liners as "Christian extremists."

Dar al-Islam, the House of Islam, embraces about one billion people of every race, from Senegal to China, from Nigeria to the former Soviet Union, and more than six million Americans as well. All are Muslims, sharing common religious beliefs, but they vary widely in behavior. Most of them are not leftists or fanatics or revolutionaries or extremists. They cannot be stereotyped in the image of one race or one kind of political or social conduct. Certainly it is absurd to identify Islam with Arabs luxuriating in oil wealth. The vast majority of Muslims are not Arabs and not wealthy. The three biggest Muslim nations are Indonesia, with about 172 million Muslims; Pakistan, with 118 million; and Bangladesh, with 100 million. The list of countries of which the population is more than half Muslim includes Mali, Afghanistan, Malaysia, Albania, and, of course, Iran—none of them Arab. And many Arabs in Syria, Lebanon, and Palestine are Christians, not Muslims.

All Muslims believe in the same God and in the same forms of worship, but that does not mean that they think alike or act in the same way toward non-Muslims. The surly customs officials at the airport in Tripoli, Libya, who took away all my books and even my Alitalia timetable as potentially subversive literature were Muslims; but so were the jovial border guards on the Pakistani side of the Khyber Pass, who plied me with weak tea and friendly questions as I crossed out of Afghanistan. The veiled, sequestered women of Saudi Arabia are not to be confused with the gaily clad women of Somalia sauntering to their government jobs.

There is technically no distinction between church and state in Islam. Islam holds itself out not just as a religion but as the source of law, guide to statecraft, and arbiter of social behavior for its adherents. Muslims believe that every human endeavor is within the purview of the faith, because the only purpose of any activity is to do God's will. For that reason, Islam as a religion invites disdain and inspires fear when its followers behave cruelly, immorally, or irresponsibly, as of course they may. But in Islam, as in Christianity, it is necessary to distinguish how the faithful behave from the way their faith teaches them to behave. Even within the community of Islam, believers frequently disagree on what is required of them. The Ayatollah Khomeini and Anwar Sadat, both Muslims, condemned each other's policies, which were all imposed in professed compliance with the requirements of the faith.

In the fourteen centuries since Islam was established, it has often been a source of conflict, violence, and fanaticism, but it has also been a source of generosity, beauty, and inspiration. Its record does not compare unfavorably with that of Christianity. The performance of the Muslim Arabs when they conquered Egypt in the seventh century, for example, is a model of benevolence compared to that of the Catholic Spaniards in Mexico and Peru.

The Koran—the Holy Book of God's revelations that is the foundation of Muslim doctrine—does not teach that violence is to be shunned. On the contrary, it prescribes violence in defense of the faith and teaches that those who join the struggle are more likely to be admitted to Paradise than those who do not. But the Koran also ordains justice, charity, mercy, self-denial, and tolerance. Those who count themselves Muslims are not, in their daily lives, any more prone to violence or aggression than non-Muslims. They are farmers, factory hands, bureaucrats, airline pilots, bank clerks, soldiers, sewer cleaners, midwives, going about their business as best they can. But it is important to remember that Islam defines the purpose of their lives and sets the standards by which they conduct their personal and communal affairs. The world of Islam is uniquely God-centered.

As a newspaper correspondent assigned to the Middle East I lived in Egypt and traveled the Muslim world from Tunisia to Pakistan. The headline events that kept me and my colleagues moving around from crisis to crisis were sometimes related to the Islamic faith of the participants, as in the Iranian revolution, and sometimes partially related to Islam, as in the Lebanese civil war and the insurgency in Afghanistan.

But economics, politics, history, and tribal memory have the same influence on Muslims as on anyone else; Islam cannot be credited or blamed for everything that happens in the Muslim world. Islam had very little to do with Sadat's determination to make peace with Israel or with the zany political theories of Libya's Muammar Qaddafi or with the pricing policies of the Organization of Petroleum Exporting Countries or even with the territorial struggle between Muslim Somalia and mostly Christian Ethiopia. If the principles of Islam were followed, every Muslim would treat every other Muslim like a brother; in fact, they have been attacking one another almost since the founding of the faith.

It has been my privilege to know Muslims of every occupation and every social level, from Iranian bankers to Palestinian plotters to Afghan intellectuals sipping tea and dreaming of revolution in the reeking back alleys of their Peshawar exile. I liked many of them and detested many others. I remember gratefully the Somali guerrilla who gave me his blanket on a cold night in the Ogaden and the Palestinian gunner in South Lebanon who gave me a cucumber when I had nothing to eat. I remember fearfully the two grim young men who accosted me on a dark street in Tehran demanding to know if I worked for that organ of imperialism, the BBC. All were Muslims, and in their own way they were carrying out the commands of their faith, caring for wayfarers or struggling against the enemy. They and a thousand others taught me every day that there is no one way to think about Muslims, no response that is always appropriate, no generalization about what Muslims do or how they react that is always applicable. Muslims believe in God, in the message of Muhammad the Prophet, in prayer, and in the Last Judgment. Beyond that, *Dar al-Islam* is more diverse than it is homogeneous.

I came to admire the Muslims in many ways and to respect their faith, but it is not my purpose here to defend them. Islam needs no defense from me. My purpose is to give a brief account of who the Muslims are, what their faith teaches, and what their world is like, in the hope that others will be spared the burden of misconceptions and misinformation that weighed upon me when I first arrived in the Middle East.

Chapter 1

Basic Beliefs and Practices

A MUSLIM is one who believes that "there is no god but God, and Muhammad is the messenger of God." A Muslim worships one all-powerful and eternal deity, called *Allah* in Arabic, who revealed His will and His commandments to the prophet Muhammad of Mecca in the seventh century A.D. Those revelations are recorded in the Koran, the Holy Book of Islam.

Allah has no physical attributes. He has no age, no shape, no mother, no appetites; but neither is He an abstraction. He is an immediate and constant presence, cognizant of every person's deeds and thoughts, aware of who follows His commands and who does not. Those commands require acceptance of Muhammad's message, social justice, personal honesty, respect for others, and restraint of earthly desires, as well as the performance of devotional duties such as prayer and fasting.

Islam (Is-LAM) is an Arabic word that means submission—submission to the will of God. *Moslem,* or *Muslim,* its participial form, means one who submits. The root is the same as that of the word for peace, *salaam.*

Membership in the community of Muslims is not conferred by man. It is acquired by a conscious act of will, the act of submission, summarized in the profession of faith: There is no god but God, and Muhammad is the messenger of God. To become a Muslim, it is sufficient to make that profession sincerely in the presence of other believers, who will witness it. But to become a Muslim is also to accept a complex, interlocking body of beliefs, practices, and ethical standards. A Muslim believes that an omnipotent, omniscient God will, on the inevitable Last Day, judge each person by his or her acts. Each person's resurrected body will be admitted to Paradise or condemed to eternal hellfire, according to God's evaluation. God is just, but God is also merciful; the sinner who repents may be welcomed into the company of the faithful in Paradise, but only if repentance is sincere and timely. On the terrible Day of Judgment repentance will be too late, and no intercession will save the doomed souls of those who disobeyed God's commands.

Because God's will is not to be determined by any human endeavor, no one, however devout and pious, can be sure of winning God's favor. But no Muslim can doubt what God expects him to do in this life if he is to have any hope of being admitted to Paradise in the next: accept the one God and the message He sent through Muhammad, pray to Him, be honest, speak truthfully, practice mercy and charity, live modestly, avoid arrogance and slander, and defend the faith against unbelievers.

All rules of belief and conduct come from God through Muhammad. Men make laws in accordance with God's commands, but there are no "commandments of the church," as there are in Catholicism, because there is no church. Islam is not an organized religion in the sense that Catholicism is, because it is theoretically a faith without clergy, saints, hierarchy or sacraments. No man stands between the believer and God.

There are men who study theology, men who lead congregational prayers and give sermons and interpret the Koran, and men who advise temporal authorities on questions of religious law. But in orthodox Islam there are no central doctrinal authorities, no equivalent of bishops or the College of Cardinals, no pope, and no intermediary between man and God. Since there are no sacraments, no one needs special standing or orders to perform them. That means there is no priesthood. Any Muslim—in practice, any male Muslim—can lead prayers and give sermons, because all Muslims are equal before God.

A Muslim confesses directly to God. No man has the power to confer or withhold forgiveness, just as no man has the power to confer or withhold membership in the community of believers. There is no sacramental entry into the faith. Because Islam does not espouse the doctrine of original sin, there is no rite of baptism to wash it away, and consequently no excommunication. Islam teaches that the sinner alone, the individual person and not his ancestors or descendants, is responsible for his actions; there is no inherited stain on the soul to be purged as a condition of entry into the faith.

The Koran, which Muslims accept as the literal revealed word of God, says, "Tell those who dread the judgment of their Lord that they have no guardian or intercessor besides Allah, so they may guard themselves against evil." (6:51) Even Muhammad, the revelator, is instructed to tell the faithful that he has no special status, no privileged association with the Deity: "I do not tell you that I possess the treasure of Allah or know what is hidden." (6:50) If he, the last prophet and the most nearly perfect of men, did not claim a special relationship with God, then clearly no other mortal does.

In Islam, as in Christianity, there are differences between what the believers are taught by their faith and what they actually think and do. For instance, while there is no Muslim priesthood, the mullahs of Iran, who are often referred to as clergy, hold a special place in the form of Islam practiced there. (See Chapter 6.) Folk practice has ascribed to various men a role analogous to that of saints in Christianity. Muslims have created shrines and devotions to these "saints" in the belief that they can do what the Koran says they cannot do—intercede with God.

In the outlying provinces of the Islamic world, where Islam is a relatively recent overlay on folk culture (as in Indonesia and West Africa), and even in Egypt and Iraq, the heartland of Middle Eastern Islam, the faithful make pilgrimages to the tombs of holy men and "martyrs." In touching appeals that would be familiar to the keepers of the shrines at Lourdes and Fatima, they ask the holy men to relay their prayers to God and they pray for earthly blessings: the safety of a son in war, a wife's fertility, even good fortune in trade.

These practices, however widespread, are aberrational, without sanction in a religion that establishes neither saints nor clergy. Islam teaches that no person or place on earth is to be worshiped, no being other than God is to be the object of prayer, and the benefits of this brief, transitory life on earth are not the proper subject for prayer.

There may have been some confusion among the Muslim masses in Pakistan and Indonesia when Pope John Paul II visited those countries in 1981, for Islam has no position comparable to the Papacy. For about seven hundred years after the death of Muhammad there was theoretically a single temporal authority who was chief executive of the Muslim community. This was the Caliph, or successor to the Prophet. Various sultans of the Ottoman Empire claimed to be Caliph of Islam as well as ruler of the Empire, but the office was dormant long before it was officially abolished by the parliament of republican Turkey in 1924, after the downfall of the Ottomans. Even at the height of its power, the Caliphate was not analogous to the Papacy, because its authority was primarily temporal, not doctrinal. In the guise of upholding Islamic law and defending the faith, caliphs did sometimes interfere in religious matters, promoting some theological views and silencing others, but they did so without divine authority.

Various international groups of religious authorities and theologians do exist in Islam. They are useful as an embodiment of the ideal of a universal faith that transcends other allegiances, but they have no authority over the way the believers practice their faith. If any of these international groups were abolished overnight, Islam as a thriving, growing faith would hardly be affected, because the individual Muslim is responsible only to Allah. Within each country or community, there are religious judges who decide how the requirements of divine law are to be enforced in specific cases, but their task is only to enforce the divine commands as revealed to Muhammad, not to reinterpret the basic creed or embellish doctrine.

The Koran, taken as the literal word of God, not written by Muhammad but only transmitted through him, is the fundamental, immutable source of Islamic doctrine and practice. A second source, inferior in authority but decisive on matters not specifically addressed in the Holy Book, is the *sunna*, "path," the way of the Prophet, his example and teaching as expressed in his deeds and words. These words of Muhammad (as opposed to those of God uttered by Muhammad in the Koran) are recorded in the *hadith* (pronounced ha-DEETH), compilations of his utterances on religious practice, social affairs, and Koranic interpretation. All Muslims accept the authority of the *hadith* in principle, but despite centuries of painstaking analysis, not all Muslims accept the same *hadith* as authentic. Most accept as valid, compilations made more than a thousand years ago, but some groups within the faith cling to their own variations and their own chains of authentication.

Islam prescribes for believers both attitudes of mind and specific duties in life. Most important are the acceptance of the uniqueness, power, and authority of God and the understanding that the objective of life is to fulfill the dictates of His will in the hope of admission to Paradise. Worldly gain and temporal power are illusory; the Koran says that "the life of this world is but a sport and a pastime." (57:20) Those who pursue riches on earth may gain them, but those who forego worldly ambitions to seek the favor of Allah—those who give alms, take care of orphans and the elderly, live chastely, and tell the truth—may gain the greater treasure, entry into Paradise.

Islam, the youngest of the world's major religions, originated in the seventh century with the life and mission of Muhammad, but it was not a totally new creed invented out of the blue. Its conceptual roots are in Judaism and Christianity. Muslims see their religion as a continuation and rectification of the Judeo-Christian tradition. The Jewish scriptures and the prophetic mission of Jesus are incorporated by reference in the Koran. The Koran teaches that God, the same God known to the Arabians as Allah, favored Jews and Christians by revealing His truth to them in holy books, but they deviated from what was revealed and fell into error and corruption.

The people of the Arabian peninsula trace their origins to the patriarch Abraham, who, according to the Koran, was neither Jew nor Christian but a kind of universal ancestor of monotheists. Hagar, the Egyptian slave-girl, and Ishmael, the son she bore to Abraham, are believed to have reached Mecca in their exile. Abraham himself is believed to have constructed the Kaaba, the sacred shrine of Mecca, which is the object of the annual pilgrimage.

Muslims believe there is and has always been since Abraham only one true religion, a consistent faith in the one omnipotent God, who from time to time has sent various messengers and prophets to reveal Himself to men and tell men what He expects of them.

These revelations were recorded in a hundred and four books, of which only four are extant: the Pentateuch, the Psalms, the Gospels, and the Koran, given successively to

Moses, David, Jesus, and Muhammad. No more are to be expected, as Muhammad was the last prophet and in the Koran, "all things are revealed."

Thus Islam is part of and traceable to the monotheistic tradition of Judaism and Christianity, and its ethical code is similar to that of Old Testament Judaism. Islam happens to be generally practiced by dark-skinned, impoverished peoples, whom Europeans in their colonial phase despised, but it is hardly the outlandish heathen cult depicted in European commentaries since the time of the Crusades.

Islam's fundamental duties, practices, and beliefs are summarized in the "five pillars" of the faith, laid down in one of the Prophet's *hadith,* and accepted by all Muslims. The five pillars are the profession of faith, daily prayer, payment of the *zakat* (alms-tax), fasting in the month of Ramadan, and the pilgrimage to Mecca. These are religious obligations. By themselves they are not sufficient to define the virtuous life, because a good Muslim must also observe a relationship of charity and justice with other members of his community, but the five pillars are the obligatory fundamentals of Islamic practice.

The Profession of Faith

The first pillar is the *shahada*, the profession of faith: There is no god but God, and Muhammad is the messenger of God. This was a revolutionary proposition when Muhammad preached it in seventh-century Arabia, for despite the Arabians' claim of descent from Abraham and their extensive contacts with monotheism, they were pagan polytheists.

The *shahada,* the basic statement of Islam, is now emblazoned on the flag of Saudi Arabia, but in Muhammad's time there was no Arabian nation. The people of the Arabian peninsula were grouped in tribes and families, some city-dwellers, some nomads, and their spiritual allegiance was parceled out to a variety of local deities and idols.

Among these pagan deities one commanded a wider loyalty than the others and was known as Allah, which is the Arabic word for god. Cesar Farah, in his book *Islam,* calls Allah "the paramount deity of pagan Arabia," recognized from Yemen to the Mediterranean. Enshrined as the principal god of the Kaaba, the pagan pantheon at Mecca, he was accorded a status above the petty gods and idols worshiped by individual tribes and local groups. He was more than equal to other gods, but less than unique.

That Allah, however, is not the God of Islam. Muhammad used the same word, Allah, but he taught that Allah is the one God, the God of Abraham and Moses, and that it was an error to worship any other. Embracing monotheism, he swept away all the lesser gods and their idols. Worshiping the one God, he taught that the local deity falsely called Allah should be abandoned and that Allah, the one God, the God of the Jews and Christians, should be worshiped.

The Koran clearly identifies Allah with the God of the Hebrews. The God who spoke to Moses during the wanderings in the desert, the God who watched over Joseph when he was betrayed by his brothers, the God who saved Noah from the deluge, is Allah, God of the Jews and God of the Muslims. "He has knowledge of all things," the Koran says. "He has ordained for men the faith He has revealed to you and formerly enjoined on Noah and Abraham, on Moses and Jesus, saying, 'Observe this faith and be united in it.' " (42:13)

Because Allah is the same God as the God of Judaism and Christianity, many Muslims disapprove of the use of the name Allah in English-language commentary on their religion. They argue that *Allah* should be translated as God, not used in the Arabic transliteration Allah, to show that this is the same deity as the one worshiped by Jews and Christians. Arabic-speaking Christians use the same word, *Allah,* to mean the Deity; therefore it is misleading to say that Muslims worship Allah, as if Allah were some God other than the God of the Jews and Christians. (In this book, God and Allah are used interchangeably.)

As described in the Koran, God is unique, everlasting, omniscient, omnipresent, omnipotent, eternal, and living. He knows everything, created everything, and controls all destiny. He is not a formed body or a substance; He is not bounded by dimensions. He sees without eyes, hears without ears, knows without a brain. (Because He has no physical attributes, there can be no portrait or statue of Him. Muslims regard all statues, icons, and representations of the Deity as sacrilegious.)

God created the earth, the heavens, the elements, men, angels, and *jinn*. The *jinn* are mysterious creatures, invisible to man, defined by the Islamic scholar Fazlur Rahman in his *Islam* as "an invisible order of creation, parallel to man, but said to be created of a fiery substance, a kind of duplicate of man which is, in general, more prone to evil and from which the Devil is also said to have sprung." The Koran says God created the *jinn,* but tells us little about them. They seem to be spirit-creatures, whose impact on the lives of men is only tangential.

The God of the Koran is never seen but always felt, because everything that exists and everything that happens is a sign of Him. He is "the Sovereign Lord, the Holy One, the Giver of Peace, the Keeper of the Faith, the Guardian, the Mighty One, the All-powerful, the Most High! He is Allah, the Creator, the originator, the Modeler." (59:23) His knowledge of all things is both universal and detailed: "Are you not aware that Allah knows what the heavens and earth contain? If three men talk in secret together, He is their fourth; if four, He is their fifth; if five, He is their sixth. Whether fewer or more, wherever they may be, He is with them." (58:17)

What God is not is progenitor or offspring. The Christian concept of the Son of God as one with God and equal to God is specifically and repeatedly repudiated in the Koran, which describes Jesus as a prophet and no more. The uncompromising monotheism of Islam is incompatible with the trinitarian deity. To Muslims, acceptance of a three-natured God is tantamount to worshiping three deities, when there is only one. The association of any person or object with the Deity is the one sin that Allah will not forgive, according to the Koran.

"Allah is one, the Eternal God," the Koran says, in Sura 112. "He begot none, nor was he begotten. None is equal to Him." As for the divine Son of God, the Koran is unequivocal: "Those who say, 'The Lord of Mercy has begotten a son,' preach a monstrous falsehood, at which the very heavens might crack, the earth break asunder and the mountains crumble to dust. That they should ascribe a son to the Merciful, when it does not become Him to beget one!" (19:88)

From time to time throughout history, Allah has revealed his power, his oneness, and his commands to men through various prophets and books. The last of these prophets was Muhammad of Mecca, whom God used as a conduit for the last revelation, the Koran, the written record of the words spoken by God to Muhammad through the angel Gabriel. The succession of prophecies ends with Muhammad, because the Koran reveals all that need be known and synthesizes all that went before.

Islam teaches that Muhammad's mission was twofold: to bring knowledge of the one God and His book of truth to the Arabians, a pagan people who had no scripture and hence no knowledge of divine truth, and to correct the errors and falsehoods into which earlier "people of the book"—Jews and Christians—had fallen.

The God who revealed Himself to Muhammad is described at the beginning of each chapter of the Koran as "the Compassionate, the Merciful." But the text makes clear that beyond mercy and compassion lies justice, in the form of inexorable, eternal damnation for sinners, unbelievers, backsliders, and those who fail to follow God's commands. On the inevitable, terrible Day of Judgment, there will be no second chance for those who waited too long to repent. While the believers are admitted to Paradise, "a garden watered by running streams," the sinners will be cast into the torment of fire, their anguish compounded by their knowledge of their guilt and the justice of their fate. They will not be able to say they were not warned.

The most arresting language of the Koran is in those sections describing the Day of Judgment, "the event which will overwhelm mankind," when the earth will be destroyed, human society will end, every soul will stand before God, and the bodies of the dead will be resurrected to dwell forever in Paradise or in Hell.

> "When the sun ceases to shine; when the stars fall down and the mountains are blown away; when camels big with young are left untended and the wild beasts are brought together; when the seas are set alight and men's souls are reunited; when the infant girl, buried alive, is asked for what crime she was slain; when the records of men's deeds are laid open and the heaven is stripped bare; when Hell burns fiercely and Paradise is brought near; then each soul shall know what it has done." (81:1)

The reference to the infant girl buried alive is an allusion to the practice in pagan Arabia of burying alive unwanted newborn females, a practice that Muhammad prohibited.

The Koran warns that "the catastrophe of the hour of doom shall be terrible indeed. When that day comes, every suckling mother shall forsake her infant, every pregnant female shall cast her burden, and you shall see mankind reeling like drunkards, although not drunk. Such shall be the hour of Allah's vengeance." (22:1)

Some translations do not use the word "vengeance," but "wrath" or "chastisement." For the sinner, the outcome is the same. On that inevitable day—the Koran does not say when it is coming; it is entirely up to the will of Allah—no last-minute repentance, no intercession, no ties of family or friendship, no desperate pleas for mercy, will save the sinners from their fate.

"Hell will lie in ambush, a home for the transgressors," the Koran says. "There they shall abide long ages; there they shall taste neither refreshment nor any drink save boiling water and decaying filth; a fitting recompense." (78:21)

The agony of the sinners depicted in the Koran is beyond imagining. The apocalyptic images vary, but all stress the physical as well as spiritual torment to which the damned will be subjected. They will drink molten metal, and when their skins are burned away they will grow new ones so their suffering may be perpetuated.

Not so the believers, those who accept God and Muhammad's message, who follow the rules of social, commercial, and personal conduct laid down in the Koran, who put humility and decency before wealth and pleasure, who pray and pay the alms-tax. Allah will "reward them for their steadfastness with robes of silk and the delights of Paradise. Reclining there upon soft couches, they shall feel neither the scorching heat nor the biting cold. Trees will spread their shade around them, and fruits will hang in clusters over them." (76:12)

In that oasis-paradise, the faithful, adorned with green silk and silver bracelets, will be attended by handsome boys and dark-eyed virgins, who will bring them refreshing drinks in silver goblets while their spirits are refreshed by the favor of God.

This is the God of Islam: Jehovah reexamined, one, omnipotent, the generous Creator who bestowed upon mankind all the blessings of earth and who demands obedience in return, the vengeful One who will extract a terrible price from those who spurn Him.

Throughout the Koran, the principal motivation for accepting God and believing in His revelation appears to be fear: fear of the last judgment and fear of eternal damnation. Though God is described as generous and beneficent, He is always the God who punishes unbelievers and destroys corrupt societies. Islam places less stress upon love of the Deity as a motivation for piety than does Christianity. So while there is a rich tradition in Islam of spirituality and love of God, it is rooted in mysticism and must be considered separately from the traditional faith. (See Chapter 6.)

Belief in the one God and acceptance of His word as revealed to Muhammad requires acceptance of the body of duties and obligations recorded in that message. These duties are both spiritual and legal, both societal and devotional, regulating each individual's relationship with God and with his fellow men. The first duty is the profession of faith. The second is prayer, the second of the five pillars of the faith.

Ritual Prayer

"Prayer," says the Koran, "is a duty incumbent on the faithful, to be conducted at the appointed hours." (4:103) It is the second of the five pillars of the faith. Those prayerful hours are not specified in the Holy Book, but in practice they are recognized as occurring five times daily: at dawn, midday, afternoon, evening, and night. The exact times vary from country to country and even, in large countries, from town to town according to the time of sunrise and sunset. In many countries newspapers print daily charts showing prayer times in the major cities, all different by several minutes.

Tradition holds that the five-a-day schedule is a compromise between the twice-daily prayer suggested in an early chapter of the Koran and the forty times a day said to have been demanded of Muhammad by God. While only five are required, Muslims are urged to pray at all times and on any occasion.

The believer may say his prayers wherever he is, alone or in a group, so long as he faces Mecca and the Kaaba.

Congregational prayer in a mosque is required only on Fridays at midday and on two major religious holidays—and then only men are required to attend—but group prayer is always considered more meritorious than individual devotion. In some countries, especially Saudi Arabia, offices and shops generally close during prayer time, but in most they do not. The individual, if he wishes to pray, simply does so, on the spot or at the mosque, while the activities of those who do not pray continue about him.

This creates situations that may strike newcomers to the Islamic countries as incongruous but that are taken for granted by the participants. In Cairo, the policeman who stands guard at the rear door of the Central Bank drops to the grimy sidewalk to worship at the appointed hour, leaving the door unwatched. The place of prayer should be clean, so he uses a battered piece of cardboard as a mat over the pavement. (Other Muslims use small rugs, the source of the term "prayer rug.") In the composing room at the newspaper *Al Ahram,* it is not unusual for some printers to walk away from their typesetting machines to pray, leaving their work to be resumed after their devotions, while their colleagues who are less devout continue to work as if nothing was happening. When President Jimmy Carter visited Saudi Arabia in January, 1978, the call to prayer went up while preparations for his arrival were still being made at Riyadh airport. All the members of the military band on duty laid down their instruments and dropped to their knees right on the tarmac for their devotions. It made a bizarre photograph in American newspapers the next morning, men and trombones prostrate together, but it did not strike the Saudis as odd in any way. It was prayer time, so they prayed, as God commands. The scene was characteristic of the prevailing lack of self-consciousness about prayer among Muslims. It insulates the faithful from cynicism. Those who do not pray may be embarrassed and apologetic, not those who do.

The believer knows when the hour of prayer is at hand because the call to prayer is sounded from the minaret, or tower, on every mosque. The call is chanted, always in Arabic, by a *muezzin*; this word is a corruption of *mu'adhdhin*, "he who recites the *adhan* (call)." Usually there is nobody actually up in the minaret. Nowadays the call to prayer is commonly tape-recorded and amplified through speakers mounted on the minarets. What is lost in charm is gained in range and volume.

The call always includes the *shahada* in a declaration such as this: "God is great, God is great. I testify that there is no god but God. I testify that Muhammad brought the message of God. Come to prayer, come to prayer. Come to prosperity, come to prosperity. God is great, God is great. There is no god but God." At dawn, the call also reminds Muslims that "prayer is better than sleep." The opening phrase of the chanted Arabic—"*Allahu Akbar*" (al-LAhu AKbar), "God is great"—is the dominant cultural chord of Islam, the declaration that punctuates all life, the reason to believe, the motive for action, inspiration for soldier and revolutionary, consolation for the oppressed.

Whether the individual is praying alone or in a group, the format and context of his prayer are the same. It is not an individual appeal to or communication with God, improvised by the believer to address his own needs, but a ritual, communal recognition of Allah's power.

The worshiper offers *rakatin*, "bendings," so called because each part of the prayer ritual is marked by a change of position: standing, bending to put hands on knees, kneeling with palms on thighs, kneeling with forehead on floor. Each *rakah* comprises a certain number of prescribed acts and words, which make up a unit of prayer; each prayer period consists of two, three, or four *rakatin*, depending on the time of day.

In the traditional prayer ritual, the positions of the hands are prescribed as well as those of the body: right over left at the chest, touching the earlobes, at the sides.

At the mosque, the worshipers align themselves in rows, spaced so that they may kneel and bow without touching those in front of them. The positions assumed in the ritual would be awkward for women if they prayed among the men, but they generally do not. In some countries, they worship in specially designated areas of the mosque and in others they are excluded from public prayer by tradition if not by law, and they perform their devotions at home.

The wording of the prayers follows established formulas of praise and obedience to God, such as this: "Glory be to Thee, O Allah, and blessed be Thy name and exalted Thy majesty. There is no deity to be worshipped but Thee. I seek the protection of Allah against the accursed Satan."

Another is this: "My Lord, forgive me. Bestow mercy upon me. Guide us right. Relieve me and absolve my sins." Passages from the Koran, which many Muslims have memorized in its entirety, are also recited.

The leader of the prayers is not a priest. His relationship with God is the same as that of the other worshipers and he has no special ritual or sacramental powers. In large mosques, the leader may be an *imam,* an individual with religious training who is learned in the Koran and who, on Fridays, gives a sermon. The title Imam is the same as that used in Shiite Islam to mean the spiritual leader of the entire community. (See Chapter 6.) The level of knowledge, eloquence, and training of the leader varies according to the size and wealth of the mosque where the prayers are said. In a poor village, he may be no more than a local artisan who has had a few years of study at a religious school.

The Koran requires that the worshiper be clean in body as well as soul when praying. Ablution is prescribed, usually a symbolic sprinkling of water but always a full washing after sexual intercourse or a long illness. Most mosques have fountains or water taps where the worshipers may clean their hands and feet, again according to a prescribed ritual, before they enter to pray. The act of cleansing is traditionally performed with the left hand, leaving the right for eating and salutation.

A mosque—*masjid* in Arabic—is not a church. God is no more present there than He is anywhere else. There is no altar, no tabernacle, no baptismal font, no statuary, no choir loft. A mosque is simply a building where the faithful gather to pray as a group. Because all men are equal before Allah, mosques have no reserved places or pews for dignitaries. As the worshipers arrive, they line up in rows behind the *imam* with no distinction by social class, wealth, or race.

The first mosque was the courtyard of Muhammad's house in Medina, the town to which he moved from Mecca when his prophetic message was rejected by his native city. (See Chapter 2.) According to Philip Hitti, in *Islam: A Way of Life,* it was a quadrangular courtyard open to the sky, partially roofed with palm branches as protection from the sun. A palm stump served as a podium for Muhammad. Later it was replaced by an actual pulpit at the suggestion of a Muslim who had seen one in a Christian church. The quadrangular open area for the gathering of believers, and the pulpit, are still characteristic features of almost all mosques.

In the early years of Islam, Muslims adapted places of worship from other religions for use as mosques. Zoroastrian temples in Persia and Christian churches in Syria were converted. The architectural variations increased in subsequent centuries as domes, porticoes, colonnades, and ornamentation were added to the basic configuration. The mosques of Islam are as diverse in style and elegance as the faith itself.

In most mosques built by the Persians and the Turks, the main congregational area is roofed or domed. Other great mosques—Ibn Tulun in Cairo, the principal mosques in Mecca, Lahore, and Delhi—are open to the air, vast patios of devotion surrounded by enclosed porches where the faithful may rest or talk, seated on the rugs or mats that cover the floor. Traditionally the mosque has served the faithful as meeting hall, shelter and library. Large mosques often contain space for religious schools, *madrasas,* where students are instructed in the Koran, religious law, and Arabic.

Two features common to almost all mosques are the *mihrab* and the minaret. The *mihrab* is a niche or indentation in the wall indicating the direction of Mecca, toward which the believers face as they pray. The minaret, the tower from which the faithful are called to prayer, is the universal architectural symbol of Islam.

Minarets vary as greatly in material, height, and style as the mosques from which they rise. In the Arabian peninsula, a village mosque may have a single unadorned cylindrical tower. A great Turkish-style mosque, such as the Blue Mosque in Istanbul or the mosque of Muhammad Ali that dominates the skyline of Cairo, will have multiple pencil-shaped minarets. Whatever the style, the minaret is to the eye what the call of *Allahu Akbar* is to the ear: a universal link in the chain of faith and culture that binds all Muslims.

The construction of mosques may be financed by governments, charitable organizations, or individuals. The person or group that finances the construction of a mosque often pays for its upkeep as well. In a poor country such as Egypt, where the government's resources are limited and the mosques overcrowded, a certain shabbiness characterizes the state-run mosques, while those endowed by the wealthy are often spotless and handsomely landscaped. The arrangements for building and maintaining mosques and for paying the salaries of those who work at religious institutions vary from country to country. Frequently the degree of political docility of the *imams* and theologians is a function of their financial dependence on the state. (One source of the political power of the Iranian *mullahs* who helped overthrow the Shah was their financial, and therefore political, independence of the government.)

Except for the Shiite mosque at Karbala in Iraq, a unique shrine where the mirror-glass interior walls seem to amplify the zealous frenzy of the pilgrims, most of the mosques I've visited were marked by a cool, restful atmosphere conducive to prayer and contemplation. At Cairo's al-Azhar, at the Umayyad mosque in Damascus, and at the great mosque in Delhi, the tranquility and peace offer physical and spiritual relief from the turmoil of the surrounding bazaars, and the Muslim can find the dignity and social equality that may not be his in the world outside.

It is customary to doff the shoes upon entering a mosque, and the function of the mosque as social and economic leveler, a place where all are equal in the sight of God, can be seen in the racks of footwear outside any mosque in Cairo or Alexandria. Battered sandals, army boots, and polished pumps are aligned side by side as their owners—separated in daily life by a vast economic and social gulf—worship together as one congregation.

Friday is the one day when attendance at a mosque for group prayer is required (though many who consider themselves Muslims attend irregularly, if at all). The Koran says, "Believers, when you are summoned by Friday prayers, hasten to the remembrance of Allah and cease your trading." (62:9) Muslims believe that the Koran is the literal word of God and therefore that the choice of Friday was dictated by God himself. Philip Hitti suggests that Muhammad made the choice for reasons more mundane than spiritual. Angry at the Jews who rejected his message, the Prophet prescribed that shops should be closed at midday on Friday because that was when Jews were stocking up for the Sabbath.

Muslim countries generally observe Friday as the weekly official holiday, though practice varies. Since Friday is not ordained as a day of rest, it is not a religious requirement that Friday be a work holiday. Until recently in Algeria, the weekly holiday was observed on Sunday, a relic of French colonial days. In Egypt, which has a large Christian minority, state-owned banks and shops, state factories, and government offices are closed on Friday, but privately owned shops are usually open on Friday and closed on Sunday, even if their owners are Muslims. In Somalia, Saudi Arabia, and Jordan, a few shops are open on Friday mornings, but no official business is transacted. Even in those countries, however, taxis and other public services operate and newspapers are published on Friday. It is not the same as Saturday in Israel, when public transit halts, restaurants close, and newspapers do not publish.

Muslims also have prescribed prayers to be said on holidays, while traveling, and on special occasions such as funerals, the most common occasion for group prayer aside from the Friday gathering.

Believing as they do in resurrection of the body, Muslims bury their dead reverently and quickly, treating the bodies with care and respect. When death occurs, the body is washed and shrouded and buried as soon as possible, preferably within a day. The standard prayer for this last journey is, "Gratitude is due to God. Prayers and peace be upon the Messenger of God. O Lord! He (the deceased) was indeed Your worshipping servant, and the son of your servants. He witnessed that there is no God but You; You alone; there is no partner for you. And that Muhammad was your servant and messenger. And indeed, you know him better than we. O Lord! If he was a doer of good, please increase the reward of his deeds. If he was misbehaving, please forgive his misdeeds. O Lord! deprive us not of his reward. And let us not be misguided after him. And forgive us and forgive him."

Though the service for the dead is standard, with minor variations according to the practices of various schools, burial customs vary. In Saudi Arabia, the body of the deceased is laid in a shallow grave scooped out of the desert. In Egypt, the body is sealed in a coffin and entombed in a mausoleum. The tombs of some wealthy Egyptians are among Cairo's most prominent architectural landmarks; some of them are so elaborate that poor families have taken up residence in them as squatters.

The ritual prayer gives oral expression to the believer's submission to God; its spiritual value is negated by misconduct or inattention. Talking, clearing the throat, moaning, laughing, and movements other than those prescribed by tradition are to be avoided, and in fact Muslims may never be more disciplined and orderly than when they are gathered for communal prayer. In Cairo, the biggest and most turbulent city of the Islamic world, where overcrowding in the mosques forces worshipers to conduct Friday prayers on the sidewalks, the men at prayer—undistracted by tourists or the whizzing traffic—perform their devotions with a deep concentration that bespeaks their sincerity.

Zakat

The third pillar of the faith is the *zakat,* "alms-tax," a mandatory donation to charity.

The Koran defines the righteous as those who "attend to their prayers, pay the alms-tax and firmly believe in the life to come." (31:4) The obligation to share what one has with those less fortunate is stressed throughout the Holy Book. Islam teaches that the riches of this world are transitory and stresses that those who have abundant blessings should share with the less fortunate. The Muslim definition of the virtuous life includes charitable support of widows, wayfarers, orphans, and the poor. The *zakat* institutionalizes that duty.

The Koran does not specify how much should be given. Nor does the Koran say how the requirement to pay the tax should be enforced, since it assumes that the command of God and the rule of the state are one and therefore the state has no enforcement power other than divine will. In some Muslim countries, the *zakat* is entirely voluntary. In others, it is enforced by the government, but according to Islamic law, it is not a state tax because it is not to be used to support the public treasury and the government does not set the rate. Some scholars argue that the *zakat* should not be collected by the state, because it has spiritual merit only if voluntary.

Islamic legal tradition, which is rooted in the Koran and in the deeds and words of the Prophet, has produced a complex set of technical regulations about how much *zakat* is due and upon what property it is to be levied. No tax is payable on a herd of less than five camels, for example. Possession of twenty-five to thirty camels requires the donation of a young she-camel; discovery of buried treasure requires the donation of one-fifth of the value. In practice, the most common measure is 2.5 percent of the amount of cash an individual holds in savings or investment for a year. An additional tax of one day's food for one person is to be paid on the occasion of Eid al-Fitr, the holiday that ends the annual month of fasting, so that the poor also may eat.

The law also prescribes the purposes for which thc state or organization that collects the tax is to use it—to help the poor, give aid to travelers and the homeless, relieve debtors, finance the propagation of Islam, and pay the wages of the collectors. These principles, which originated in early Islam, before the disintegration of the purely Islamic state, do not necessarily prevail in contemporary Muslim nations. Laws and practices vary; what remains constant is the obligation of the good Muslim to do what he can in the name of God to help those less fortunate. The particular duty of paying the alms-tax is part of the general requirement to be charitable and generous and to live in a way that contributes to the general welfare of the community.

Fasting

The fourth pillar of the faith is the fast of the month of Ramadan. Ramadan is one of the twelve months of the lunar calendar, used by Muslims since the seventh century, the first century of the Islamic era. Because it is set according to the lunar calendar, Ramadan occurs on different dates in each year of the Gregorian calendar. It is the month in which the first Koranic verses were revealed to Muhammad and in which Muhammad's small band of followers achieved their first important military success, at the Battle of Badr in 624 A.D. During Ramadan, Muslims are obliged to refrain from eating, smoking, drinking, and the pleasures of the flesh from first light to last light unless they are ill, traveling, nursing, or pregnant.

Islam is not an ascetic religion. The Koran encourages the use and enjoyment of the blessings that God has bestowed on mankind. But Islam does teach control of the appetites and discipline of the passions. The requirement of fasting, laid down in the Koran, contributes to the Muslim's mastery of his worldly concerns and to the community's collective sense of conforming with God's commands. The fast fosters compassion for the hungry and thirsty.

The time of fasting begins, according to the Koran, when it becomes possible to tell a white thread from a black one in the first light of dawn. During the daylight hours, Muslims are urged to pray at the mosque and commanded to avoid all food and drink. Sexual intercourse is also prohibited in daylight.

These requirements affect the pattern of life in the entire Muslim world, disrupting the normal schedules of work and study. Public life, commerce, and government slow to a crawl, especially when Ramadan falls in the long, hot days of summer, because the rigors of the fast inevitably result in curtailed work hours. Many a Western businessman has learned the hard way that Ramadan is the wrong time to travel to Kuwait or Libya; not only are work hours shortened but also influential officials with the authority to make decisions and sign contracts often leave for Europe when Ramadan arrives.

The strictness with which the fasting requirement is enforced varies from country to country, some governments and societies being more easygoing or secular than others.

In Kuwait, where I once spent a week during a Ramadan that fell in September, when daytime temperatures were over 110 degrees, cafes, restaurants, and juice bars were closed during the day. A few hotels that cater to Westerners were allowed to serve food and drink, but even the ground-floor coffee shop at the Sheraton Hotel, a popular gathering place for young men about town, was closed until evening. In Egypt some restaurants and snack bars stay open but discretion is advisable, and most of the Muslims who choose not to fast take their refreshment in private.

In the latitude of Amman or Jeddah, daylight during a summer Ramadan can last as long as sixteen hours. The fast is onerous and difficult. The people compensate after dark for the rigors of the day with a feast called the *iftar,* "breakfast." When radio stations broadcast the cannonshot that signals the sunset and the evening prayer that follows, the *iftar* brings sweet relief as families dig in and children run through the dark street, singing and waving lanterns.

At the end of the month, Muslims celebrate a holiday known as Eid al-Fitr, after which, life returns to normal. The end of Ramadan and the start of the holiday are proclaimed officially only when the new moon—the rising of which marks the start of the next month—has actually been sighted by the appropriate religious authorities. The rising of the new moon is of course predictable with mathematical certainty through astronomical observations that Muslim scholars helped to develop, but tradition holds that human sightings are required before events keyed to the calendar can begin. Printed calendars and schedules list future events and holidays as "tentative" or "subject to official confirmation." This tradition usually makes little practical difference, but occasionally it results in confusion, when the people of one community observe an event a day earlier or later than the people of another or make a false start on a holiday that is rescheduled at the last minute because the moon has not been sighted.

The Muslim calendar, which in a few countries is also the official public calendar, consists of a 354-day year divided into twelve lunar months. A day is added to the last month eleven times in every thirty years, so that in a century the Muslim calendar diverges from the Gregorian calendar by just over two years.

The first day of the first year corresponds to July 15, 622 A.D., the year in which Muhammad and his followers migrated from Mecca to Medina. The months are Muharram, Safar, Rabi al-Awwal (Rabi I), Rabi al-Thani (Rabi II), Jumada I, Jumada II, Rajab, Shaban, Ramadan, Shawwal, Dhu'l-Qadah, and Dhu'l-Hijjah. The years are designated "A.H.," *Anno Hegirae*, "after the *hijra*" (the Arabic word for the migration).

The extent to which these months and the Muslim calendar are used in contemporary life varies from country to country. In general, business and international affairs are conducted by the Western calendar, and religious affairs according to the Muslim calendar. Sometimes they are used side by side. In Cairo, a new bridge over the Nile is named "Sixth of October," and a new town in the nearby desert is called "Tenth of Ramadan," both dates marking the same event, the start of the 1973 war against Israel.

Ramadan is a collective and unifying experience, in which workers fast together and families and friends feast together in affirmation of their obedience to God. The other great annual event that inspires mass participation is the *hajj,* the pilgrimage to Mecca, the fifth pillar of the faith.

The Pilgrimage

The *hajj*, which all Muslims are obliged to make once in their lives, is the unifying force of Islam. It brings together in the experience of faith the polyglot peoples of a multiracial, international religion; it is the event in which all sects within Islam participate side by side.

Rich and poor, herdsman and tycoon, scholar and illiterate, man and woman, Arab, Persian, and Turk, African and Asian journey to the sacred shrine. Some camp in tents, others stay in new hotel suites at exorbitant prices, but all are equal before Allah as they kneel in prayer, indistinguishable in the white raiment of pilgrimage.

Non-Muslims are banned from Mecca, but the pilgrimage, which for centuries was a closed book to outsiders, can now be observed in detail, because the principal rites are televised to Muslim countries, with commentary in English provided by the Saudi Arabian state broadcasting service. The Saudi Ministry of Information also provides detailed color slides of the rituals.

The events of the pilgrimage are a mass commemoration of the story of Abraham and of the lessons to be learned from it: Abraham's obedience to God's command to sacrifice his son Ishmael (not Isaac, as Jews and Christians believe), God's compassion in sparing Ishmael, the expulsion of both Hagar (Abraham's concubine and Ishmael's mother) and Ishmael from the community of the Hebrews because of the jealousy of Abraham's wife, Sarah, and God's mercy in caring for them in their exile. The pilgrimage teaches that God is merciful and just to those who obey him. The spiritual objective of the pilgrims is to put off worldly concerns and things of the self, to commune with God, and contemplate His oneness. The rites of pilgrimage involve physical comings and goings, but these are a means, not an end. They enhance the spiritual purpose, which is to achieve a purity of the soul and a communion with God that will exalt the pilgrim for the rest of his days. Once a *hajji* (pilgrim), always a *hajji;* in some countries the word is even added to a pilgrim's name when he returns from Mecca.

At pilgrimage time, the airports of the Middle East, North Africa, and South Asia are crowded with travelers waiting for special flights to Saudi Arabia. For many it will be the only journey of their impoverished lives beyond their native village or province. The jet airliner and cooperation among governments have eased the difficulties of the pilgrimage, but memories linger of the arduous struggles of past generations to fulfill the Koran's commandment to go to Mecca. North African folklore tells of pilgrims from the medieval empire of Mali wending their way along the caravan trails of the Sahara for years to reach and cross the Red Sea. Every Egyptian village contains a house or two the walls of which are adorned with pictures of the modes of travel used by the occupant to reach the sacred city—camel, ox-cart, and boat.

As recently as 1945, when Saudi Arabia was still a remote outpost and the pilgrimage was the kingdom's chief source of income, the number of persons making the pilgrimage was officially put at 37,630, many of whom came from within the Arabian peninsula. By the end of the 1980s, the number sometimes reached two million a year, and they were coming from every continent. Many Muslims make the journey several times. All are obliged to make it at least once if they are able.

Until recently, making the *hajj* was dangerous. Pilgrims set out knowing that they might not return, but that was not a deterrent—to die in the sacred city is considered a blessing. Even now, newspapers in Egypt (which is only a short distance from Mecca across the Red Sea, not a continent away) carry anxious reports about the health and safety of pilgrims. But the risks have been in fact minimal since the Saudi government put some of its wealth to work providing medical care and sanitation for the pilgrims and eliminating the banditry that traditionally plagued the weary travelers.

Making the pilgrimage means more than taking a plane ride. Once at Mecca, the pilgrims perform a complex, often grueling series of rites and prayers lasting several days. The hours when no specific rites are scheduled have traditionally been used for religious discussion and study among Muslims from different races and cultures. These informal meetings enhance the spirit of brotherhood, which Muhammad preached, and the interaction of scholars and thinkers from different communities who have met at the pilgrimage has led to the development of some of the great works of Islamic theology.

The central place of devotion is the Kaaba, the chief shrine of Islam, which stands in the courtyard of the Great Mosque at Mecca. The courtyard is a vast enclosure the size of a football field, surrounded by a two-story, arched colonnade, where tens of thousands of worshipers may pray simultaneously. The Kaaba, standing in the center of the open area, is a stone structure forty feet wide, thirty-five feet long and fifty feet high, which is usually covered by a cloth. Nothing in its appearance is inherently inspirational. The religious significance of the Kaaba lies in its history.

Worship at the site predates Islam. Muslims believe that Abraham *(Ibrahim* in Arabic), the patriarch of the Arabs, built the original Kaaba and a house of worship on the site. In Muhammad's lifetime, the Kaaba was the object of annual pilgrimage by pagan Arabians, who had turned it into a pantheon for their tribal and regional deities. These deities and their idols were swept away by Muhammad's monotheism, but the custom of the pilgrimage—in remembrance of the true God and of Abraham, not of pagan idols—was incorporated into Islam.

A door leads to the interior of the Kaaba, but there is nothing inside. The only specific object of veneration is the Black Stone, a stone about eight inches in diameter, which is mounted in a silver frame set into the east corner of the exterior. This stone is believed to be the only remnant of the house of prayer built on the site by Abraham, and it is traditional for pilgrims to kiss it.

Muslim tradition holds that Hagar, the handmaiden of Sarah, and Ishmael, the son she bore to Abraham, were saved from the agony of thirst in their exile by the waters of the well of Zamzam, which was opened for them by the angel Gabriel. This well, which is still giving water, is outside the Kaaba but within the confines of the Sacred Mosque. It is customary for pilgrims to drink from the well and to carry bottles of its water home with them. In Muslim tradition, Hagar and Ishmael remained at the site, and the community of Mecca grew around them. It was on a visit to his exiled son living at Mecca that Abraham agreed to the sacrifice from which God then spared him, and Abraham and Ishmael built the Kabba on God's command as a place of worship.

Just outside the Sacred Mosque is the Masa, "running place," a covered arcade that extends a quarter-mile between the two rocky hills of Safa and Marwah; it commemorates Hagar's run back and forth searching for water.

Pilgrimage is of two kinds. One is *umrah,* "lesser pilgrimage," which can be performed at any time of year and includes worship only at the Kaaba and other shrines adjacent to the Great Mosque. The greater pilgrimage, the *hajj* proper, adds to the rites of *umrah* others performed outside Mecca. The *hajj* is the event that inspires the great annual migration of the faithful. It takes place only during the specified days, the first part of the month of dhu'l-Hijjah.

The process of cleansing the soul in preparation for the sacred rites of pilgrimage begins as soon as the believer sets out on his journey. The Koran instructs those undertaking the pilgrimage to refrain from sexual intercourse, angry words, and obscenities while traveling, and prohibits the killing of game while on pilgrimage. The restriction on hunting is said to emphasize that the *hajj* is a time of peace and harmony with all of God's creation. A pilgrim who violates the ban is required to bring to the Kaaba a sacrificial offering of a domestic animal similar in value to the animal he has killed or to atone for his offense by fasting or giving food to the poor. (5:98)

Muhammad of course envisioned the pilgrimage as an overland migration of the Arabian people, to whom his prophetic message was addressed. The ban on the killing of game was a test of their self-discipline while on that trek. Today most pilgrims arrive in Saudi Arabia at the airport in Jeddah, which is on the Red Sea about fifty miles from Mecca.

There they are taken into the charge of pilgrimage authorities assigned by the Saudi government, men who have mastered the complex logistics of the event and provide, for a fee, every service, everything from transportation and sleeping tents to food and guides who see to it that each pilgrim performs the rites correctly. The guides know the sacred sites, the languages of the pilgrims, and the customs of worship, which vary slightly from group to group. The guides' services are not mandatory; those who speak Arabic and know the terrain can dispense with them.

The pilgrim should arrive at Mecca by the seventh day of the month. Upon arrival—in practice, often before leaving his native country—the pilgrim removes his regular clothes and puts on the traditional garb of the *hajj.* For men it consists of two seamless white wrappers, one about the lower part of the body, one about the upper. Most pilgrims leave one shoulder bare. There is no special dress for women, but most wear full-length white dresses that cover the arms. Whatever their custom at home, they are forbidden to veil their faces while on pilgrimage, and the hands are ungloved. The uniformity of dress contributes to the collective sense of community, to the sense of rising above distinctions of color and class in the spirit of religious brotherhood to which the pilgrims aspire.

During his journey, up to the time he enters Mecca, the pilgrim chants a short formula acknowledging his acceptance of God's command: "Here I am in answer to your call, O God. Here I am! Here I am! You have no associate. Here I am! All praise and favor and kingship are yours. Here I am!"

Upon arrival at Mecca suitably attired and removed from mundane concerns, the pilgrim proceeds directly to the Sacred Mosque, where he performs a ritual ablution and enters the courtyard through the Gate of Peace. There he kisses the Black Stone and performs seven counterclockwise circumnambulations of the Kaaba, three at a rapid pace and four at a normal walk. On each pass round the Kaaba, the pilgrim touches the Black Stone, though in practice the size of the crowd often makes that impossible. Chaos would be inevitable if each of the tens of thousands of pilgrims making the rounds of the Kaaba contested with the others for access to the stone, so a gesture toward the stone on each pass becomes an acceptable substitute.

A *Handbook of Hajj*, prepared for American pilgrims by the Islamic teaching center in Indianapolis, advises, "A big rush and some confusion is very natural when hundreds of thousands of people assemble. Try your best to perform ceremonies and make movements in a calm and quiet way . . . Prophet Muhammad (peace be upon him) has taught us to be calm and quiet in Hajj ceremonies."

The veneration of the Black Stone seems aberrant in a religion that professes to have avoided anything resembling idol-worship since the time of Muhammad. Muslims say they do not worship the stone but only honor it as a symbolic link to their spiritual ancestors. A book distributed by the government in Saudi Arabia gives this explanation: "Muslims in no wise worship the Black Stone. They kiss or touch it because it is known that the Prophet Muhammad did so and thereby they establish a link between themselves and the Prophet.

And he did so because it was a link between himself and Abraham."

There follows in the succeeding days of the pilgrimage a prescribed series of sometimes arduous rites and treks to holy places. In years when the *hajj* season falls in high summer, the pilgrims are exposed to relentless sun and searing heat which make the rites especially hard for the elderly and infirm.

The first of the prescribed rituals is a trek, made seven times, back and forth through the arcade joining the summits of the hills of Safa and Marwah, to commemorate Hagar's search for water. On the eighth day of dhu'l-Hijjah, all the pilgrims again perform the circumambulation of the Kaaba and then assemble for noon prayers at Mina, five miles outside Mecca. They remain at Mina, praying through the night and early on the morning of the ninth of the month, they migrate to the Plain of Arafat, about thirteen miles southeast of Mecca.

There they gather at noon for prayers and for a sermon, which is delivered from the spot where Muhammad is believed to have preached his Farewell Sermon (described in Chapter 2). The entire afternoon of the ninth day is spent standing in prayer on the Plain of Arafat; it is the most important ritual of the pilgrimage. Those who are not physically able to stand in the sun may sit or seek shade, but it is more meritorious to remain standing, bareheaded, throughout the afternoon reading the Koran and praying: "Here I am, O God, Here I am!"

According to *Handbook of Hajj*, "The day of Arafat is the day of exaltation, reverence, glorification and perception. It is the day when our Merciful Lord manifests His glory on the heaven and takes pride in the people of the earth before His angels, making them witnesses to His forgiveness and the welcome awarded to His worshipers. This is the greatest hospitality to the pilgrims and the most valuable reward from the Gracious Lord. In the vast square of the plain of Arafat, tears are shed, errors are corrected, sins washed out and faults redressed for those who ask the Lord for forgiveness and offer sincere repentance for their wrongdoings in the past. Happy is the person who receives the Mercy and Pleasure of Allah on this particular day. This is why the prophet (peace and blessings be upon him) said, 'the Hajj is Arafat.' "

Prayer continues until sunset. Then the entire throng, nearly equal to the population of Houston, goes on the move again. The pilgrims spend that night camped at Muzdalifa, an open plain between Arafat and Mina. They pass the night in prayer and rest, and each pilgrim gathers pebbles to be used in the rites the following day (though the *Handbook of Hajj* says it is "not necessary to pick pebbles from Muzdalifa, as is believed by many. The pebbles can be picked up either from Mina or on the way to it"—a reminder that there are still disagreements over details of these age-old rituals).

On the morning of the tenth of the month, the pilgrims return to Mina, where there are three stone pillars. Each pilgrim casts seven pebbles at one of the pillars, saying, "In the name of God Almighty I do this, and in hatred of the Devil and his pretense." This ritual is said to commemorate Abraham's act of driving away a tempting Satan by throwing stones at him on this spot.

This ceremony is followed by the ritual sacrifice of an animal, usually a sheep or goat, the concluding rite of the pilgrimage. The sacrifice commemorates Abraham's submission to God's command to sacrifice Ishmael and the decision of a merciful God to allow an animal to be offered in the boy's place.

This day, the tenth of Dhu'l-Hijjah, is celebrated as the Eid al-Adha, the festival of the sacrifice, or the Eid al-Kabir, the great feast. Throughout the Muslim world, it is a day on which the heads of families in their homes, whether a big-city apartment or a hut in some remote village, duplicate the sacrifice at Mina with the sacrifice of a sheep or goat, half of which is consumed at a family feast, the other half of which is given to the poor. It was this day that President Anwar Sadat of Egypt was celebrating when he prayed at al-Aqsa mosque in Jerusalem during his history-making visit to Israel in 1977.

After the sacrifice at Mina, male pilgrims have their heads shaved and female pilgrims have their hair cut and their nails are clipped. The pilgrims resume their normal attire and all normal activities except sex. The formal ceremonies are concluded, though prayer-gatherings continue and many pilgrims make a side trip to Medina for further prayer. Each participant has taken part in a mass human migration and collective spiritual exercise that knows no parallel in Western faith. He has done what God commanded—accept, believe, pray, visit the Sacred Mosque, partake of the brotherhood of Islam—and the spiritual benefits of the pilgrimage will sustain and comfort him as he returns to daily life. Forever a *hajji,* the pilgrim is secure in knowing that death cannot overtake him with the duty to make the pilgrimage unfulfilled.

The side trip to Medina is undertaken by many Muslims as part of the pilgrimage, but its motivation and purpose are different. Medina is the city where the Prophet lived for the last ten years of his life. He and his most prominent early converts are buried there. A visit to Medina is therefore an act of tribute and respect to men, not an act of worship of God, an essential distinction in Islam.

The *Handbook of Hajj* warns pilgrims that while it is permitted to visit these sites and salute the memories of the men buried there, "it is not permitted to ask the prophet to fulfill any need or to remove any distress, or to heal any patient or to make rich anyone who is poor. All such acts are the acts of polytheism. And Allah does not forgive polytheism."

This is a reminder that Muhammad and all other prophets before him and all the believers who came after him were but men, mere mortals who have died. They have no power of intercession with God, they are not associated with God, they are not exalted above other men, they do not work miracles. A Muslim prays to no man, and in making the pilgrimage to Mecca, follows the command of Allah and prays to Him. In visiting Medina, however, the pilgrim pays respect to a man.

The orderly management of the *hajj* each year has been a source of pride to the Saudi government, but the excessive zeal of Shiite pilgrims from Iran provoked clashes with Saudi security forces in 1987 in which about 400 people died. This incident led to a nasty feud between Saudi Arabia and Iran that tainted the pilgrimage for years. In September 1989, the Saudis beheaded 16 Kuwaitis accused of setting off bombs to disrupt the pilgrimage at Iran's behest. The *hajj* also has provided cover for men from poor countries to enter Saudi Arabia and stay on to look for work. And although the Saudis have performed prodigious feats of organization, sanitation, and logistics to make the *hajj* more of a spiritual adventure and less of a physical ordeal than in the past, they have not succeeded in controlling the hucksterism and price gouging that victimize the inexperienced and often illiterate pilgrims.

After the 1987 incident, Saudi Arabia restricted the number of Iranian pilgrims it would admit each year, and Iran responded by boycotting the *hajj*. But to most pilgrims, who are apolitical, the *hajj* continues to represent a spiritual triumph that brings together more than a million souls, united in their exaltation and their devotion to Allah and his prophet. They come together in piety and self-abnegation, as their religion commands. Dropping all other concerns, Muslims of every station in life, generals and shepherds, housewives and cabinet ministers, unite in a spiritual exercise that elevates them above the realities and rivalries of daily life.

Social and Legal Duties

Those five pillars of the faith—the profession of faith, ritual prayer, *zakat,* fasting, and the pilgrimage—encompass the fundamental beliefs and practices common to all Muslims, but they do not represent a comprehensive list of the spiritual duties, standards of conduct, beliefs, and attitudes that are required of a good Muslim. Islam is not a series of disjointed rites and practices but a continuum, an all-encompassing social, ethical, and spiritual system in which all parts and all participants are interrelated. The gates of Paradise are not opened to those who go here and there or who say this prayer or that, but to the virtuous, the sincere, the charitable, and the dutiful. Beyond the pillars of the faith there is a demanding list of obligations that true believers undertake to show their obedience to God.

These obligations are of two kinds. One kind is spiritual and mental, involving the attitudes and states of belief that God demands of those who believe in Him. The other is legal and social, involving the rules of conduct and codes of law that exemplify the proper spiritual attitudes and put them into practice in daily life. Such well-known rules of Islam as the prohibition of alcohol and usury fall into this category. They were not imposed to make life difficult for believers but to enable believers to know how to act and what to do in their daily lives to fulfill God's commandments.

Some of the obligations were laid down in the Koran,

others derived from study of the Prophet's words and example. Obedience to the rules does not, by itself, constitute the virtuous life. To gain Paradise, the believer must first achieve submission of his soul to God's will. Submission of his daily life to God's rules of conduct is meritorious only if it is a manifestation of his spiritual condition. Belief and behavior are both judged on the Last Day; neither has merit without the other.

The Koran says, "Those who surrender themselves to Allah and accept the true faith; who are devout, sincere, patient, humble, charitable, and chaste; who fast and are ever mindful of Allah—on these, both men and women, Allah will bestow forgiveness and a rich reward." (33:35) And again the Koran teaches, "The true believers are those whose hearts are filled with awe at the mention of Allah and whose faith grows stronger as they listen to His revelations. They are those who put their trust in their Lord, pray steadfastly, and bestow in alms of that which We have given them." (8:2)

Similar passages throughout the Holy Book define the Muslim conception of the virtuous life: believe in God, pray to Him, act in His name, accept His prophet, live modestly, be charitable and truthful, refrain from mockery and falsehood, defend the faith against attack by unbelievers, and recognize that the life of this world is but a transitory preparation for the awesome final judgment. To help orphans, refrain from gambling and fortune-telling, and give true weight in commerce are required. But they are meritorious in the sight of God only if done in His name. The Prophet himself is recorded in the *hadith* as having said, "Actions are but by intention and every man shall have but that which he intended. Thus he whose migration [from Mecca to Medina] was for Allah and His messenger, his migration was for Allah and His messenger; and he whose migration was to achieve some worldly benefit or to take some woman in marriage, his migration was for that for which he migrated." Thus the Prophet taught that deeds done for the sake of Allah are the virtuous deeds, not those done for worldly ends.

The required spiritual attitudes and earthly conduct are mutually reinforcing and form a system of behavior in which submission to God requires certain types of conduct and living by those rules of conduct is a manifestation of spiritual submission. A good Muslim refrains from drinking alcohol because God commands it, not because liquor is prohibited by his government; the government prohibits it because it is God's command. The logical extension of this relationship is that Islam seeks to obliterate the distinction between religious and secular law, between duty to God and duty to the state. In Islam, religion and state are one. *Sharia,* the code of law based on the Koran and the *sunna,* is both religious and secular at the same time. The distinction between what is Caesar's and what is God's is alien to Islam.

How the law of Islam developed and how it works in practice in modern nation states must be examined separately. (See Chapter 4.) For the individual Muslim, the choices are easy. He may live in a country that permits alcohol and gambling, but he knows it is better not to partake. He may live in a society where the alms-tax is voluntary, but he knows it is better to give. He may work in a place where the machines keep running during prayer time, but he knows it is more meritorious to stop and pray. He may be in a gathering in which spiteful gossip dominates the conversation, but he knows it is better to refrain. The code of the vendetta may prevail in his community, but he knows that in the Koran, the righteous are defined as those who "curb their anger and forgive their fellow-men. Allah loves the charitable." (3:134) On all occasions, the Muslim is free to make his own choice, but he cannot be ignorant of which course is in conformity with God's command and which is not. Obedience to the law of God is required even if no temporal authority is enforcing it.

In situations that are not explicitly dealt with in the Koran, Muslims look for guidance to the life and words of the Prophet. Muhammad was only a man, but Muslims believe he lived a nearly perfect life. His life and words represent the standards of devout, pious, and upright behavior by which Muslims measure their own morality and that of their fellow men. The Koran itself is interpreted according to what is known of the Prophet's life: such and such an action cannot be prohibited because we know that Muhammad did it. Because he was mortal and not divine, because he was a man who loved women, engaged in trade, made enemies, fought bravely, and cherished his family, he can be a flesh-and-blood model, emulated as no deity or supernatural being could be.

Chapter 2

The Prophet Muhammad

ISLAM is like Christianity in that it originated in the life and works of one well-known historical figure and is inseparable from him. The fundamental difference is the humanity of Muhammad.

The most basic tenet of Islam is that Allah is the one God and that no person, creature, or thing may be associated with him or accorded divine attributes. The Koran stresses that Muhammad was a mortal, born of earthly parents, destined to die and be judged by the Creator. Muhammad worked no miracles and raised no one from the dead. His achievements were a manifestation of the will of God, not of any supramortal essence in himself.

Muslims never refer to themselves a Muhammadans, because the word implies that they worship Muhammad as Christians worship Christ, which they do not. As an inspired man, the vessel of divine revelation, prophet, guide, leader, commander, exemplar, and lawgiver, Muhammad is revered, admired, and imitated, but he is not worshiped.

There are times and places where this distinction seem to be eroded by an excess of zeal among Muhammad's followers. At the great mosque in Delhi, the attendants who display putative relics of the Prophet, including a sandal he is said to have worn, exhibit an unctuous reverence inappropriate for any mortal.

The reason *Handbook of Hajj* advises pilgrims who visit Medina not to pray to Muhammad for any miracles or earthly benefits is precisely that Muslims have a traditional tendency to invoke the Prophet's aid as if he in fact had supernatural powers. Edward W. Lane, in the 1836 classic *Manners and Customs of the Modern Egyptians,* noted that "the respect which most modern Muslims pay to their Prophet is almost idolatrous. They very frequently swear by him;

and many of the most learned, as well as the ignorant, often implore his intercession"—even though the Koran teaches that no one, not even Muhammad, can intercede with God on behalf of men. Lane reported that one Imam Ahmad Ibn-Hanbal "would not even eat watermelons because, although he knew that the Prophet ate them, he could not learn whether he ate them with or without the rind, or whether he broke, bit or cut them." I never encountered any imitation of the Prophet quite so absurd, but it is certainly customary to invoke his name at any time and on any occasion—even giving directions to a cab driver. ("To the university, by the Prophet!") These, however, are pious irrelevancies, derived not from any Islamic claim of Muhammad's divinity but from the tradition of devotion to a holy, divinely guided man.

The Prophet, whose name means "highly praised," was born about 570 A.D. in Mecca, a trading post in the Arabian peninsula, well outside the mainstream of contemporary events in Europe and around the Mediterranean. Arabia was a violent and licentious semi-primitive corner of the world, where religion took the form of pagan worship of tribal gods and idols. Many Jews and Christians lived in what are now Saudi Arabia and Yemen, but most of the population had not adopted monotheistic beliefs.

Mecca was not only the commercial but also the religious center for the tribes of the peninsula. They all had their own gods and idols, but some gods were common to all of them, and the shrine of those deities was in Mecca. That shrine was the Kaaba, from which Muhammad would soon expel all idols and images and which he would establish as the central shrine of Islam.

The world beyond Arabia, at the time of Muhammad's birth, was entering an era of violent transition. Europe was descending into the Dark Ages. The Merovingian descendants of Clovis I were dividing the Frankish kingdom. The Lombards invaded Italy, meeting little resistance, and established a capital at Pavia. Rome was reduced to a minor duchy, important only as the seat of the Papacy. New ideas and cultures were rising in parts of the world untouched by the decay of the Roman Empire; the Mayan empire flourished in Mexico, and Buddhism spread through China and Japan. It is an instructive period of world history for those of us accustomed to a Ptolemaic view of civilization in which all other cultures are thought to revolve around our own.

Shortly before Muhammad's birth, the Byzantine Empire, based in Constantinople, reached the zenith of its power under Justinian. Throughout the Prophet's lifetime, the lands of the eastern Mediterranean and western Asia were ravaged by wars between Byzantium and Persia. The Persians captured Damascus in 613, sacked Jerusalem in 614, and briefly took Egypt. Then the tide was reversed, and in 625, seven years before Muhammad died, the Byzantines scored a decisive victory over the Persians at Nineveh. Southern Arabia was a Persian satrapy for a time, but most of these events on the northern fringes of the peninsula had little direct impact on the Prophet. Their importance to him was that they left both Byzantium and Persia exhausted and vulnerable to the advance of the inspired Arabians who were to overwhelm them within a generation.

It is often said that Muhammad was the only great religious leader to live in the full light of history, meaning that his life and works are known to us in detail, recorded by himself and by contemporaries whose works survive. But it is difficult to distinguish facts about Muhammad from pious tradition passed down as fact.

Scholars do not even agree on the year of his birth. Information about the years before he undertook his prophetic mission is almost as scanty as information about the young manhood of Jesus. There are wide variations in accounts of such crucial events as the Battle of Badr and the *hijra,* and the bias of each narrator influences his account. Muslim biographers and hostile commentators have irreconcilable views about Muhammad's character and motivation and about the nature of his mission.

What Muslims believe was divine inspiration and a command from God has been ascribed by some Western writers to epilepsy or fakery or insanity. Dante, in *The Divine Comedy,* consigned Muhammad to the ninth circle of the Inferno, with the "sowers of schism and of discord," as if Muhammad were a renegade Christian. Henry Treece, in his history of the Crusades, attributed Muhammad's revelations to the sun-crazed musings of a semiliterate trader lulled into a trance by the swaying of his camel. Because of the tradition that Muhammad actually fell down, groaning and sweating, as the revelations came upon him, Tor Andrae, a sympathetic biographer, observed, "It has long been thought that Mohammed was an epileptic. Even certain Byzantine writers made this discovery, and for a long time past western writers have edified their readers with this compromising fact about the archenemy of Christianity. Even in recent times some authors have held fast to this idea, influenced by the scientifically superficial and hasty theory, which the medical psychology of the past century has made fashionable for a while, that the inspired state is 'pathological.' " However, Andrae says there is no evidence that Muhammad was clinically epileptic; even if there were, that would not necessarily undermine his claim to have received divine revelations.

Edward Gibbon, who devoted a long section of his history of the decline of Rome to the rise of Islam, said that Muhammad was an "eloquent fanatic" who "assumed a false commission to inculcate a salutary doctrine" in his countrymen. J. M. Rodwell, in the preface to his translation of the Koran, called Muhammad a "great though imperfect character, an earnest though mistaken teacher," who was subject to "morbid and fantastic hallucinations, and alternations of excitement and depression, which would win for him, in the eyes of his ignorant countrymen the credit of being inspired." Rodwell naturally displayed the cultural arrogance of Victorian England. Those who do not think that Muhammad was, in Rodwell's word, "mistaken," interpret differently the events of the Prophet's life. The light of history is shed by different lanterns.

This account of Muhammad's life and work is derived from both western and Muslim accounts, including the Koran, which is the only source of detail about many episodes in the Prophet's career. Dates and events that are presented as factual are those on which all accounts, Muslim and non-Muslim, agree.

Muhammad's father was of the Hashem (or Hashim) family, a minor but respected clan within the powerful tribe of the Quraish. Later generations of Hashemites, collateral descendants of the Prophet through the line of his great-grandfather, claimed the status of nobility among Arab families. (The link to the family of the Prophet is what shored up the questionable royal claims of such modern day Hashemite rulers as King Hussein of Jordan and before him King Faisal of Iraq.) The Quraish, who dominated Meccan commerce and controlled the lucrative traffic in pilgrimages to the idols enshrined in the Kaaba, later became Muhammad's most determined opponents and are condemned in the Koran as unbelievers.

Muhammad's father, Abdullah, died before Muhammad was born. The Prophet's mother, Amina, died when the boy was six, and he was entrusted to the care of his grandfather, Abdel Muttalib. The grandfather was a distinguished personage, said to have been a descendant of Ishmael, and was the custodian of the Kaaba. Abdel Muttalib is honored in Muslim tradition as the man who rediscovered and excavated the well of Zamzam, which had been filled during a tribal dispute.

Abdel Muttalib died only two years later, and the boy Muhammad was passed on again, this time to an uncle, Abu Talib. The Koran's stress on justice and charity toward orphans is apparently attributable to these events of Muhammad's childhood, though of course those who believe that the Koran is entirely and only the eternal revealed word of God would minimize the extent to which its contents were influenced by the personal experience of the man chosen as the conduit for the revelation. (See Chapter 3.)

The Unlettered Prophet

The Koran calls Muhammad "the unlettered prophet," and Muslims believe he was indeed illiterate. That is an essential point, because if Muhammad was unable to read or write, that reinforces his claim to have received the revelations of the Koran directly from Allah. In the Koran, Allah says to Muhammad, "Never have you read a book before this, nor have you ever transcribed one with your right hand. Had you done either of these the unbelievers might have justly doubted." (29:48)

The unbelievers who scoffed at Muhammad accused him of cribbing his material, especially those parts incorporating lessons and episodes from Jewish and Christian scriptures. Even if Muhammad could read, he could not have had firsthand knowledge of those scriptures, because they had not then been translated into Arabic. But there was abundant opportunity for exposure to Jewish and Christian teachings. Many Jews lived in the towns of Arabia, the Arabians had extensive mercantile commerce with Christian Syria, and Arabians had traveled across the Red Sea to Christian Abyssinia. An Abyssinian army under the Christian King Abraha invaded Arabia at about the time of Muhammad's birth, a campaign recounted in the chapter of the Koran entitled "The Elephant."

Tradition holds that Muhammad, though trained only to herd sheep and goats, was a handsome youth, distinguished by honesty and trustworthiness, who refrained from participating in pagan rituals. But modern historians say all that is known with certainty is that when Muhammad was twenty-five he married Khadija, a wealthy widow. She is said to have been so impressed by his shrewd business judgment on a caravan trading-trip and by his handsome features that she offered him her hand, though she had resisted other suitors.

Most accounts say Khadija was forty years old at the time of the marriage, but that may be questionable, since she bore Muhammad six children: al-Qasim, Abdullah, Zainab, Ruqayyah, Umm Kulthum, and Fatima. Only the girl Fatima survived her father, a misfortune for the Prophet, because it left him without sons in a society that prized male offspring, and a misfortune for Islam, because it led to disputes over the succession to Muhammad's temporal authority, which continue to divide the community of believers to this day.

Apparently the marriage was otherwise a great success. Muhammad, who later would have nine other wives, had none but Khadija while she lived. She gave him her unstinting support when the revelations came to him and he began sending the Meccans a message they chose not to hear. Khadija believed, and her belief sustained and comforted Muhammad.

What Muhammad actually did during the years between his marriage and the call to prophethood is not known. But he is said to have had the custom of retreating from time to time to a cave on Mount Hira, outside Mecca, for meditation. It was there on the "Night of Qadr" (night of glory or night of power), the night in the month of Ramadan in the year 610, described in Sura 97 of the Koran, that Allah called Muhammad to be His messenger.

According to Muslim tradition, the revelation came in the form of an appearance by the angel Gabriel, who commanded, "Recite!"

Muhammad asked, "What shall I recite?" The angel replied, as recorded in Sura 96 of the Koran, "Recite in the name of your Lord who created, created man from clots of blood! Recite! Your Lord is the most bountiful one, who by the pen taught man what he did not know." (Some translations use "proclaim" instead of "recite"; others, less plausibly if Muhammad was illiterate, use "read.")

The Koran is not precise about the way in which the angel made himself known. It says that "a gracious and mighty messenger, held in honor by the Lord of the Throne," revealed himself to Muhammad. (89:19) "He stood on the uppermost horizon; then, drawing near, he came down within two bows' length or even closer, and revealed to his servant that which he revealed." (53:7)

Fazlur Rahman, a prominent scholar of Islam, maintains that it was not a physical encounter at all but an entirely internal mystical experience. "This idea of the externality of the Angel and the Revelation," Rahman says, "has become so ingrained in the general Muslim mind that the real picture is anathema to it."

Tradition holds that Muhammad was so shaken by the revelation that he ran home, chilled and trembling, and asked Khadija to cover him with a blanket or cloak. But the prophetic mandate was not to be denied. The messenger angel insisted, "You that are wrapped up in your vestment arise and give warning." (74:1)

Each revelation is said to have caused Muhammad to fall down in groaning, sweating fits. These reports have contributed to the epilepsy theory advanced by debunkers, although the occurrences are consistent with the physical symptoms exhibited by some Christian saints who have claimed to have had mystical experiences. At first some of Muhammad's fellow Meccans accused him of madness, fakery, and flights of poetic fancy. The Koran, however, says he was not a poet, not mad, and not faking, only conveying a message he clearly heard from a God-sent emissary he clearly saw.

Muhammad was about forty years old when the revelations began, an obscure man of no known personal or professional distinction aside from a reputation for probity and intelligence. It is hardly credible that he could have achieved what he did in the remaining one-third of his life if he had not been at least sincere and dedicated in his mission, inspired by some force or faith that sustained him and ultimately persuaded his compatriots. The hostile European commentators who dismiss his entire career as charlatanry underestimate the people of Arabia.

To the few Meccans who took him seriously Muhammad preached a simple message. He said they must abandon their pagan idols and their licentious ways and repent before the one true God, Allah, lest they be condemned at the Last Judgment to eternal hellfire. From the beginning, his message was tied to a program of social reform. Prayer and belief alone were insufficient; it was necessary to trade honestly, treat women better, care for orphans, forego usury, and abandon infanticide.

At first Muhammad evidently saw himself not as the founder of a new religion but as a reformer and restorer of monotheistic truth as he understood it had been revealed to the Jews and Christians before him. But his attempt to curb the traditional practices of an unruly society marked him as a new kind of voice, a social agitator prepared to challenge as much as preach, which no doubt contributed to the hostility of the ruling Quraish.

This hostility was passive at first, because Muhammad was thoroughly unsuccessful at attracting followers and appeared to pose no threat to the established order. The Meccans scorned and mocked him, taunting him with demands that he work miracles or produce supernatural signs to demonstrate the authenticity of his claims.

Muhammad always declined to traffic in miracles to satisfy the doubters. He argued that it was for Allah, not for him, to give signs, if He chose, and that earlier prophets, including Jesus, had given supernatural signs, only to be rejected by unbelievers anyway. Furthermore, Muhammad argued, all life and nature—the sun and the moon, the wind and the rain, the cow and the palm tree—were signs of Allah's power and grace, if man would but recognize them. "Do they not see the birds that wing their flight in heaven's vault? None sustains them but Allah. Surely in this there are signs for true believers," says the Koran. (16:79)

So few were the believers, so paltry the flock that gathered about him in the first few years that Muhammad evidently had moments of doubt and wavering. But he was sustained by the comforting words of Allah: "We know well that what they say grieves you. It is not you that they are disbelieving; the evil-doers deny Allah's own revelations." (6:33)

In three years the Prophet is said to have made only thirty converts, including Khadija. The most important of the others were his cousin Ali; Abu Bakr, a wealthy merchant later to be the first Caliph, or leader of the Muslim community; and Zaid ibn Harithah, a former slave and Muhammad's adopted son.

Muslim biographers say the band of believers was so small because Muhammad kept his mission secret, but this is hard to reconcile with the clear instructions he received to spread God's word and the Koran's accounts of how he did speak out and was spurned. The more probable explanation is that few people believed him. Then as he began to preach more widely, the community of believers grew, but so did the hostility of the Quraish. Muhammad was denouncing the gods who represented tradition and order. He was espousing a faith that chose religious brotherhood instead of tribal identity for the foundation of society. And he threatened the commercial profitability of the pagan activities centered on the Kaaba, which the Quraish controlled.

Bernard Lewis, in *The Arabs in History,* says that the opposition of the Quraish was "largely economic in origin," but they evidently also resented the pretensions to leadership of one who was not of the ruling classes.

"Now that the truth has come to them," says the Koran, "they say, 'It is witchcraft. We will not believe in it.' They also say, 'Why was this Koran not revealed to some mighty man from the two [chief] towns?' Are they the distributors of your Lord's blessings?" (43:30)

The Quraish ostracized Muhammad and his followers, refusing to trade or associate with them. Muhammad Abdul Rauf, in his brief sketch of the Prophet's life, says the Quraish also subjected the early Muslims to severe torture. "They did not hesitate to apply the most appalling methods of persecution against the believers. Each tribc undcrtook to deal with its own members who became Muslims. They tortured them by fire and by heated rods of iron. The bodies of their victims were chained, exposed naked to the heat of the burning midday sun, and they were made to lie with heavy rocks placed on their chests. Some of them died and some lost their sight but none gave in."

The persecution was so intense that Muhammad was

obliged, in the year 615, to allow some of his followers to flee to Abyssinia (now Ethiopia), and he himself appears to have been virtually under house arrest protected only by the refusal of his uncle Abu Talib to turn him over to his adversaries.

One of the most vigorous of those adversaries was another of his uncles, Abu Lahab, who was rigidly hostile to the new faith. Abu Lahab earned the distinction of being the only individual cursed by name in the Koran: "May the hands of Abu Lahab perish! May he himself perish! Nothing shall his wealth and gains avail him. He shall be burnt in a flaming fire [a play on the meaning of Abu Lahab, father of flame] and his wife, laden with faggots, shall have a rope of fibre round her neck." (111)

This was a low period in Muhammad's mission and in his personal life. Although Umar (also spelled Omar), an influential opponent, who was later to be chosen second Caliph, embraced Islam in 617, Muhammad's failures and disappointments far outnumbered his successes. Khadija died in 619, then Abu Talib. The Prophet was stoned during a month-long sojourn at Taif, a mountain town southeast of Mecca (now the summer capital of the Saudi monarchy) and forced to slink back into a hostile Mecca.

In 620 Muhammad made what Muslims call his night journey, in which he was transported to Jerusalem and ascended from there into the heavens. This was probably a mystical experience or vision but many Muslims believe Muhammad was actually transported physically, by a miracle, to Jerusalem, the sacred city of monotheism, and thence through the seven heavens to the Divine throne. The Koran does not claim that Muhammad's journey was corporeal. The details of popular belief are embellishments of the Koranic text, which says (in the Yusuf Ali translation, clearer on this point than the Dawood), "Glory to Allah, Who did take His servant for a journey by night from the Sacred Mosque (i.e, Mecca) to the Farthest Mosque (in Arabic, *al-masjid al-aqsa*) whose precincts We did bless in order that We might show him some of our signs." (17:1) That blessed Farthest Mosque, al-Aqsa, on Jerusalem's Temple Mount, is regarded by most Muslims as the third holiest site in their religion, the first two being the Kaaba and the Great Mosque of Medina.

Jerusalem, the Holy City of the Jews and Christians, had an important symbolic place in Muhammad's nascent religion. His followers in Mecca faced Jerusalem when they bowed in prayer, which he instructed them to do either because the Quraish excluded Muslims from the Kaaba or because he was trying to establish the continuity of Islam with the faith of the Jews or both. But there is no evidence that Muhammad ever actually went to Jerusalem, despite the rich tradition of folk tales describing the means by which he was supposedly transported and the details of his sojourn.

The Egyptian scholar Ahmad Galwash, in *The Religion of Islam,* which was published with the approval of the religious authorities at Cairo's al-Azhar University, says of the night journey (as it is called), "All that Muslims *must* believe respecting this journey is that the prophet saw himself, in a vision, transported from Mecca to Jerusalem and that in such vision he really beheld some of the greatest signs of his Lord. However, some trustworthy tradition insists that this journey was a real bodily one and not only a vision."

In either case, it was an exalting spiritual experience, which consoled Muhammad in his darkest hour and marked the beginning of a change in his fortunes. Shortly after the night journey, the Prophet was at a pilgrim fair outside Mecca where he met a group of men from Yathrib, an important town to the north, some of whom were probably Jews. It was an encounter that changed the history of Islam and of the world.

It was evidently not a chance meeting; the men from Yathrib sought him out. According to Tor Andrae, in his study of Muhammad's life, the historical or traditional explanation for their approach to Muhammad is that many Jews lived in Yathrib and therefore people there were more receptive to monotheism and the call of a prophet, but there was probably a political motive as well. Unlike Mecca, which was ruled by the Quraish and prosperous in its stability, Yathrib was exhausted by a power struggle among two Arab and three Jewish tribes, and its citizens were looking for a unifier and mediator. Fazlur Rahman suggests that they sought out Muhammad because even though he had failed to convert the Meccans word of his "moral prestige and statesmanlike ability" had already spread beyond his native city.

The men went back to Yathrib, about 280 miles north of

Mecca, and told of their meeting. At the fair the following year, 621, a delegation of twelve returned to Mecca and entered into an agreement with Muhammad. They pledged to refrain from idolatry, promiscuity, and infanticide, and they offered a welcome to the Prophet and his followers. Muhammad dispatched one of his disciples to Yathrib to instruct the people in his teachings. In 622, a delegation of seventy-five citizens of Yathrib formally invited the community of Muslims to move to their town.

The Migration to Medina

Muhammad was not primarily interested in Yathrib. His objective was the conversion of Mecca, which was in effect the religious capital of Arabia. But he was making little headway there, and practicality dictated that he accept the invitation, which would enable him to establish a useful power base at last. This decision prepared the way for the seminal event in Islamic history, the *hijra* (or *hegira,* as it is usually spelled in English), the migration of Muhammad and his followers from Mecca to their adopted city. The Muslims left Mecca in small groups, so as not to arouse suspicion. The migration was completed on September 24, 622.

According to the Koran, Muhammad and Abu Bakr were the last to leave Mecca. Bernard Lewis, in his history of the Arabs, says their departure was unopposed by the Quraish, but Muslim historians record elaborate ruses devised to ensure the Prophet's escape from determined pursuers. His cousin Ali is said to have slept in Muhammad's bed, at great risk to himself, to delude the Quraish into thinking the Prophet was still at home. Muhammad and Abu Bakr eluded the Quraish by hiding in a cave. An Arab legend says that after they entered, two pigeons laid eggs at the entrance and a spider wove a web across the opening, so that the pursuers thought that no one was inside.

Yathrib, the new home of Islam, was renamed al-Medinat al-Munawara, "the illuminated city," or al-Medinat al-Rasul, "the City of the Messenger" (accounts vary), and has been known ever since as Medina, the Arabic word for city.

There Muhammad was in wholly different and more promising circumstances than he had been in at Mecca. He was free to preach openly and was heard with respect. The scorned outcast of Mecca was welcomed by the Medinese, who had no tribal hostility to him and no vested interest in the commerce of the pilgrimage to the Kaaba. Muhammad was no longer a solitary troublemaking mystic; he was the leader of a growing community, its judge and lawgiver, and soon would be its military commander as well.

In the absence of a strong ruling power at Medina, Muhammad's temporal authority grew rapidly. It was reinforced by Koranic revelations that put the seal of divine authority on his position as "Commander of the Faithful" and equated Muhammad's instructions to the community with the divine will: "He that obeys the Apostle obeys Allah himself." (4:80) In the *hadith,* Muhammad is quoted as telling the Muslims, "What I have forbidden to you, avoid; what I have ordered, do as much of it as you can. It was only their excessive questioning and their disagreeing with the prophets that destroyed those who were before you."

The basic doctrines of the faith had been established at Mecca. Now, at Medina, the Koranic revelations and Muhammad's teachings dealt less with eschatology and more with the social and legal issues confronting the community. The mundane supplanted the mystical in the revelations. The exalted prophetic visions gave way to long lessons on social behavior, family life, justice, law, prohibited conduct, and the obligation of the faithful to fight for their beliefs. Muslims, having learned what to believe about God and the Last Day, were now taught how to act on earth in accordance with that belief.

Muhammad's first act of governance is said to have been the issuance of a charter establishing the relationship of the three groups that made up the population of Medina: his followers from Mecca, the indigenous Medinese *ansar* (helpers), and the Jews. The charter guaranteed religious freedom for the Jews, urged cooperation and unity among the Muslims, and declared that Muhammad should be the arbiter of disputes. With that the Prophet established two principles that were revolutionary in their time and place and had been rejected at Mecca. One was that Islam was the source of temporal as well as spiritual authority, and the other was that faith, rather than tribe, should be the bond that regulates the affairs of men.

Both principles are still basic to Islam. The brotherhood

of Islam, the *umma,* or community of believers, has existed ever since in a bond of faith that transcends race and politics. "The believers," says the Koran, "are a band of brothers." (49:10)

The working agreement with the Jews, however, did not survive long. Muhammad naively expected them to accept his religious message as well as his temporal authority and he was angry when they did not. The Jews mocked his revelations and scorned him for his imperfect understanding of the Jewish scriptures, to which he frequently alluded. Muhammad suspected that the Jews were giving secret support to the Quraish of Mecca, whose hostility to him did not abate after the *hijra.*

This tension with the Jews is said by some authorities to account for decisions the Prophet made early in his sojourn at Medina, which effectively Arabized the new faith. Islam became less an extension of Judaism and more a specifically Arabian creed.

In accordance with new instructions from Allah, Muhammad changed the *qibla,* the direction of prayer, from Jerusalem to Mecca, and he incorporated into Islam the pilgrimage to the Kaaba. Friday replaced Saturday as the day of congregational prayer. "We will make you turn toward a qibla that will please you," says the Koran. "Turn toward the Holy Mosque [of Mecca]; wherever you be, face towards it." (2:144)

Those who accept the Koran as the literal word of God need look no further than this expression of the divine will for the source of such decisions as the change of *qibla.* But the Koran was not revealed in a vacuum, and it is hard to avoid the conclusion that this and other Koranic commands of the Medinese period were tailored to suit Muhammad's circumstances. Those chapters that justify or rationalize peccadilloes in his personal life or military decisions that violated tribal codes hardly permit any other judgment. This is not necessarily inconsistent with the belief that the Koran is the word of God; if Muhammad was God's messenger, it was natural for God to help him carry out his mission. But the changing of the *qibla* and the incorporation of the pilgrimage into Islam were not done in accordance with abstract celestial commands and clearly had political as well as religious motivation that went beyond spiting the Jews.

Muhammad still viewed Mecca as his objective and still

hoped to convert the Quraish. In dropping the Jewish Sabbath and in making Islam a faith focused on Mecca instead of Jerusalem, he may have been making overtures to the hostile Meccan rulers. The Koran emphasizes the Arabness of Muhammad's mission, his role as prophet to a people who had no scripture of their own; and to the Arabs, Mecca was the traditional center of worship. Even at Medina, Muhammad referred to Mecca as "the sacred city." Medina was only a temporary sanctuary, from which he sought to implant Islam in the city that had denied it. The change in the *qibla* and the inclusion of a pilgrimage to the sites of Abraham (not to the pagan gods of Mecca) could only make Muhammad's faith less alien to the Meccans.

Before resuming his mission to Mecca, however, Muhammad had first to consolidate his power at Medina.

Aside from the Jews, his chief source of difficulty was a group of Medinese Arabs who resented his influence and sought to sabotage him. Their tactic was to pretend to embrace Islam while secretly working in concert with the Jews against Muhammad. They were known as the Hypocrites. Muhammad and his sincere followers are said to have known perfectly well what the Hypocrites were up to, but Muhammad accepted their false professions of faith and even allowed them to fight with his troops, saying that it was up to God to determine what is in men's hearts. He adopted that policy, according to Muhammad Abdul Rauf, because "had he rejected the Hypocrites, he would have established suspicion as a principle of judgment, thus opening the gate to future despots who would liquidate their adversaries on suspicion or accusations, claiming to be following the example of the prophet." Unhappily, the history of Islam down to the present includes all too many despots who have liquidated adversaries on suspicion, but as Rauf says, they can find no justification for their actions in Muhammad's teachings or in his example.

When the leader of the Hypocrites died, Muhammad is said to have attended the funeral and led prayers for him, thus winning over into genuine faith many of those who had been secretly opposed to him.

The last ten years of Muhammad's life is a story of government and diplomacy more than a story of religion. The fundamentals of the faith were well established; but if Islam was to survive its founder, it had to become irreversibly ascendant in Arabia within his lifetime, and it was to that objective that the Prophet devoted his energies in conflicts with the Jews and Hypocrites of Medina that alternated with recurring military skirmishes against the Quraish of Mecca.

The skirmishes evidently originated in the need of the Muslim community in Medina for food and money, which impelled them to resort to the traditional kind of caravan-raiding that was indistinguishable from banditry except perhaps in motive. Even if the Muslims had not been obliged to raid, however, armed conflict with the Quraish was probably inevitable, given the Prophet's determination to implant Islam in Mecca.

The Battle of Badr

Two years after the *hijra,* a small band of believers attacked a caravan and carried off the spoils. Muhammad himself did not participate, but he was criticized for allowing the attack to take place during a month regarded as holy by the Arabians when, by tradition, a truce was in effect. Thus, this first Muslim skirmish was a tactical success but a political liability for Muhammad.

His justification for the breach of taboo is recorded in the Koran: "They ask you about the sacred month. Say, 'To fight in this month is a grave offense; but to debar others from the path of Allah, to deny Him, and to expel His worshippers from the Holy Mosque is far more grave in His sight. Idolatry is worse than carnage.' " (2:217)

The Prophet and his followers were city-dwellers, not bedouin, and any analysis attributing the behavior of Muslims to bedouin tradition is specious. But the Muslims evidently adapted themselves quickly to the techniques of desert warfare. Their next recorded encounter, a real battle with lasting significance, was a spectacular success. It was the Battle of Badr, which took place in March, 624. It is analyzed in Sura 8 of the Koran, which says that Allah caused Muhammad to underestimate the enemy's numbers so he would not shrink from the encounter. Muslims still give thanks for that today.

Ten accounts of Badr by Muslim and Western chroniclers may give ten different versions of the details, but there is no dispute about the scope of the incident or its outcome. The

Muslims prepared to raid a caravan that was passing southward on its way to Mecca. The Meccans, alerted, reinforced. Muhammad and about 300 followers encountered a Meccan force of nearly a thousand at Badr, eleven miles southwest of Medina, and routed them.

To the Muslims and to other Arabs of the peninsula, this demonstrated that Allah was indeed on the side of Muhammad. The victory, against such great odds, reinforced Muhammad's claim to be the true prophet, built the confidence of the community, and prepared the way for decisive encounters with both the Quraish of Mecca and the Jews of Medina. A Koranic revelation told the Muslims that Allah had sent a thousand angels to help them and would always ensure the triumph of the believers. Other revelations instructed the believers in their obligation to join the fight when the call to do so was issued. It was not their arms but the power of God that achieved the victory, the Koran told the Muslims, and God will always be with those who fight for the faith.

During the war between Iran and Iraq in 1980, Professor Fouad Ajami of Johns Hopkins University told a Washington lecture audience, "Islam is a martial civilization. If you succeed, that means God is on your side." So it was with Muhammad after Badr, the victory that epitomized oppressed Islam rising against its foes with the help of Allah. When Egypt and Syria staged their joint attack against the Israelis in 1973, they called it "Operation Badr," and all Muslims understood.

The year after Badr, the Quraish sought revenge. They counterattacked with 3,000 men. Muhammad organized a defense on a slope at Uhud, north of Medina, but his troops were defeated when archers on the flank left their posts, apparently fearful that they would be cut out of the booty. Muhammad himself was wounded in the rout.

Then in one of those unaccountable blunders that fill the pages of military history, the Meccans withdrew after the battle instead of entering Medina, failing to press their advantage. Perhaps they believed that the defeat they had administered to the Muslims would suffice, but the result was to leave the community of the faithful intact and to leave Muhammad's authority over the Muslims unchallenged. Far from losing control because of the defeat, Muhammad chastised his followers for their weakness and laid down regulations for the division of the spoils in future engagements, which were not long in coming.

The Quraish sent another expedition northward in 627. Muhammad foiled it by ordering a trench dug around Medina. When the Meccans withdrew their siege after this Battle of the Trench, the nature of the military struggle between the two communities changed. The Quraish were never again able to challenge the Muslims at Medina, and the initiative passed to Muhammad, who resumed his efforts to implant Islam in the sacred city.

Between skirmishes with the Quraish, Muhammad pressed his campaign against the Jews of Medina. The olive branch that he had held out to the Jews in the early days of Islam, when he still believed the Jews would accept his message as a continuation of their own beliefs, he withdrew in disillusionment. He saw them as treacherous, supporting the Quraish and violating their charter with the Muslims. The Jews not only rebuffed his message, they also ridiculed him. Muhammad retorted that they had corrupted and rejected their own scriptures. Koranic revelations spoke of the Jews in harsh terms.

In the Koran, God says, "Because of their iniquity, we forbade the Jews good things which were formerly allowed them; because time after time they have debarred others from the path of Allah; because they practice usury—though they were forbidden it—and cheat others of their possessions." (4:160) Respect for Jews as "people of the book" gave way to excoriation and contempt; the Koran denounces the Jews as blasphemers and corrupters, and even associates them with pagans as the strongest enemies of Islam. (5:85) "Those to whom the burden of the Torah was entrusted and yet refused to bear it" says the Koran, "are like a donkey laden with books." (62:5)

Two of the three Jewish tribes of Medina were expelled from the city. The third, the Qurayza, supported the Quraish during the Battle of the Trench, and when that engagement ended, the Muslims extracted a terrible vengeance. All the men, six hundred to eight hundred in number, were beheaded; the women and children were sold into slavery. That is one of the few recorded incidents of its kind in the early history of Islam; the Prophet preached tolerance and compassion, not blood lust, and generally conquered groups were treated with mercy. The mass execution of the Jews of

Medina is justified by Muslim commentators on the ground that they had not only rejected Islam but actually conspired against the Muslims in violation of a solemn agreement. In effect, Muhammad made a distinction between the religious teachings of Judaism, which he professed to admire, and the actions of the Jews who lived around him, to which he responded with violence. That is roughly analogous to the distinction made by most contemporary Muslims between Judaism, for which they profess respect and Zionism, which they abhor.

After the Battle of the Trench and the elimination of Jewish opposition, events moved swiftly, as Muhammad felt himself strong enough to challenge the Meccans. Rather than undertake direct military confrontation, he devised a political strategem.

He and a large band of the faithful, said to number more than a thousand, set out for Mecca not as an army but as pilgrims desirous of visiting the sacred shrine. As the Muslims approached the city, the Meccans sent out a delegation to negotiate with Muhammad. The outcome was a pact known as the Treaty of Hudaibiya. Muhammad and his followers agreed to put off their pilgrimage until the following year, and the Meccans acknowledged their right to make it. The Quraish accepted Muhammad's right to preach and in effect acknowledged his legitimacy.

This diplomatic compromise upset some of Muhammad's more zealous followers, but it demonstrated once again that Muhammad was a flexible pragmatic leader, not a fanatic. He was willing to see blood shed when necessary, as at Badr, but he was also willing to negotiate and compromise to minimize violence, as he did when he agreed to the Treaty of Hudaibiya, which served his objectives to establish himself and Islam in Mecca. The pact with the Meccans was evidently seen by members of other Arabian tribes as authorization for them to embrace Islam, and it is said that more people then did so than had accepted the faith in all the preceding years of Muhammad's mission.

The treaty was signed in 628. The following year, as agreed, Muhammad and some of the Muslims did make the pilgrimage. They spent three days in Mecca, and by all accounts the citadel of idolatry began quickly to crumble when confronted with the power of Islam. The Muslims won some illustrious converts who had formerly opposed Islam.

Among them was Amr ibn al-As, who a few years later was to conquer Egypt in the name of Islam.

Muhammad's was not a mission of half measures or partial successes. He wanted Mecca. Though the Muslims and the Meccans were technically at peace under the terms of Hudaibiya, Muhammad either believed that the Quraish violated the agreement or perhaps concocted some breach of the treaty to justify a decisive confrontation. According to Bernard Lewis, "The murder of a Muslim by a Meccan for what appears to have been a purely private difference of opinion served as a *casus belli* for the final attack and conquest of Mecca."

In January, 630, Muhammad assembled an army of 10,000 men and marched on Mecca, where he met little resistance, either because the Meccans finally accepted the message of Islam or because they bowed to superior numbers. The Quraish were undone when their leader, Abu Sufyan, embraced Islam and threw in his lot with Muhammad. The Muslims marched into the city, and Muhammad personally directed the destruction of the pagan idols in the Kaaba. He himself is said to have wrecked the wooden image of a pigeon that was hanging from the shrine's roof.

The ascendancy of Islam in Arabia was assured, if not yet complete. It was manifest that Islam was the true religion of Allah. How else could the scorned upstart Muhammad and his few persecuted followers have overcome not only the Quraish but also the power of all the tribal gods and all the idols of the Kaaba? It was just as Muhammad had been saying all along; the power of the true God would reveal itself, and when it did, all the false gods would crumble. With the acceptance of Allah and of Islam by the Meccans and the neighboring tribes, Muhammad's mission was nearly complete.

The occupation of Mecca appears to have been a model of mercy and charity. Muhammad pardoned most of his foes, and if they embraced Islam, he shared with them the tribute that began to flow in from tribes of the peninsula who submitted to Muhammad's temporal authority, if not entirely to his creed. The Prophet preached tolerance, equity, and piety, and he evidently practiced what he preached. The brief time remaining in Muhammad's life was devoted mostly to consolidating details, such as the exclusion of non-Muslims from the holy places—a rule that is still enforced by the government of Saudi Arabia—and a ban on visiting the shrines except in proper raiment. Those who accepted Islam were welcomed into the faith; those who did not were excluded from power and booty, but not killed or exiled.

Historians say there is evidence that Muhammad would next have directed his attention northward from Medina, to begin the dissemination of Islam outside the Arabian peninsula, but he had not long to live. In February, 632, he undertook a last pilgrimage to Mecca. On the Plain of Arafat he preached a farewell sermon still admired by Muslims for its virtuous tone and effective delivery.

He reminded the faithful, "Ye shall have to appear before your Lord Who shall demand from you an account for all your actions." And he told them again, "Know that all Muslims are brothers. Ye are one brotherhood; no man shall take aught from his brother unless by his free consent. Keep yourselves from injustice. Let him who is present tell this to him who is absent. It may be, that he who is told this afterward may remember it better than he who has now heard it."

With that final restatement of his message—remember Allah and the Last Judgment, shun injustice, spread the word, and embrace all Muslims as brothers—Muhammad's mission was completed. He returned to Medina and died there in the arms of his favorite wife, Aisha, on June 8, 632.

Muhammad's Character

The historical details of Muhammad's career, remarkable as they are, reveal little about the character of the man. They are a testament to his courage and determination, but they do not lead to unarguable conclusions about his virtue or his motivation. Muhammad was probably not the perfect individual of flawless character and transcendent virtue revered by Muslims. Who could be? But he certainly was not the mad, licentious heretic and opportunist described in much Christian commentary.

In an unflattering biography published in 1921, R. F. Dibble said that Muhammad's character was "a fusion of the furthest limits of charlatanism, demagoguery, bombastic egotism and general intellectual incompetency with the opposite extremes of willing martyrdom, unaffected simplicity and sincerity, and lightning flashes of divine poetry." But could the work of a demagogue, charlatan, and intellectual incompetent have survived and prospered for more than a thousand years, inspiring uncountable millions of followers and guiding an entire culture?

It seems safe to say that Muhammad was sincere, dedicated, courageous, generous, compassionate, and committed to social justice and reform. The uncritical admiration of him that one hears from ordinary Muslims however, overlooks the evidence that the Prophet was also sometimes vengeful, spiteful, and duplicitous. He was, after all, human and ambitious too.

Among many Western commentators, who until recent times seem to have been motivated largely by hostility toward Muhammad and a desire to discredit him, the Prophet has a reputation of being a voluptuary, based on his many marriages. Muslims reject this characterization.

It is true that Muhammad spurned asceticism. The Koran teaches Muslims to enjoy fully those pleasures of life that are permitted to them. Muhammad certainly did not teach Muslims to refrain from the enjoyment of sex, nor did he do so himself; but his attitude toward women was hardly one of unrestrained hedonism.

Living in a society where plural marriages were common and casual sex with slave-girls was taken for granted, Muhammad was monogamous until after Khadija died. Among the (at least) eight other wives he had later, some were the widows of companions who had fallen in battle, women who needed care and shelter and were taken into the Prophet's establishment out of kindness. But charity was not the only stimulus. Aisha, daughter of Abu Bakr, whom Muhammad married late in life, is said to have been a virgin with whom he had a physical relationship, and his marriage to his cousin Zainab provoked an outright scandal.

Zainab was the wife of Zaid ibn Haritha, Muhammad's adopted son, one of the first converts. Zaid divorced her and Muhammad married her, a violation of custom that required a Koranic verse to justify it: "When Zaid divorced his wife, We gave her to you in marriage, so that it should become legitimate for true believers to wed the wives of their adopted sons if they divorced them. Allah's will must needs be done. No blame shall be attached to the prophet for doing what is sanctioned for him by Allah." (33:37)

Muslims argue that Zainab always preferred the Prophet and never wanted to be married to Zaid in the first place. But even if we assume the worst about this incident—that Muhammad defied taboo and abused his power to steal a woman who belonged to a loyal follower—one stain ought not to negate a life's work marked by respect for women and efforts to improve their legal and social standing. Muhammad imposed rules limiting polygamy, restricting divorce, and providing for the care of divorced women, all major reforms in the context of seventh-century Arabia.

Few men have left so great a mark on history as did Muhammad. He exercises direct daily influence over the lives of the approximately one billion people who follow his faith and over the policies of their governments. In a public career of just over twenty years, he established a major world religion that flourishes thirteen hundred years later. He espoused the principle of a community of the faithful united by their beliefs, which transcend tribal, ethnic and family loyalties. He instilled the virtues of mercy, justice, integrity and self-restraint into a pagan society that placed little premium on any of them. And he left the Koran, the revealed book, guide, beacon, inspiration, law, and consolation to the Muslims who would follow him.

Chapter 3

The Koran

THE GLORIOUS KORAN, the Holy Book of Islam, the religion's fount of faith and giver of law, is not easy to read. Especially in translation, where it inevitably lacks the compelling resonance and subtlety of the Arabic, it seems disjointed, repetitive, and stylistically inconsistent. Its 77,934 words (as counted by Philip Hitti) are punctuated by references to historical events and by oblique asides about Muhammad's own life that are meaningless to the uninitiated reader without some commentary or guide to the text.

When the text asks, for example, "Have you not considered how Allah dealt with the army of the Elephant?" the answer is that God sent a plague of birds to pelt this army with stones of baked clay, but there is no explanation of what army is being discussed. (105:1) The reader must learn from other sources that the reference is to the campaign of Abraha, the Christian ruler of Abyssinia, who invaded Arabia about the time of Muhammad's birth and marched on Mecca, only to be foiled by a plague that destroyed his army.

The Koran is often didactic and tediously detailed; it is seldom amusing. It recounts—in different form from that of the Jewish scriptures—the stories of Moses, of Joseph and his brothers, of the sacrifice of Abraham, of Noah and the flood, and of the destruction of Sodom, but the use of narrative is exceptional. The Koran generally lacks the dramatic stories and stirring tales of heroes and miracles that enliven Jewish and Christian scriptures.

But the Koran—or, in the more accurate transliteration, Qur-an (which means "recitation")—is comprehensible in its context, and needs no apology. It is the essential core of Islam. To Muslims, it is the literal word of God, handed down directly from the Creator to man through Muhammad. The Koran is unchanged and unchangeable since it was transmitted. Muhammad died, and all other creatures will die, but Allah and the Koran are eternal.

As the word of Allah, the Koran is the source of doctrine, law, poetic and spiritual inspiration, solace, zeal, knowledge, and mystical experience. As the wellspring of the Arabic language, it is the model of linguistic purity and stylistic elegance. Committed to memory by schoolchildren, recited on every important occasion, it is a ubiquitous spiritual and cultural force, unequivocal, chastening, comforting. In a religion that spurns statuary, tabernacles, and images, the Holy Book is the physical symbol of the faith, illuminated by calligraphers and carried on dashboards by cab-drivers.

American children who are taught in school that the Koran is the "Muslim bible" are misled. The Koran purports to be the successor and continuation of the Jewish and Christian scriptures, incorporating their teachings in a new revelation that gave the people of Arabia an enlightenment previously accorded only to Jews and Christians. But the Bible was written by men, in several languages, and compiled by men over many centuries. Some Christians reject entire books as spurious, and of course Jews reject the entire New Testament. Muslims believe the Koran was not written by man but dictated by God. It was uttered by one man, the man chosen by God to transmit His word, in a single language in just over twenty years.

The Koran is the only divine scripture in Islam and is self-contained, not subject to addition. There could be no Koranic equivalent of the elevation to scriptural status of the letters of St. Paul. All Muslims accept all verses of the standard text, which has existed unchanged in its original idiom since the seventh century. The Book, rather than any person, is the earthly manifestation of the Divine existence. It is not written by divinely inspired humans but reproduced from God's original text—in Hitti's words, "an exact replica of a heavenly prototype."

The Arabness of the Koran is stressed in the text. The purpose of the revelation to Muhammad, it says, is to bring to the polytheistic, pagan Arabians an understanding of the true God and of His inexorable judgment in order that they might change their evil ways. The Arabians, like the Jews and Christians before them, were to have a divine book, even if they chose to reject its message or disobey its commands, as the Koran says Jews did in falling away from the Torah.

"We have revealed the Koran in the Arabic tongue that you may grasp its meaning," the text says. "It is a transcript of Our eternal book, sublime, and full of wisdom." (43:2) And again: "This is revealed by the Compassionate, the Merciful; a book of revelations well expounded, an Arabic Koran for men of understanding. It is good news and a warning." (41:1) And again, "The Book of Moses was revealed, a guide and blessing to all men. This book confirms it. It is revealed in the Arabic tongue to forewarn the wrongdoers and give good news to the righteous." (46:12)

Because of these verses stressing the Arabic language of the revelation, and because the linguistically rich, poetic style of the Arabic is almost impossible to reproduce, Muslims have traditionally resisted the translation of the book into the many tongues of the non-Arabic faithful. Christian missionaries learn local languages in order to translate the Bible into them; Muslims recite the Koran only in Arabic. Islamic education stresses the learning of Arabic as the key to reading the Koran, rather than adaptation of the Koran to the vernacular.

Most of the world's Muslims today, though, are not Arabs and cannot read Arabic. Religious authorities in the non-Arab countries have had to make some concessions to that reality. In schools and libraries, they use translations, usually accompanied by the Arabic text in adjacent columns or on facing pages. Arabic only is used in communal prayer and in public ceremonies. The translations are for instructional purposes, not for devotional ones. These translations are usually called "interpretations." The translators acknowledge that they cannot reproduce the style, grace, or linguistic richness of the original, and in any case the Koran, having been handed down by God in Arabic, cannot actually be translated, Muslims believe.

The earliest translations into English were made from the Latin and the French, not from the original Arabic text. The work was done by scholars and by debunkers of Islam, not by admirers or supporters of the faith, and Muslims have long chafed at what they regard as the inaccuracies and distortions built into European language and English editions of the Koran. A. Yusuf Ali, in the preface to his translation prepared at Lahore in the 1930s, calls it incomprehensible that the eighteenth-century translation of George Sale, based on a Latin text that had been "carefully selected and garbled" by the Italian Maracci to "give the worst possible impression of Islam to Europe" should have been so long accepted as the standard edition of the book in English. (Sale's was the translation used by Edward Gibbon in preparing his *Decline and Fall of the Roman Empire*, to give but one example of its influence.) Maracci, says Ali, "was a learned man, and there is no pretense about the object he had in view, *viz.*, to discredit Islam by an elaborate show of quotations from Muslim authorities themselves." To protect the integrity and reputation of the Koran and of Muhammad, Muslims began to prepare their own translations into English in the early years of the twentieth century, always adding the disclaimer that the Koran, by its divine nature and the uniqueness of its language as the literal word of God, cannot actually be reproduced in any tongue but Arabic.

During prayers at the mosque, at public events, and on television, Koranic verses are recited in Arabic, whatever the local language. The verses are not merely read or spoken; they are chanted by men who spend years studying their art. Any traveler in the Middle East who turns on a radio or television set quickly becomes familiar with the unique sound of the Koran as it is chanted in slow cadence and high, quavering tones by a robed *imam* or *mullah* holding his hands up to his ears in a ritual posture. These recitations convey the power and allure of the verses even to those who cannot understand the words. The sounds, if not the literal meaning, form a cultural bond among Muslims as the Latin Mass once did among Catholics.

Koran recitation is an established profession, the members of which have an international association and review one another's credentials. Many of the reciters are blind, especially among the older generation in poor countries such as Egypt, because memorization and recitation of the Koran constituted one of the few trades open to the blind. In modern times, the best and most popular reciters have become rich through command performances, television appearances, and tape recordings. Egyptian television sponsors Koran-reciting contests for young boys, and a promising career awaits the winners.

Islam's Arabian origins and Muhammad's mission of bringing revelation to the people of Arabia are reflected in the Koran's Arabic language and in the uniquely Arabian vision of Paradise that the Koran promises to believers.

On the bleak Arabian peninsula, an unforgiving landscape of sun, sand, and rock, where the oasis and the date palm meant life itself, what could be more appealing than the promise held out by the Koran of "gardens watered by running streams," rich in fruit? The reward of the believers will be an abode in gardens of palm trees and fruit, shade and cool water, where they will be adorned with silks and brocades and drink from silver goblets, attended by "dark-eyed virgins." Even now, in an Arab world vulgarized by vast wealth and crude politics, men of integrity ask for no more; the Koran teaches that all the wealth and power of this world will avail the sinner nothing on the Day of Judgment.

In keeping with the Arabian tradition, the Koran originated not as writing but as recitation. Muhammad did not write down what he heard from the angel or preach from a text. He communicated orally, speaking to different people at different times, though often about the same subjects. That helps to explain the repetitiveness of the written compilation that was made later—certain formulas about Allah, the Last Judgment, prayer, and the authenticity of the message naturally had to be reiterated as the audience changed. The effect is similar to that of formula repetition in Greek epic poetry, which was also rooted in oral tradition. In place of "rosy-fingered dawn," the reader of the Koran finds "gardens watered by running streams," or "Allah is forgiving and merciful," phrases and themes that recur throughout the text.

In uttering each revelation as it came to him, Muhammad was without any text of the earlier revelations to which he could refer. Even if such a transcription existed, he could not have read it if, as the Koran says, he was unlettered. Since the revelations came over a twenty-year period in changing circumstances, it is not surprising that there are inconsistencies in the text compiled after Muhammad's death.

Critics evidently reproached Muhammad for saying different things at different times, especially since he claimed to be relaying the word of Allah, but the Koran explains, "If We abrogate any verse or cause it to be forgotten, We will replace it by a better one or one similar. Do you not know that Allah has power over all things?" (2:106) In other words, who are you, mortals, to question the word of Allah?

Muhammad was interested in results, not in rigid adherence to unenforceable dicta, and the Koran reflects the pragmatism that characterized Muhammad's public career. The consumption of wine, for example, is first tolerated, then discouraged, then banned, the last step coming only when Muhammad's moral authority in the community is well established.

Compilation of the Text

No text of the revelations was compiled in Muhammad's lifetime. He established Islam as a new religion of the Book, but at his death there was no Book—only fragments of what Muhammad had been heard to say, scribbled on bones and skins and recorded in the memories of men.

Disputes arose almost immediately about what Muhammad had actually said. As those who had known or heard the Prophet began to die or to be killed in the wars by which the new faith was spreading, it became apparent that an authentic text would have to be established that all believers could accept, a text that contained all the divine revelations as distinguished from the human utterances of Muhammad the man. The task was begun under Abu Bakr, the first caliph, or successor to the temporal authority of the Prophet, but not completed until the time of the third caliph, Uthman (644–656).

A committee headed by Zaid ibn Thabit, a Medinese who had been Muhammad's secretary, gathered all the fragments of text and memory extant, collecting pieces of parchment and bone on which verses had been recorded, and produced a text which the Caliph, Uthman, proclaimed official. All others were ordered destroyed. This work of Zaid and his associates remains the only and unchallenged version of the Koran, never to be revised, exempt by its divine origin from the tinkering to which the Bible has been subjected. Because the book is taken to be the literal revealed word of God and because it is the foundation of the Arabic language, it is not to be "modernized," simplified, revised, or updated. The textual integrity of the book—whether lovingly illuminated in gilt-edged works of art or smudgily printed in cheap mass-produced copies—is the strength of the religion, familiar and unchanging, identical from West Africa to China. When the novelist Salman Rushdie suggested in *The Satanic Verses* that a scribe had taken advantage of Muhammad's illiteracy to tamper mischievously with God's revelation, the collective outrage of the faithful was not surprising.

The text consists of 114 *suras,* "chapters," which vary in length from three verses (three lines of English text) to 286 verses (more than thirty pages of English text). Each *sura* has a brief title, which may refer to its subject matter ("Man," "The Cataclysm," "Joseph," "Divorce") or may be just a word to which an allusion is made in the text ("The Fig," "The Cow," "The Pen," "The Greeks," "Light").

Zaid and his associates evidently devoted their editorial efforts to ensuring the accuracy of each individual *sura* by interviewing believers who had heard Muhammad and checking differing versions against this testimony. They did not compile *suras* in any logical order, or at least not in any order readily apparent to the reader. They generally placed the longest *suras* first and the shorter ones at the end, without regard to subject matter, date, or relationship to the events in Muhammad's life. Literalists argue that the order of the *suras,* as well as their content, was dictated by God. They claim to find thematic and stylistic consistency in the traditional arrangement but for the nonspecialist, the standard arrangement by length is only confusing.

It obscures the clear stylistic difference between the lyrical, inspirational *suras* of Muhammad's Meccan years and the prosaic, lawgiving *suras* of his Medinese period. It also tends to discourage new readers, because the longer *suras* are more mundane and specific in subject matter and less exalted, stirring, lyrical, and universal than the shorter, Meccan *suras.* In the traditional arrangement, the *sura* that comes first after the opening invocation is "The Cow," the longest and perhaps most difficult, ranging over the story of Adam and Eve, God's warnings to the Children of Israel, the story of Moses, God's covenant with Abraham and Ishmael to sanctify the Kaaba, the placement of the *qibla,* the prohibition against eating pork, the Ramadan fast, the pilgrimage, and the rules for divorce. To the uninitiated reader, it seems a dismaying jumble.

To surmount those problems, Western translators have tried to rearrange the *suras* in chronological order, and the standard English translations issued by commercial publishing houses generally use the chronological sequence, in which "The Cow" comes near the end. Putting the verses in approximately chronological order shows how the Koran evolved in style and subject matter to reflect the course of the Prophet's life. A pattern emerges from the erratic changes of theme and inconsistencies of style that seem to characterize the traditional text. The early, shorter *suras* evoke the preacher of mystical revelations in Mecca, exhorting unbelievers to acknowledge the one God and the certainty of His terrible judgment. The longer, didactic, later *suras* reveal the Commander of the Faithful in Medina, handing down laws, admonitions, and rules of social behavior to a community that has already accepted Islam.

Throughout the text, there are verses that justify and authenticate the revelations, often by challenging unbelievers to produce a better book if they reject this one.

Other verses serve to rationalize actions in the Prophet's life that drew criticism from his opponents. Besides the *sura* putting a curse on Abu Lahab and the one giving divine approval to his marriage to Zainab, there is a *sura* validating some of his other marriages, another approving his violation of the traditional month of truce, and another calling down punishment on gossips who spread a scandalous tale about his wife Aisha. (24:11) One entire *sura,* number 66, is described by scholars as a justification for Muhammad's failure to keep a promise to another wife, Hafsa, that he would refrain from dallying with a Christian slave-girl. Muslims see these passages not as manipulation of revelation on the part of the Prophet for his own purposes but as continuing signs of God's special favor to Muhammad, His chosen messenger.

The Koran defines itself. It is "a book in which all things are written." (50:4) It is "a scripture revealed since the time of Moses, confirming previous scriptures and directing to the truth and to a straight path." (46:30) It is "no invented tale, but a confirmation of previous scriptures, an explanation of all things, a guide and a blessing to true believers." (12:111) It "could not have been composed by any but Allah. It confirms what was revealed before and it fully explains the scriptures. It is beyond doubt from the Lord of the Creation." (10:37)

Despite its disjointed format, this "explanation of all things" does present a cohesive picture of the universe and man's place in it. All matter, all creatures, and all events are part of God's divine work. Nothing in the cosmos is accidental, and no order of being determines its own place in the cosmic scheme. Man is the highest of God's creatures, free to use and enjoy the fruits of the earth, but he is still subject to Allah's absolute will and must exercise his privileges within the limits set by Allah.

God has manifested His divine power in every function of the universe, as man can see if he will contemplate the signs abundant in nature. Man knows what God expects of him, because he has been told in a series of prophecies and revelations. But mankind is weak and inconstant, compelling God to send plagues and disasters upon the earth to correct its errors. Kings and empires, cities and temples have been brought down by God's wrath, and a similar fate awaits all those who ignore His message. The message is transmitted by prophets—Abraham, Moses, Jesus, and finally Muhammad—who are tested by adversity and scorned by men but vindicated by Allah in testimony to the truth of their message.

The revelations of the Koran are presented in a style usually described as rhymed prose. The verses are not metrical, but they generally end with rhymes or similar sounds. Read aloud in the Arabic, the Koran commands attention and is more powerful in spiritual impact than the mere meaning of the words can convey.

It was on the Night of Qadr that Allah sent down the first revelation to the Arabians through Muhammad. "We revealed the Koran on the Night of Qadr. Would that you knew what the Night of Qadr is like! Better is the Night of Qadr than a thousand months. On that night the angels and the Spirit by their Lord's leave come down with His decrees. That night is peace, till break of dawn." (97)

Though it is not known which revelations actually came first, the "decrees" and commands from God that began on the Night of Qadr, in the standard Arabic text, start with the Exordium, the opening, the Mother of the Book. The first chapter is instilled in every schoolchild's memory and repeated at every session of prayer: "In the name of Allah, the Compassionate, the Merciful. Praise be to Allah, Lord of the Creation, the Compassionate, the Merciful, King of Judgment-day! You alone we worship, and to You alone we pray for help. Guide us to the straight path, the Path of those whom You have favored. Not of those who have incurred Your wrath, nor of those who have gone astray."

That opening phrase, "In the name of Allah, the Compassionate, the Merciful," which also introduces each subsequent chapter of the Book except the ninth, may be the most recited group of words in the history of language. In the Muslim world it is in constant use, not only on religious occasions.

Public officials begin speeches with it. Officers use it in exhorting their troops. It is imprinted at the top of official documents in Egypt and chalked on blackboards in Saudi Arabian classrooms. Radio announcers open news broadcasts with it. Throughout the Middle East the sound of the Arabic—*bismillah ir-rahman ir-rahim*—is to the ear what the minaret is to the eye, a link in the chain of Islamic brotherhood, a sound as familiar and comforting as a father's reassurance.

The revelations of the Holy Book are laid out in a variety of styles, techniques, and expository approaches, which can be illustrated with a few examples.

> By the Fig, and by the Olive!
> By Mount Sinai, and this inviolate land!
> We moulded man into a most noble image and in the end We shall reduce him to the lowest of the low: except the believers who do good works, for theirs shall be a boundless recompense.
> What, then, can after this make you deny the Last Judgment?
> Is Allah not the best of judges?

That is Sura 95, one of the early Meccan *suras,* showing the evocative, lyrical style and the emphasis on the inevitable judgment that characterize the early chapters. The judgment is described many times, in imaginative and apocalyptic terms, like this: "On that day the heavens shall become like molten brass, and the mountains like tufts of wool scattered in the wind. Friends will meet, but shall not speak to one another. To redeem himself from the torment of that day the sinner will gladly sacrifice his children, his wife, his brother, the kinsfolk who gave him shelter, and all the people of the earth, if then this might deliver him." (70:8)

As Muhammad preached to the Meccans, the Koran often took the form of instructions to him from Allah on how to answer the questions and arguments of the unbelievers: "They question you about the Hour of Doom. 'When will it come?' they ask. But how are you to know? Your Lord alone knows when it will come. Your duty is but to warn those that fear it." (79:42)

In the later Medinese *suras,* rules and regulations for the community are handed down, unembellished by rhetorical flourishes: "Believers, kill no game whilst on pilgrimage." (5:98) "Do not usurp one another's property by unjust means, nor bribe with it the judges in order that you may knowingly and wrongfully deprive others of their possessions." (2:188) "You shall not wed pagan women, unless they embrace the faith." (2:221)

Long passages are devoted to precise rules concerning inheritance, divorce, and slavery. The text specifies, for example, "A male shall inherit twice as much as a female. If there be more than two girls, they shall have two-thirds of the inheritance; but if there be one only, she shall inherit the half. Parents shall inherit a sixth each, if the deceased have a child," and so on, through other family situations and degrees of consanguinity. (4:11)

Neither the beliefs of Islam nor the rules of behavior for the community are codified in the Koran. They probably could not have been codified, given the oral development of the revelations and the Prophet's changing circumstances. But in the aggregate, the verses of the Holy Book are sufficient to their purpose. They tell the believers what they need to know about God, judgment, Paradise, and sin. They tell Muslims what to do and what not to do to find favor with Allah. They tell Muslims what to think about everything from war to menstruation. And they establish the practices of devotion, prayer, and pilgrimage that still define Islam in the modern world, practices that are largely the same after thirteen centuries of schism, war, and theological disputation as they were when the Koran was first compiled.

While the Koran imposes unequivocal rules and obligations, it also encourages intellectual and scientific inquiry—

inquiry which, the Holy Book says, will surely result in reaffirmation of Allah's truth.

During the long centuries when the Islamic world was mired in intellectual torpor, doctrinal rigidity, and obscurantism, Westerners generally seem to have believed that these were inherent characteristics of Islam. But the political and technological advances made by Muslim societies in this century show that that is not the case. The Koran gives ample scope for intellectual exploration of natural phenomena and for scientific study, if not for systematic philosophy.

The Holy Book is dotted with passages such as this, on The Bee: "From its belly comes forth a fluid of many hues, a medicinal drink for men. Surely in this there is a sign for those who would give thought." (16:69) The same *sura* invites men to contemplate how it is that the cow gives milk and the date palm gives food and the rain gives life to the parched earth. Signs of God's truth can be found, the Koran says, in the wind, the clouds, and the crops, if man will but study them.

Many contemporary Muslims urge the acceptance of that challenge. Rather than opposing scientific inquiry and technological development as inconsistent with revelation, they argue that study will demonstrate the existence of a cosmic order of which the creatures and objects on earth form only a part and which can be understood only in the context of a supreme being. If the Koran invites men to study the phenomena of nature and to enjoy what God has given them on earth, how then can it be wrong to do so?

This new outlook is seen in practice in the technological revolution stimulated by oil wealth that has occurred in Saudi Arabia in the past twenty-five years. The physical appearance of the country has been transformed and life revolutionized by desalination plants and computers and microwave communications systems and air-conditioned pickup trucks, but the society remains firmly Islamic in purpose and law. Islam provides continuity, stability, and reassurance in the face of overwhelming change.

In Libya, which was one of the most backward of Muslim countries at the time of the 1969 revolution that overthrew the monarchy, Qaddafi has devoted long passages of his speeches to arguing that Islam is not incompatible with technical progress. In Egypt, President Sadat, whose world outlook was otherwise totally different from Qaddafi's, modified the constitution to adopt "science and faith" as the official motto of the state. In his view, now prevalent in the Muslim world, the Koran shows that it is not necessary to reject the one in order to embrace the other.

The use of the holy text to make convenient political or legal points is an irresistible temptation to Muslim leaders. While all Muslims accept the authority of the Koran, they do not all agree on the meaning of each passage and can find a verse to justify any public policy. The Koran's meaning is not absolute. The text says of itself, "Some of its verses are precise in meaning—they are the foundation of the Book—and others ambiguous. Those whose hearts are infected with disbelief follow the ambiguous part, so as to create dissension by seeking to analyze it. But no one knows its meaning except Allah." (3:7)

Commentaries on the Koran

The injunction against debate over ambiguous passages did not inhibit the development of Koranic commentary as a scholarly discipline or the creation of a vast library of textual analysis, which examines the Koran historically, etymologically, mystically, and legally. There is hardly a word in the text that has not been pored over by scholars seeking to wring from it the last drop of significance, real or imagined.

The first commentator is said to have been the Prophet himself. Muhammad heard that one of the faithful was literally sitting up at night during the month of Ramadan, holding before his face a white thread and a black one, in order that he might pray and begin his fast at the very moment when he could tell them apart, as the Koran prescribes. Muhammad said that was not necessary. What the Koran meant was the "thread" of black and white light that appears in the sky at early dawn. Recorded examples of Muhammad's explanations of Koranic passages are included in the compilations of his sayings that form one of the foundations of Koranic law.

It is understandable that scholars would seek to fathom obscure references, such as that in Sura 83 to a place called Illiyun where the "register of the righteous" is kept. But commentary for its own sake, commentary that obscured rather than illuminated, overwhelmed useful intellectual endeavor. So much legend was attached to the Koran in the guise of analysis that the greatest commentators, such as ibn-Jarir al-Tabari (838–922), had to devote much of their energy to weeding out what the Koran did not say before explaining what it did say. Of Tabari it is related that he was asked to expound upon the question of how much money Joseph's brothers received when they betrayed him. He replied that since the Koran does not give the amount, it is irrelevant, and time should not be wasted trying to figure it out. Taha Hussein, the greatest writer and educator of modern Egypt, recalled in a memoir that his boyhood at Cairo's al-Azhar (pronounced AZ-har) was consumed by endless lectures about one generation's commentaries on the previous generation's glosses on the commentaries of antiquity on the Koran, its grammar and its rhetorical style—a sterile curriculum that led him to support the establishment of Egypt's first secular university.

Commentary is still a staple of the religious curriculum and religious debate. As Fazlur Rahman notes, "whatever views Muslims have wanted to project and advocate have taken the form of Qur'anic commentaries." Fortunately for the people of Islam, however, the traditional scholars have no monopoly on the Koran. Anyone can read it. Its verses were revealed through Muhammad to ordinary folk who lived in the workaday world, not to learned specialists, and the text still provides guidance and lyrical inspiration to the most humble of people, the people who represent the vigorous and living faith.

Chapter 4

Law and Government in Islam

THE BASIC principle of Islam that emerges from the Koran and from Muhammad's life is that the religion is based upon behavior as well as belief. To be a Muslim is to believe in God, the prophecy of Muhammad, and the Last Judgment; but it is also to live in a prescribed way. The soul's submission to God's supremacy has its indispensable earthly counterpart in the individual's submission to God's code of conduct.

Islam tells its adherents not only what to believe about God, angels, and the afterlife, but also how to live on earth in such a way as to find favor with God. Within the principles of social justice, communal peace, and individual dignity, Islam lays down rules governing daily life, commerce, the family, and society that are the basis for the common observation, "Islam is more than a religion, it is a way of life."

Because the spiritual beliefs and the specific rules are equal parts of the faith, there is no distinction in Islam between doctrine and law or between church and state. At least in theory, Islam is all-encompassing. No thought, act, contract, or relationship is beyond its scope. Christ's injunction to "render unto Caesar the things that are Caesar's and to God the things that are God's" is alien to Islam—in fact, its opposite. In the words of Bernard Lewis, "Such pairs of words as Church and State, spiritual and temporal, ecclesiastical and lay had no real equivalents in Arabic until modern times, when they were created to translate modern ideas; for the dichotomy which they express was unknown in medieval Muslim society and unarticulated in the medieval Muslim mind."

Muslim rules of conduct and social action are based on the Koran and on the *sunna,* the true path or way of the

Prophet, which consists of the words and deeds of Muhammad as remembered and recorded by his followers. The precepts are incorporated in a body of law called *sharia,* translated by Fazlur Rahman as "the path or the road leading to the water, i.e., a way to the very source of life." *Sharia* is the code of law based on religious principles that regulates the conduct of all Muslims, a code that covers social, commercial, domestic, criminal, and political affairs as well as devotional practices.

The Koran, which was handed down by God, and the *sunna,* which was fixed by the life of the Prophet, are unchanging, but *sharia,* which is made by men, evolves with history. While the Koran and the *hadith,* the written record of Muhammad's pronouncements, which is the foundation of the *sunna,* are elaborately specific on some points, such as the rules governing inheritance, they are vague and sometimes contradictory on others, such as the kind of government an Islamic society should have. The issues that were left undefined, either because Muhammad had no occasion to address them or because they were unknown and unanticipated in seventh-century Arabia, have been the subject of a continuous and frequently unsuccessful effort to codify *sharia* in a way that all believers would accept. Islamic jurisprudence, which attempts to apply *sharia* to specific situations, must by its nature change with time and circumstance, and therefore is as subject to dispute and disagreement as any other jurisprudence.

Fazlur Rahman defines *sharia* as "the assembly of Divine imperatives to man, imperatives which are frankly admitted to be primarily of a moral character. The *sharia* is thus not an actual code of particular and specific enactments but is coterminous with the 'good.' " Technically, *sharia* is not the same thing as jurisprudence, legal science, or legislation, but as a practical matter the word is commonly used even by Muslims as synonymous with Islamic law, including all its sources and its subsidiary principles and disciplines. A call for a return to *sharia* means a return to a legal system based on the Koran.

All Muslims recognize the existence of *sharia* and the five broad categories into which it divides human conduct: required, encouraged, permissible, discouraged, and prohibited. But Muslims disagree over the details, over which acts and practices should be grouped in the middle category—

should divorce, for example, be considered "permissible" or "discouraged"?—and they disagree over the extent to which *sharia* is applicable in a modern nation-state.

In the absence of any central doctrinal authority in Islam—there is no Supreme Court of *sharia*—individual Muslim countries have tailored *sharia* to their own purposes and found room within its principles for their own customs. Just as there is no one book that comprises *sharia,* so there is no one formula for the application of *sharia* in running a modern country.

In Saudi Arabia, *sharia* is the only code of law and the only constitution (though even there administrative regulations are issued by secular authorities to deal with activities that have no religious implications, such as traffic rules or entry visas). In Egypt, the constitution, a European-style document adopted by parliament, was amended in 1979 to make *sharia* "the basis" instead of "a basis" for legislation. The change upset the country's Christian minority but had little actual impact on government; the administration of justice is in the hands of civil courts enforcing secular law, because *sharia* courts were abolished in Egypt under Nasser. In Iraq, *sharia* has been subordinated to secular law and the doctrines of the ruling party. In Turkey, government policy since the Kemalist revolution has excluded *sharia* entirely from the state's legal and administrative codes; Turks are Muslims, but the Turkish state is secular. Morocco, Jordan, and Saudi Arabia are monarchies that claim to be based on Islamic principles and traditions, but many Islamic scholars and legists believe that *sharia* actually prohibits hereditary rule.

Said Ramadan, in his book *Islamic Law,* notes that the existence of *sharia* as an integral part of the Islamic faith does not mean that most Muslims in the contemporary world are governed by it. Most, in fact, are not, in the sense that the constitutions and laws of most modern post-colonial countries are derived from or mingled with European legal traditions. But *sharia* is neither a dead letter nor an abstraction. It provides a measuring stick by which the faithful judge the performance of their rulers. Islamic concepts of morality and justice are rooted in *sharia,* so that even when *sharia* is not formally incorporated into a state's legal system, the state must coexist with it. Political appeals in the name of *sharia* are difficult to ignore, because *sharia* by definition represents justice, and it is politically risky for the ruler of any Muslim society to act in violation of what his people understand *sharia* to require. The usual test is one of compatibility: Is this action or that rule or this other new program compatible with the principles of *sharia?* The introduction of mechanized farming, for example, is clearly compatible; but what about the introduction of birth control or organ transplant surgery?

Muhammad laid down general principles to which Muslims should adhere, such as honesty and modesty. But he did not legislate in the abstract. He dealt with specific situations as they arose, rather than laying down broader rules. Pagan Arabians, for example, practiced infanticide, killing baby girls, so Muhammad prohibited it. They did not practice euthanasia, so Muhammad did not rule on it. The Arabians frequently quarreled over the division of spoils from caravan raids, so Muhammad regulated them. In the absence of rivers, they did not quarrel about water rights, so they are not dealt with, except through the general statement of the principle of social justice and equity.

Nor did Muhammad try to ban practices so deeply ingrained in the society that attempts at suppression would have caused rejection of his entire message. He was a practical man, who sought to convert his contemporaries, not merely lecture to them. Just as our own courts avoid issuing orders they lack the power to enforce, Muhammad refrained from banning slavery and polygamy outright, because many in the community would not have obeyed him. The Koran discourages those practices, but it does not prohibit them.

Therefore, in the interpretation of contemporary, liberal Islamic scholars, laws based upon the Koran and upon Muhammad's life and words are liberating, not confining, banning only what must clearly be banned. According to this school of thought, which is now dominant, Islam does not prohibit for the sake of prohibiting. Islam permits, in accordance with God's command, and therefore is not the narrow, restrictive force in life that it was made to be for centuries. In this view, a small number of activities, specifically dealt with in the Koran and the *hadith,* clearly fit into one of the four limiting categories of human behavior. Prayer is required, forgiveness of debt is encouraged, polygamy is discouraged, usury is prohibited. But most human activity is grouped into the fifth, neutral, category, neither required nor prohibited, and therefore decisions about it are left up to the individual or the society.

According to A. K. Brohi, the Pakistani legal expert who wrote the introduction to Ramadan's treatise, Islamic law evolved from the few precepts handed down to untutored semi-primitive Arabs into a sophisticated code of law because scholars have interpreted the Koran and the *sunna* as guidelines, not as a closed book from which no deviation is permitted. These guidelines have enabled Islam to develop as the world developed, its legists applying the principles of the religion to situations and concepts beyond the imagination of Muhammad's contemporaries. In doing so, they have of course exposed themselves to differences of interpretation and to vigorous dissent, but they have saved the religion from fossilization. Their work represents Islam's best effort to tell the faithful what the Koran or the Prophet would have decided if called upon to judge new subjects and changing societies.

The view that *sharia*—and therefore Islam itself—is flexible and culturally adaptable has not always prevailed. For centuries *sharia* was a reactionary, introspective discipline, the main purpose of which seemed to be to insulate Muslim societies from the modern world. In the words of Fazlur Rahman, "The actual legislation of the Koran cannot have been meant to be literally eternal by the Koran itself . . . very soon, however, the Muslim lawyers and dogmaticians began to confuse the issue and the strictly legal injunctions of the Koran were thought to apply to any society, no matter what its conditions, what its structure and what its inner dynamics."

The modernist view is that *sharia* is and must be an evolving code rather than an immutable set of rules. Contemporary arguments dwell less on whether *sharia* is flexible than on how to apply its principles to new situations, given that *sharia,* as a code of laws embodying the right way for a Muslim to live, must exist. Since Muslims generally believe that although God is omniscient and everything happens according to His will, the ultimate fate of the individual is not predestined, the religion must provide a code that tells each person how his faith requires him to act.

Predestination and Fatalism

The question of predestination is as old as the faith. In the eighth and ninth centuries it was taken up by a group called the Mutazilites, who held that predestination, the idea that man's fate is fixed before his birth, was irreconcilable with doctrine of divine justice and mercy. They said that God was only essence, without the human attributes of knowledge or will; therefore in the domain of moral action, it was up to men to determine rationally—with the aid of revelation—what was good and to act accordingly. They also rejected the dogma that the Koran was the uncreated word of God, coeternal with Him. The Mutazilites said that view compromised the oneness of God.

In the ninth century the Caliph al-Mamun elevated Mutazilism to the status of official creed. He proclaimed that the Koran had been created by God and was not coeternal with Him. The test of orthodoxy was the answer to the question whether God created all things, including the Koran. A "no" answer brought torture and imprisonment, and the Caliph decreed that all judges must subscribe to the new doctrine. Mutazilism, which originated in rationalism, thus manifested itself as illiberal and repressive, and after al-Mamun's death his successors repressed it as vigorously as he had imposed it. The argument over the eternality of the Koran is of little relevance to the practice of ordinary Muslims today; but it shows the extent to which Islam, basically a straightforward and unequivocal faith, has undergone the same process of self-analysis as Christianity. The issues of rationalism and spirituality, divine omniscience and human freedom, have never been finally settled.

Many passages in the Koran can be taken to mean that the fate of every individual is sealed from the moment his soul is created:

> Every misfortune that befalls the earth, or your own persons, is ordained before We bring it into being. (57:22)

> We have made all things according to a fixed decree. We command but once: Our will is done in the twinkling of an eye. (54:49)

> Say: 'Nothing will befall us except what Allah has ordained. He is our Guardian. In Allah let the faithful put their trust.' (9:51)

Islam has struggled to reconcile this belief that God has foreknowledge and that all events on earth occur in conformity with a divine plan with the instructions of the Koran and the Prophet to do good works and live virtuously to find favor with Allah. In short, if everything is predestined, why make the effort? Ahmad Galwash, the Egyptian scholar, says the companions of the Prophet put this question to Muhammad himself.

"Since God has pre-appointed our places, may we confide in this belief and abandon our religious and moral duties?"

He replied, "No, because the righteous will do good works and the wicked will do bad works."

This dialogue has its counterpart in an Arab tale about a man who, traveling with Muhammad, asked as they stopped for the night, "Should I tether my camel, or trust in God?"

Muhammad replied, "Trust in God—and tether your camel."

It has often been suggested that the backwardness and stagnation that afflicted the Muslim world between the fall of Baghdad to the Mongols in the thirteenth century and the renaissance of the twentieth century resulted from a collective fatalism and indifference, which grew out of belief in predestination. But that fails to explain why Muslims today are not fatalistic, indifferent, or intellectually backward. The Iraqis who nationalized the oil fields and the Egyptians who took over the Suez Canal were Muslims, like their ancestors, but not inclined to leave the fate of their national resources in the hands of Allah; they trusted in God, but they tethered their camels. The Koran teaches submission to the will of Allah, but it also teaches that God will not change the fortune of a people unless they change it themselves.

The more probable cause of the backwardness of the Muslim world over centuries was the venality and corruption of the rulers, the brutality of successive conquerors, and the economic and cultural disruption caused by the Europeans' discovery of a seaborne trade route around Africa, leaving western Asia isolated from the traditional invigorating influences of trade and cross-cultural contacts.

The vitality of Islam in this century demonstrates that fatalism and passivity are hardly inherent. A taxi driver given an address or a secretary making an appointment will respond, as the Koran commands, "*Insha'allah*," "If God wills it." But the submissive Arab who accepts any misfortune with a resigned sigh of "It is written" and the reactionaries who oppose long-range planning because it implies lack of trust in the divine order have been overtaken by events. The prevailing view is that belief in divine order and will does not relieve a society of the obligation to better itself or the individual of his obligation to lead a virtuous life. At the Last Judgment, each person is to be held accountable for his own life, and *sharia* embodies the standards by which that judgment will be made.

"Things do not happen haphazardly," says Muhammad Abdul Rauf in *Islam: Creed and Worship,* but according to a divine order that regulates the workings of the universe as it regulates the "harmonious functioning" of the parts of the human body. It is "not correct" to say that Muslims are fatalistic. "If fatalism means the acceptance of every thing or condition as inevitable, and assumes an attitude of apathy, or implies a denial of human freedom, it is certainly something different from our concept of 'qadar,' " or the workings of the universe according to God's predetermined order. "God's foreknowledge of what we shall do is not inconsistent with human freedom."

God has foreknowledge of everything, and no earthly power can control His judgment, but the Koran teaches that each individual still has the responsibility to act, to do, to live in obedience to God's command. "Each soul is the hostage of its own deeds. Those on the right hand will in their gardens ask the sinners: 'What has brought you into Hell?' They will reply, 'We never prayed or fed the hungry. We engaged in vain disputes and denied the Day of Reckoning till death at last overtook us.' " (74:38)

Even if the fate of a man's soul is predetermined, he has no way of knowing what that fate is, and therefore it behooves him to strive for Allah's favor. While on earth, he has freedom of choice and he is obliged as a believer to exercise that freedom in accordance with God's law, embodied in *sharia.*

"A sinful man," writes Galwash, "can on no account shun the moral responsibility for his deeds, on the plea of having acted upon irrevocable divine predestination, of which he was totally ignorant . . . Belief and faith in divine predestination can neither necessitate denial of human consciousness of freedom of will, nor eliminate the factor of individual responsibility from human conduct."

The individual Muslim is sustained in adversity by the belief that whatever has happened or will happen is in accordance with God's master plan; but he still faces the duty to live, work, and conduct his social and commercial life in obedience to God. Through *sharia,* he knows what God requires of him. The details missing from the general precepts of the five pillars of the faith may be filled in by *sharia.*

The first source of *sharia* is the Koran. While the Holy Book is not a legal document and makes no attempt to codify its commands and prohibitions, its pronouncements on many points were incorporated into Islamic law: Give correct weight in trade; give debtors extra time to pay; punish both partners in a homosexual relationship; enlist witnesses when entering into contracts; do not commit adultery; do not gamble; do not eat pork; do not give the feeble-minded custody of money.

The second source of *sharia* is the *sunna,* or way of the Prophet: What did Muhammad do in such a situation? What did he say? What did he tolerate by his silence?

As military commander, ruler of the community of the faithful in Medina, husband, preacher, legislator, and judge, Muhammad left behind a body of actions and sayings, which are used as examples by later generations of Muslims seeking to follow the virtuous path. The precepts of the *sunna* are extra-Koranic and therefore not directly attributable to God's command; but the Prophet is believed to have been a man of total virtue and integrity whose actions always accorded with the divine will. Therefore, in the absence of a specific Koranic instruction, Muhammad is to be emulated.

The Example of the Prophet

The principle of following Muhammad's example is laid down in the Koran itself. The principle was useful to Muhammad's followers because it gave them guidance about how the Holy Book's instructions were to be carried out. The

Koran, for example, instructs the believers to pay the alms-tax, but it does not say how much or to whom. The answer is to be found in the *sunna.*

Muhammad said, "Let him who is present carry this to him who is absent" and his command was obeyed. Thus, his family and other companions recorded his sayings, instructions, and proclamations—the *hadith*—which are the basis of the *sunna* and second only to the Koran as the source of doctrine and practice. But while all Muslims accept the Koran as one immutable unit handed down by God, about the authenticity of which there can be no question, debates about the authenticity of various *hadith* have been going on since the beginning of Islam. Some Muslims accept only those sayings and traditions traceable directly to Muhammad and members of his family, others accept those traceable to the Prophet's companions.

An elaborate set of standards was developed for examining purported sayings of the Prophet and for sorting out the genuine from the spurious. In orthodox, or Sunni, Islam, six books of *hadith* are generally accepted, all compiled in the first three centuries after Muhammad's death. The two considered most trustworthy are those of al-Bukhari, who is said to have validated only seventy-five hundred sayings or traditions out of the half-million that he studied, and of Muslim ibn al-Hajjaj. Each saying that was accepted is said to be traceable in a direct line to someone who heard it from Muhammad or saw what the Prophet did. Putative *hadith* that were perceived to conflict with basic tenets of the Koran, such as those that promised earthly as opposed to heavenly rewards for good deeds, were excluded. The personality and motivations of the narrator were also examined.

In compilations of the *hadith,* the name of the source or authority upon which the authentication rests is included with each saying, as in this: "On the authority of Abu Hamza Anas Ibn Malik (may Allah be pleased with him), the servant of the messenger of Allah (may the blessings and peace of Allah be upon him), the Prophet said: 'None of you truly believes until he wishes for his brother what he wishes for himself.' It was related by al-Bukhari and Muslim."

Other examples of the Prophet's sayings, reproduced in Kamil Avdich's *Survey of Islamic Doctrine,* are:

> You may recognize a hypocrite by three distinguishing qualities: when he speaks, he does not tell the truth; when he promises anything, he breaks his promise; and when you trust him, he betrays you.
>
> Every Muslim has six obligations toward his fellow Muslim: he greets him whenever they meet; answers his call; wishes him well when he sneezes; visits him when he is ill; follows in his funeral when he dies; and wishes for him what he wishes for himself.
>
> The strong man is not the one who knocks people down; the truly strong man is the one who can control himself in anger.
>
> Whatever you dislike doing in front of people, do not do it when you are alone.
>
> God has no mercy for those who have no mercy for their fellow-men.

The *hadith* provide useful moral and social guidance. They are indispensable in applying the principles of the Koran to daily life and thus in the development of *sharia*. Study of the *hadith*, the Koran, commentaries on the Koran, and Arabic, is the foundation of the curriculum at the *madrasas* (religious schools), where Muslim boys learn the precepts and traditions of the faith to carry them back to their homes and villages. Through those students, the Prophet's words are a living presence in the Islamic world.

Revelation ceased with the death of Muhammad. The community of Muslims grew rapidly, however, expanding out of western Arabia into Asia Minor and Africa within a few decades, and assimilating societies, customs, and intellectual experiences that were never addressed in the Koran or in the *hadith*. It was obviously necessary to adjust the body of rules and laws to encompass those new realities. Since religion and the state were the same in Islam, the religion had to adjust as the state expanded. The law had to evolve. Since the Koran was fixed and the guidance of the Prophet no longer directly available, the Muslims developed secondary sources of law, on which they relied when no specific Koranic verse or *hadith* was available. These secondary sources are human, not divine, in origin. Law based on them must conform with the Koran, but it is still man-made law and thus not immutable. Over many centuries of Islamic intellectual decline, *sharia* based on these sources came to be regarded as absolute and inflexible, as if handed down like the Koran itself, but modern reformers have reestablished the principle that law can be amended as circumstances change.

Other Sources of the Law

The secondary sources of law, as given by Said Ramadan and other Muslim writers, are *ijma* and *qiyas*.

Ijma means consensus or unanimity. It refers to the principle that believers cannot agree on error; if the members of the community accept some point of rite or doctrine, that is Islam. This principle can be traced back to the Koran and to the Prophet himself. In the early centuries of Islam, it was used to validate practices of peoples who came into the faith that were not authorized by revelation but too deeply ingrained to be uprooted. Later *ijma* came to mean agreement not of the community at large but of the *ulama,* or learned scholars and doctors who represented the religious authority of a given country.

Qiyas is reasoning by analogy, in which principles or rules clearly laid down in the Koran or the *hadith* are applied to matters that seem similar. Since the Koran prohibits the drinking of wine, for example, *sharia* by extension prohibits the drinking of all alcoholic beverages. The Koranic ban on usury becomes, by analogy, a ban on sharecropping.

The application of *qiyas* by an individual is called *ijtihad,* (individual reasoning). It has been recognized since the time of the second caliph as a source of decision-making by believers in cases for which there is no applicable Koranic text and no precedent in the *sunna.*

Ijtihad represents intellectual freedom in Islam. The gradual retreat of Islamic religious scholarship into pedantic hair-splitting and stultifying reaction is viewed by modern commentators as synonymous with "closing the gates of *ijtihad.*"

With the rejection of *ijtihad,* the *ulama* became custodians of dogma. Legal formalism became entrenched. The self-appointed guardians of consensus converted a process of intellectual expansion in early Islam—the development of *sharia* through reasoning—into a tool of doctrinal absolutism controlled by precedent, ushering in long centuries of stagnation that marked the decline of Islamic thought and Islamic power.

Contemporary Muslim writers such as Fazlur Rahman and Muhammad Nowaihi of the American University in Cairo recognize that Muslim theology and thought decayed and ossified over several centuries. In their view, the more closely the *ulama* held the right to interpret and analyze, the more rigid Islamic thinking and law became. They attribute the intellectual decline to many causes. One such cause was the early argument over the eternality of the Koran, which drove traditional thinkers into rigid positions. Another is the destruction of Baghdad and the Abbasid Caliphate (see Chapter 5). That catastrophe focused the work of the *ulama* on preserving social cohesion in a time of turmoil and thus discouraged the intellectual innovation that had been a hallmark of the religion.

The legal scholars, like the custodians of any discipline, tended toward rigidity and formalism anyway, because that enhanced their status in the community. With the collapse of the Abbasid Caliphate, which represented the zenith of Muslim cultural achievement, Islam turned inward, closing itself off from new ideas, and remained in that posture until the "gates of *ijtihad*" were reopened by reformist thinkers and modernizers in the nineteenth century. *Ijtihad* does not mean each person is free to do or think as he pleases; it means that Muslims need not address new issues according to rigid old formulas.

The Schools of Law

Even at its most inflexible, *sharia* was never monolithic. There have been since early Islam different schools of law, accepting the same general principles of faith, but differing on details of practice and on intellectual and theological issues. The schools are not mutually exclusive, and Sunni Islam considers them equally legitimate.

The four principal schools of law that have survived to the present day are: Hanafi, named for Abu Hanifa (died 767),

Maliki, named for Malik ibn Anas of Medina (died 795), Shafi'i, founded by Muhammad ibn Idris al-Shafi (died 820), and Hanbali, named for Ahmad ibn Hanbal (died 855).

As a practical matter, it makes little difference to the ordinary worshiper which school is prevalent among the legal scholars and ritualists of his town. At al-Azhar in Cairo, the greatest center of Muslim learning, students and teachers from all four schools have traditionally worked together. Yet there are differences in approach to important theoretical problems. The Shafi'i school, for example, accepted the technique of establishing law by *ijma* and found *hadith* to justify it, while the Hanbali school rejected *ijma* and resorted to *qiyas,* in Philip Hitti's words, only in "rare cases of sheer necessity." The Hanafi school is described as tolerant of the exercise of individual opinion, while the Shafi'i school subordinated it to the principal sources of doctrine, namely the Koran, the *hadith, ijma,* and *qiyas.*

Outside the learned academies and doctoral dissertations, these schools are only variations on a universal religion, their differences embodied in variations of ritual that are of negligible spiritual significance. M. A. Rauf gives these examples as they apply to the ritual of ablution before prayer. The Shafi'i and Hanbali schools do not regard semen emitted by a male as a pollutant that must be washed away before prayer, but the others do. The Maliki school exempts a newly wed bride from the requirement of immersing her head in the bath that must precede prayer if she has had sexual intercourse.

The schools differ on technical points of prayer rituals. During congregational prayer on feast days, practitioners of three schools recite the phrase "prayer unites the worshipers together." The Maliki school rejects that pronouncement. During prayers for the dead, which all schools require, *imams* of the Maliki and Hanafi schools stand opposite the shoulders of a female corpse and at the abdomen of a male one; in the Shafi'i and Hanbali schools, the positions are reversed. The Maliki permit the prayers to proceed as long as the body of the deceased is somewhere in the room; the others require that the body be in front of the mourners. For Friday congregational prayers, the minimum number of adult males who must be present is three in the Hanafi school, twelve in the Maliki, forty in the Shafi'i and Hanbali.

To dismiss these as trifling distinctions that mean little to the ordinary peasant or factory hand going about his prayers is not to minimize the earnestness with which they have been debated by Muslim legists and scholars. Vast libraries have been filled with learned treatises on the origins of the schools, on the authority of the various sources of law and doctrine, and on the details of ritual. If Islam had a Papacy or a College of Cardinals or a format for holding doctrinal conferences such as those of Nicaea or Trent, these matters might have been settled as they arose. But since there is no such central authority the arguments went on, creating a kind of academic growth industry in Islam that has little to do with the fundamental tenets of the faith.

The absence of a central authority in the religion does not mean that the religious leaders of the community do not try to guide or control the believers. In any country, the leading Islamic authorities—the *ulama,* the Minister of Religious Affairs, the senior religious judges, theology professors, Koranic scholars—give sermons, address the faithful on radio and television, publish newspaper and magazine articles, and teach classes designed to instruct Muslims about the issues of the day as well as about the principles of the faith.

The Friday religious sermon is a staple feature of Arabic newspapers. The degree to which the sermon deviates from the government line on any given point is a function of the degree to which the government controls the press and the religious authorities. In general, the learned elders who have access to space in the newspapers and time on television are those who can be counted on to cooperate with the government in power. If, for example, a government is committed to nationalization of industry, the religious leader authorized to preach on state-owned television and write in state-owned newspapers is likely to find that Islam endorses state ownership. His counterpart in the next country, a private-enterprise regime, can be expected to conclude the opposite.

This is not to question the sincerity of Muslim religious leaders, though Islam no doubt has as great a share of sycophants and opportunists in its leadership as does any other religion. But Islam is a flexible creed, and there is room for different interpretations; the religious leaders have vast influence and they have to use it judiciously. If they withdraw or withhold their support from any regime or policy, they can create an unstable situation in the country, and that is not done lightly.

Because each nation sets its own rules for the extent to which religious considerations will affect its policies (making the distinction between church and state that Islam theoretically eliminated), the *ulama* have almost no real power as an international group.

In 1977, the Second Islamic Ulamas Conference met in Cairo for twenty-six days and issued the predictable recommendations: that *sharia* be enforced in Muslim countries, that a uniform Islamic constitution be drawn up to serve those countries seeking to implement *sharia,* and that Islam should defend itself against communism. Politically it was a sterile exercise; the resolutions were printed in some newspapers and that was the end of it. But *sharia* itself and the *ulama* as a body have a higher function. They represent the collective religious conscience of the community, and the ruler of any country is well advised to maintain at least the appearance of harkening to the *ulama*'s counsel. The *ulama* are not clergy; they cannot excommunicate. But they can obstruct and agitate if a ruler embarks on a course clearly incompatible with Islam. They themselves can be the targets of repression if they refuse to give their endorsement of some policy when the ruler asks it, and they can be the targets of agitation from the public if they show themselves too compliant with a regime that espouses un-Islamic policies.

From time to time the religious authorities will issue a *fatwa,* a legal decision or opinion that represents their view on some controversial point that is not before the religious courts. In 1964, when the religious authorities and princes in Saudi Arabia concluded that it was necessary to depose the ailing King Saud, the *ulama* ratified the palace coup that installed Faisal as king by issuing a *fatwa* declaring it to be in the public interest. A more recent example was provided by the Grand Sheik of Cairo's al-Azhar mosque and university. When President Sadat signed the Camp David peace agreement with Israel, the Grand Sheik issued a *fatwa* endorsing the accord and saying that it conformed with the principles of Islam. Many Muslims believe that it did, but the credibility of the Grand Sheik had to be weighed against his position as a presidential appointee whose salary is paid by the state. The *fatwa* was useful to Sadat in protecting him against criticism at home, but it did little for him outside his own country. Egypt was promptly banned from international Islamic conferences.

Law and Government

The importance of *sharia* lies in the relationship between religious and secular law in the modern state and the extent to which one forms the basis for the other. Except in Saudi Arabia, where in theory *sharia* is the only law, generally what has happened is that a *de facto* distinction has developed by which *sharia* principles apply to family matters and form the basis of a society's moral code, while purely secular matters are left to secular governments. *Sharia* is the moral basis of society; where no moral questions are raised, *sharia* is applied only to the extent of ensuring that secular laws do not conflict with it. Nothing in the Koran or the *sunna* is directly applicable to such contemporary problems as industrial pollution and traffic control, so regulations for those matters can be set according to nonreligious criteria. To conform with Islamic law, the regulations must be just, equitable, and imposed after consultation with the community, but there is considerable leeway within those standards.

How do these balances of interest work in practice? The answer varies from country to country. On this question, as on most others, it is impossible to generalize about Muslim societies.

In Egypt, during the 1970s, religious conservatives mounted a campaign against alcohol, demanding that *sharia* be applied to outlaw the consumption of beer, wine, and hard liquor. But Egypt as a practical matter is not in a position to impose such a ban. Tourism is a major industry, and the government tries to do nothing that would discourage visitors. Besides, since the nationalization of Egyptian industry in the 1960s, the state has owned the breweries, wineries, and distilleries, which provide jobs for thousands of workers. After much debate in parliament and the press, a tacit agreement was reached. The government accepted the enactment of legislation that confined the public consumption of alcohol to establishments designated as tourist sites, which meant hotels and Western-style restaurants in Cairo, Alexandria, Luxor, and Aswan. The practical effect was negligible, since ordinary working Egyptians seldom drink alcohol anyway, but the principle of deference to *sharia* was reaffirmed.

In Saudi Arabia, the sale of life insurance is still banned, because it is often thought of as betting on human life, which *sharia* prohibits. But the rush of oil wealth and the boom in commerce have forced the Saudis to make some adjustments on other issues. Banks, for example, are barred from charging interest, which is perceived as a violation of the Koranic ban on usury; but they are allowed to charge a "commission" on loans and to take a percentage of equity in projects being financed. Some practical distinctions have developed between matters that are within religious jurisdiction and those that are not. Civilian police investigate traffic accidents and determine responsibility, but the Saudis leave it to the *qadis,* or religious judges, to determine the amount of compensation to be paid to the victims' families. The custom of compensation predates Islam. It originated in tribal law centuries before the motor vehicle was dreamed of, but it was incorporated into *sharia* and thus is still applicable.

Saudi rulers have shown themselves politically adroit at working within *sharia* to encourage technological innovation and commerce, which they support, and to discourage political innovation, which they find threatening. In Egypt, political parties were banned for many years as corrupt and disruptive, but in Saudi Arabia they are banned for ostensibly religious reasons, as a violation of the Koranic injunction against divisive sects. That is a motivation less open to debate and more durable than the purely political motivation employed in Egypt under Nasser. Conversely, the Saudis have brought matters essential to the flow of commerce —immigration, civil service, social insurance—out of the purely religious sphere and into the area of administrative regulations. These are called rules rather than laws, to avoid conflict with *sharia*'s exclusive claims, but it is a distinction without a real difference. The effect is to take crucial matters out of the jurisdiction of the religious establishment.

Abdul Aziz, the first king of modern Saudi Arabia, showed how to use religion to validate technological innovation when he persuaded the *ulama* to accept the satanic invention, the radio. He did it by arranging for a reading of the Koran over the air. If the instrument could accurately disseminate the holy word, the *ulama* ruled, it must be permissible.

Modernization meant bringing in foreigners—non-Muslims. Abdul Aziz imposed that too on the *ulama* by turning religious argument to his advantage, overriding the objections of the traditionalists in order to encourage oil exploration.

James P. Piscatori, in an essay in the anthology *Islam and Development,* reports uncovering a story that shows how the King worked his will. When an elder named Abu Bahz criticized him for yielding to the inducements offered by the infidel Americans, the King invited him to make his accusations publicly at the royal court. Abu Bahz did so. Then, as reported by an American diplomat, "The King left his throne seat and stood beside Abu Bahz and said, 'I am now not the King, but only a Muslim, like you a servant of the prophet, Abdel Aziz, appealing for judgment to the ulama, the judges of the Islamic law which binds us both equally.' . . . Showing a thorough knowledge of the prophet's life and traditions, the King cited several well-attested cases when the Prophet employed non-Muslims individually and in groups. 'Am I right or wrong?' The judges replied unanimously that he was right. 'Am I breaking Sharii law, therefore, when I follow in the footsteps of the prophet and employ foreign experts to work for me? The Americans at el-Kharj and other foreigners who operate machines are brought here by me and work for me under my direction to increase the material resources of the land and to extract for our benefit the metals, oil and water placed by Allah beneath our land and intended for our use. In so doing, am I violating any Muslim law?' The judges returned a verdict of not guilty."

In countries more diverse and politically complex than Saudi Arabia, religious issues cannot be resolved by dramatic performances on the part of the ruler.

Malaysia, which is only about half Muslim, has been grappling for years with the issue of *khalwat* (close proximity between the sexes). The word actually means sexual relations between unmarried men and women, a frequent occurrence in Malaysia's urban slums, but evidently it is also sometimes applied to mere proximity, or circumstances that could lead to sexual relations. *Khalwat* is prohibited not just by the religious authorities but also by the laws of the Malaysian states, with punishments of a month in jail or a fine of about $100 (U.S.). The questions that stir vigorous political debate are whether the state should enforce this prohibition and whether the ban should be applied to non-

Muslims. The country's highest court ruled in 1962 that it did not apply to non-Muslims, but the issue is revived periodically, especially during the sporadic outbreaks of religious agitation, when the country's Muslims press for the imposition of *sharia* on the entire nation.

In Nigeria, according to S. S. Richardson in the anthology *Islam in Africa,* at the time of independence the question arose of what kind of criminal code was to be applied in the country's northern region, where Muslims predominate. In the colonial era, matters of criminal justice, personal status, and family life had been within the jurisdiction of the local "native courts," which were religious tribunals that judged according to *sharia.* But nations must govern. What was acceptable under British rule was not conducive to the development of national unity. Independent Nigeria did not want one code of laws for one group of citizens and another for the rest.

In search of a legal system acceptable to Muslims and non-Muslims, the regional legislature in Northern Nigeria in the 1950s sent panels of prominent citizens to Libya, the Sudan, and Pakistan, three other post-colonial Islamic nations, to examine their legal systems.

"Upon their return," Richardson writes, "these missions reported that conflict in criminal matters was avoidable by the adoption of a secular code uniformly applied to all classes of the population irrespective of tribe, race and creed, and that such a code was acceptable to the Muslim majority provided that it did not offend the injunctions of the Holy Koran and Sunna. Diversity, however, was the rule in family matters in mixed communities and in general Islamic law governed such matters for the Muslim majority."

Called upon to put this principle into practice, another panel of distinguished Muslims, including non-Nigerians, recommended that neither religious law nor the British-inspired Nigerian Criminal Code be imposed. They suggested the adoption of a uniform penal code and code of criminal procedure based on the so-called Sudan Code. While not specifically Islamic, it could be guaranteed by the religious authorities on the panel not to contain anything that conflicted with *sharia*. Eventually a modification of the Sudan Code was adopted, but only after long negotiations with the *ulama* on its provisions governing capital punishment, other forms of traditional *sharia* penalties such as lashing, and the applicability to non-Muslims of the ban on alcohol.

In murder cases, for example, "The admission of grave and sudden provocation as a mitigating factor was conceded only after the learned intervention in person of the Mufti (or religious judge) of the Sudan, who invoked the support of Maliki texts which referred to the killing of adulterers in the heat of passion," Richardson said.

It would probably not be difficult for a Western-trained secular lawyer to write a commercial code and inheritance law that are, like the Sudan Code, not specifically religious but still in conformity with the spirit of *sharia.* In commerce, the Koran requires fair trading and honest weight. Debts are to be recorded in writing, along with the date repayment is due, and scribes should record the agreement. In case of dispute, it is prohibited to bribe the judges.

The Koran is even more specific and detailed on questions of estates and inheritance and on the fiduciary responsibilities of orphans' guardians. Like other principles of Islamic law, these are not merely legal requirements; they are divine requirements. The law is the religion, and vice versa. Like Jewish law and Christian canon law, Islam holds that it is indeed possible to legislate morality; violation of the law is sin.

Those entrusted with the care of orphans must protect their property, holding it in trust for them until they are of marriageable age. If a guardian is rich, he should pay for the orphan's care with his own funds; if he is poor, he should use only as much of the orphan's inheritance as is necessary to raise the child. To steal the property of an orphan or betray that trust is a serious offense.

As for inheritance, Chapter Four of the Koran lays down rules as to how an estate is to be divided in almost every combination of family circumstances. Women, whose property rights are guaranteed in Islamic law, are entitled to their share of every estate. If a man and woman stand in the same degree of kinship to the deceased, the man's share is twice as large as the woman's, but that is not necessarily to her disadvantage. Her share is entirely her own, but if she is unmarried, the law requires him to take responsibility for her support.

Since inheritance rights and portions are spelled out in the Koran, it is often argued that land reform laws of the kind imposed in Egypt under Nasser and in Afghanistan before the Soviet invasion are un-Islamic; they interfere with the dictates of the religion. That may be so, but the political requirements of the state took precedence over *sharia,* as often happens.

Criminal Law

It is when Islamic law moves out of the fields of commerce and inheritance into personal conduct, family life, the status of women, and criminal conduct that it becomes more difficult for non-Muslims to understand it. Of all the elements of Islam that have inspired contempt and fear among Westerners, those parts of the law dealing with criminal conduct and the status of women have seemed most alien to us. Yet Muslims credibly defend their traditions on these matters, holding to them as a source of social strength, moral firmness and family cohesion. If Islamic law is harsh and retributive, it is probably no more so than our own, and our distaste for the apparently inferior status of women in Islamic law often fails to recognize the very real rights and protections accorded to women in *sharia*—rights broader, in many cases, than those women had until recently in many American states.

One reason the government of Saudi Arabia and many other Muslims objected to the British film *Death of a Princess,* which depicted the execution of a princess for marrying a commoner, is that it perpetuated the Western stereotype of Islam as some kind of barbaric force that lives on cruelty and retribution, extracting blood from innocents in the name of Allah. The execution of the princess, apparently on the insistence of a powerful uncle in the ruling family, embarrassed many Saudis when it occurred. The film, with its images of a sexually-repressed society steeped in cruelty and suspicion, was clearly an exaggeration, as I can attest after several visits to the country. To Muslims seeking understanding in a world community long dominated by European concepts of justice, however, the film was a nasty setback.

The Koran, like the Torah from which many of its principles derive and like our own criminal codes, does command "retaliation" for murder and it calls for flogging for adultery and maiming by cutting off the hand as punishment for theft. In practice, not only today but historically, the so-called traditional penalties have rarely been carried out; courts have interpreted the requirements for witnesses and corroborating evidence so as to spare most defendants from the maximum penalties.

The Koran was issued in primitive times to primitive peoples who were controlled more by tribal traditions than by any code of law. Putting a high value on the family and faith as the foundations of human society, the Koran proposed to deal harshly with offenses that undermined them—adultery, fornication, homosexuality, and apostasy. In establishing the community of Muslims as the source of temporal authority, the Koran gave that community the power to deal with infractions in a way that Muhammad's contemporaries would respect.

In a world of violence, it would have been futile for the Prophet to teach Muslims to turn the other cheek, but it seems clear that Islam sought to control violence, not encourage it. The Koran stresses mercy and forgiveness. It prescribes retaliation for bloodshed, but only on a one-for-one basis, not in vendetta. The family of a murder victim is entitled to "satisfaction," but it is the duty of the community to see that satisfaction is given so that it need not be taken by force. In a society where incest, infanticide, polygamy, banditry, slavery, and vendetta were common, the criminal code of Islam can be seen as one of moderation and progressive reform, not as the dark regimen of cruelty and reaction often depicted in the West. Attempts to apply it literally today, as in Pakistan, are criticized even by many Muslims as misguided because circumstances have changed.

As a practical matter, history and politics have altered conditions in the Muslim world, so that the authority of the state, backed by a written code of laws expressed in nonreligious language and often influenced by European legal models, has generally supplanted the Koranic formulas for punishment. Rapists are still occasionally beheaded, and hands might be cut off for theft, but in the worldwide community of Islam, about one billion people, such cases are extremely rare. Most Muslim countries have civilian tribunals and prisons to mete out punishment without applying the specific penalties that are prescribed in the Koran. What remains in place is the Koranic view of what constitutes sinful—and therefore illegal—conduct: murder, theft, sexual offenses, gambling, drunkenness, cheating orphans out of their patrimony, abuse of wives and slaves, dishonesty in trade, and neglect of aged parents.

There is a difference between religion and politics in Muslim countries, as there is everywhere else, regardless of Islam's claim to be an all-encompassing system. Recent history in the Muslim world has been marked by bloody incidents of drumhead justice that certainly clash with our standards of legal fairness: mass hangings in Damascus, summary executions in Iran, mass executions of suspected Communists in Iraq. Even when the forms of trial and verdict have been followed, as in the cases of the Saudi princess and Prime Minister Zulfikar Ali Bhutto in Pakistan, the result has seemed unpalatable. But these events grew out of the political context of the countries in which they occurred. They cannot be seen as examples of Islam in action, and in fact it is safe to say that many Muslims were just as distressed by them as many non-Muslims.

Muslim criminal law emphasizes the guilt of the transgressor, not the responsibility of society or the potential for rehabilitation. But the general principle is one of equity. The punishment should fit the crime and give what satisfaction is possible to the victims, and it should uphold the basic values of the Muslim community.

Individual rulers and governments behave differently. An example is made of some wrongdoers, especially if their crimes threaten the stability of the state, for example, the Communists who fomented unrest in the Iraqi army, the band of fanatics who murdered a former religious affairs minister in Egypt, and the extremists who gunned down a class of military cadets in Syria. Their crimes were serious, and their punishment was swift. So was that of the insurgent gang who seized the great mosque at Mecca in 1979. They violated the most solemn of Islamic laws by shedding blood in the holy place, and it was in keeping with the principles of Islamic justice that they be executed. In all these cases, the absence of a prolonged appeal process may have made Westerners uncomfortable, but Bhutto had an appeal process that seemed endless, and the Pakistani government was still criticized in the West for executing him.

In any case, capital punishment is hardly unique to Islam. It is doubtful that the Muslim countries collectively are guilty of more violations of the fundamental principles of justice than are non-Muslim countries, but even if they are, the reasons are more political than religious. The Koran is no more to blame than the Bible is to blame for the excesses of some Latin American juntas.

The Status of Women

There is probably no issue that has more unfavorably influenced the Western world's image of Islam or more preoccupied lawmakers in Muslim countries than the status of women. Films such as *Death of a Princess,* with its images of repressed Saudi women cruising desert highways in search of sex, and stories about apartments in Jeddah that stand empty because the builder neglected to include separate elevators for women leave indelible impressions.

No brief treatment can do justice to an issue as old as Islam. The fact that it took Egypt's parliament thirteen years to debate and enact minor changes in that country's Law on Personal Status is an indication of the complexity of the subject and the intensity of the feelings it arouses.

To understand the social pressures that wealth, communications, education, and contact with the West have created in the Muslim world, it is necessary to recognize that there is more to the Islamic view of women than polygamy and easy divorce. Rules governing the status and conduct of women in Muslim countries have their roots as much in local and tribal tradition as they do in Islam, and there is a difference between public and private conduct. I have been a guest in homes of Saudi Arabian businessmen where unveiled Saudi women mingled with male guests just as they would in London, but those same women would not appear unveiled on the street.

That it why it is difficult to generalize about the status of women in Islam. Even the casual traveler in Muslim countries can recognize that what is true of women in one country is not true of those in another and that the differences are based more on economics, education, and local custom than on religious doctrine. The robed, veiled Afghan village woman following meekly behind her husband has little in common with the woman in blouse and skirt who runs the tourist information office at Tunis airport and who chats in French and English with any traveler who approaches.

In Tunisia, Egypt, Iraq, and Somalia, women work as flight attendants on the national airlines, waiting on men and serving them liquor. Gulf Air, the airline of the Gulf Emirates, imports women from Europe to do that work. In Egypt, the universities are coeducational. In Saudi Arabia, men and women are educated separately, and women generally see male instructors only on closed-circuit television.

Inconsistency is the rule even within individual countries. In Egypt, as recently as 1976, a female cabinet minister was denied permission to board a flight to Europe at Cairo airport because she could not prove that she had her husband's consent. In Saudi Arabia, where photographs of adult females are rarely seen, foreign women were permitted to read the news on television in the 1970s. In Damascus, it is common to see a young woman dressed in European style shopping downtown with her mother, whose face is concealed behind a black veil and whose body is hidden in a shapeless, monochromatic coat.

When President Jimmy Carter visited Saudi Arabia in 1978, his wife, Rosalynn, was obliged to walk behind him when going down the airport reception line and to dine separately with the women of the royal family while the President ate with King Khalid and the princes. (The U.S. Embassy was obliged to bring in a female information officer from Sanaa, Yemen, to handle Mrs. Carter's part of the program.) Yet after dinner, King Khalid's brother Crown Prince Fahd, the country's leading political figure, received Barbara Walters and gave her an interview. The rules that say Fahd could be interviewed while the King could not and that Fahd could talk to Barbara Walters but not to Rosalynn Carter may be found in the book of Saudi protocol, not in the Koran.

An American woman journalist who is Jewish told me after she had gone to Saudi Arabia to report on a visit by Secretary of State Henry A. Kissinger that her biggest problem in Riyadh was not her religion but the shortage of toilet facilities for women. The Saudis assume that women will not be going to—much less working in—government buildings. I knew a Lebanese architect in Riyadh who designed several buildings for the Saudi government. He said his plans always included extra utility closets with plumbing that could be converted to women's rest rooms when the inevitable day came that they were needed. But even though many Saudi women now are educated and employed, the workplace still is segregated by sex.

The Koranic vision of women is both liberating and confining, uplifting and degrading. In a society in which women were possessions, taken and put aside like trinkets, often held in conditions approaching bondage, the Koran imposed rules and prohibitions that curbed the worst abuses, ensured women's property rights, and encouraged men to treat women with kindness and generosity.

Women are equal in the faith. The Koran stresses that the women of Islam have the same religious duties as men and the same hope of being admitted to Paradise, although there are exemptions from such obligations as the Ramadan fast granted to women who are menstruating or nursing.

In defining the virtuous—those who are "devout, sincere, patient, humble, charitable, and chaste"—the Koran uses the feminine as well as the masculine form of each word. (33:35) But it would be disingenuous to claim that the Koran accords women an equal place with men in earthly society. A monograph by Gamal Badawi entitled "The Status of Women in Islam," published by the Muslim Students' Association of the U.S. and Canada, makes the crucial point: "In consideration of the physiological and psychological make-up of man and woman, both have equal rights and claims on one another, except for one responsibility, that of leadership."

The Holy Book takes for granted, as indeed it had to in seventh-century Arabia, that men lead the community, fight, hunt, preach, and make law. Women raise children and tend to domestic duties. Women are equal before God and will be judged on the last day by the same standards as men; but the Koranic vision of Paradise, where the faithful will be attended by "dark-eyed virgins," is certainly one that appeals to men. The delights awaiting women are not specified.

The Koran repeatedly belittles women. Referring to the pagan association of female goddesses with Allah, the Koran says, "Would they ascribe to Allah females who adorn themselves with trinkets and are powerless in disputation?" (43:18) The Holy Book teaches, "Men have authority over women because Allah has made the one superior to the others, and because they spend their wealth to maintain them. Good women are obedient. They guard their unseen parts because Allah has guarded them. As for those from whom you fear disobedience, admonish them and send them to beds apart and beat them." (4:34) The Koran says nothing about circumcision, though Muslim boys traditionally are circumcised, but it is specific about menstruation. It is an "indisposition," and men should refrain from intercourse with menstruating women until they are "clean," just as is prescribed in Orthodox Jewish law. After women are "clean" again, men are free to have relations with their women as God instructed them. "Women are your fields. Go, then, into your fields as you please." (2:223) Women are to dress modestly, cover their finery with cloaks, avert their gaze, and reveal themselves only within the home. The Koran does not require that women veil their faces in public. Saudi Arabia imposes this restriction on women, but most Muslim countries do not. Local custom prevails.

The Koran ratified the traditional roles of men and women in society: men hunting and trading while women keep house, men strong and free, women somehow tainted by the reproductive process God created, dependent upon men, available for use upon demand. Still, the Koran's dictates on women's legal status (as opposed to their social status) were quite advanced for their time, and Islamic law gives women some rights more liberating than those found in Western legal codes.

The Koran teaches, "We shall reward the steadfast according to their noblest deeds. Be they men or women, those that embrace the faith and do what is right We will surely grant a happy life." (16:97)

Other verses are in the same spirit: there is no distinction between men and women in religious duty, and no ancestral Eve is held responsible for the imperfections of mankind. The Koran and the *hadith* laid down rules ensuring for women the respectable and dignified status that had been denied them, and they emphasized the stability of the family. Although many Muslim women now hold jobs and work in the professions, the traditional role assigned to them was domestic. As in many Orthodox Jewish communities and in most Western societies, men made the decisions and controlled the economy; women kept house, raised children, worked in the fields, and limited their employment to cottage industries. The principles of Islamic law ensure that a woman who performs her duties faithfully is ensured a life of dignity; her husband is obliged to treat her decently. The law may often be violated or ignored, but that is hardly unique to Islam.

The Koran prohibited the practice of taking mothers and other female relatives in marriage. Plural marriage was tolerated, but the maximum number of wives allowed to any man other than Muhammad was four. Divorce was permitted, but men were prohibited from casually putting women aside and taking them again and again, as they had been in the habit of doing.

Islamic law does permit a man to divorce a woman by pronouncement, saying three times, "I divorce you," but it also permits women to initiate divorce proceedings, often on more grounds than are permitted in the United States. If a woman is not supported financially, if she is abused, if her husband refuses to have relations with her or is impotent, she may divorce him.

Contrary to the general impression in the West, Islam does not encourage divorce or permit it to be undertaken lightly. In the words of the Egyptian writer Galwash, "There is no justification for permanently yoking together two hostile souls," but from the Koran he says, "It is clear that Islam discourages divorce in principle and permits it only when it has become altogether impossible for the parties to live together in peace and harmony."

Divorced women may retain their personal property and anything their husbands have given them. Whatever property the husband agreed in the marriage contract to convey must be fully conveyed if there is a divorce, even if it was not fully conveyed at the time of the marriage. This is one of many examples of the way in which *sharia* ensures women's rights over their own property. A woman's money, land, and property are her own, regardless of her marital status.

Adultery and fornication are prohibited by the Koran. In cases of adultery, the man as well as the woman is to be punished with a hundred lashes, and women are protected from reckless or unfounded accusations against them by a Koranic provision, "Those that defame honorable women and cannot produce four witnesses shall be given eighty lashes." (24:4)

Four *suras,* numbers 2, 4, 24, and 65, give in complex detail the rules governing sexual conduct, marriage, and divorce. A divorced woman must wait three menstrual cycles before she may remarry. A man who has twice pronounced his intention to divorce a woman must then either make the third pronouncement and let her go or take her back in honor—he may not leave her in suspense. Having divorced a woman a third time a man may not, under the law, remarry her unless she has married and been divorced by another man in the meantime. (To view Islam as permitting easy divorce is misleading; the cumulative effect of the regulations is to restrict what previously had been a casual practice.)

Children and close female relatives are not to be taken in marriage. Sex with slave-girls is permitted, but the slave-girls may not be sold into prostitution. A Koranic injunction against marriage to unbelievers has meant, in legal practice, that Muslim men may marry Muslim women or women from among the "people of the book," but they may not marry polytheists or pagans. Muslim women may marry only Muslim men.

Whatever the circumstances, men are cautioned to treat women with kindness and respect, and to honor all terms of the marriage contract. Men and women both are instructed to "turn their eyes away from temptation," curb their sexuality, and live modestly.

The law is equivocal on the subject of polygamy. Plural marriage was common in Muhammad's time, and as a practical man seeking to enlist converts, he could not abolish it outright, especially since he himself had nine wives, though not all at one time. The Koran permits polygamy, but in terms that discourage and limit the practice.

I once watched a rich Saudi arrive at a hotel in Damascus with his entourage: four wives, veiled, trailing dutifully behind him. The scene fitted the stereotype perfectly, but the reason I remember it is that it was actually a rarity. Polygamy is practiced in some countries, and Islamic law does permit it, but it is by no means the norm, and some Islamic countries have simply outlawed plural marriage altogether.

Countries that prohibit polygamy by legislation cannot be accused of violating *sharia;* rather than violating it by prohibiting plural marriage, they are carrying its provisions to their logical conclusion. But those apologists for Islam who say that the Koran actually prohibits plural marriage—by the famous limitation that polygamy is permitted only to those who can treat all their wives equally, and since nobody can do that, polygamy is never permitted—are on shaky ground.

The Koran says (in the Yusuf Ali translation, clearer in this passage than the Dawood), "If ye fear that ye shall not be able to deal justly with the orphans, marry women of your choice, two, or three, or four; but if ye fear that ye shall not be able to deal justly (with them), then only one." (4:3) Elsewhere the Koran says that it is not possible to treat several wives equally. But to interpret these passages as a ban on polygamy reads too much into them.

As Galwash and other commentators point out, it is not possible to believe that the Koran bans as sinful something the Prophet himself is known to have done. Galwash argues that there are times and places in which social conditions make polygamy desirable, as in Muhammad's day, when widows of slain Muslim warriors needed to be cared for in dignity. Islam limits polygamy, rather than encouraging it, but it is going too far to say that it actually prohibits the practice.

Sharia and Contemporary Society

It slanders Islam to think of it as a vengeful, primitive religion characterized by polygamy, the execution of adulterers and apostates, and the cutting off of hands. To walk the streets of Alexandria, Isfahan, or Lahore is not to enter some feverish world of scimitar-wielding vigilantes on guard against infidels and fornicators. Muslims have a well-developed sense of right and wrong, but mostly they go about their daily business like any other people, recognizing God's dominion but more concerned with putting food on the table than with punishing fornicators. The revolution in Iran made other Muslims uncomfortable precisely because of its relentless zealotry.

The Prophet said, "The blood of a Muslim may not be legally spilt other than in one of three instances: the married person who commits adultery; a life for a life; and one who forsakes his religion and abandons the community." This instruction is permissive, not mandatory. Execution for these offenses is not standard. Adulterers generally are not put to death (even when four adults can be found to testify that they witnessed the event, as required before punishment may be administered), and death for apostasy is rare—so rare that many Muslim leaders were shocked when Ayatollah Khomeini endorsed a call for the murder of Salman Rushdie, the renegade Muslim author of *Satanic Verses*. The spirit of Islamic law emphasizes justice for transgressors, equity for victims, and mercy for the unfortunate. Only unreconstructed literalists argue that justice today requires adherence to practices that applied in the seventh century.

Even when the law is specific and unequivocal it is not uniformly applied, because jurisprudence is made and changed by men and is not characterized by unanimity. It is clear, for example, that Muslims are forbidden to eat pork. But how does a modern government enforce that rule, if at all? In Saudi Arabia, no pork products are produced and none may be imported. In neighboring Qatar, the same rules apply, except that in the rear of a big supermarket there is a "pork room," where non-Muslim foreigners may shop for ham and sausage. In Egypt, swine are raised, and pork is openly sold in butcher shops. Most of the pork trade is carried on by Christians. Muslims avoid it, but not because of any action by the government.

As for apostasy, the Koran pledges punishment for it in the next world only, not on earth. In 1977, zealots in the Egyptian parliament introduced a bill to require the government to impose capital punishment on apostates, which they said was required by *sharia*. That touched off a public debate including long editorials in the newspapers, which concluded that abandonment of Islam, while sinful and reprehensible, does not require death for the apostate. If it did, there would be a bloodbath in upper Egypt, where there is a large Coptic Christian population. Christian men embrace Islam because it permits divorce, but then return to Christianity once they have shed their wives. They are apostates, but they are not executed, although in recent years they have been attacked by Muslim vigilantes.

The individual Muslim must be guided in his conduct by thc principlcs of *sharia,* which shows him how to live in a way pleasing to God. The purpose of rules and regulations devised by humans is to put those principles into practice in order that God's will be done. The rules are not an end in themselves, they are not the same in all countries or societies, and they are not carved in stone. While retaining the *sharia* rule that a man may divorce his wife by pronouncing three times his intention to do so, for example, many countries have modified it by requiring that the pronouncement be made before a judge or that the divorce be granted only on showing cause.

The era of flexibility follows a long period of absolutism, in which the art of amending the law to reflect changes in the world while conforming to the spirit of the Koran is said to have been nearly lost. Islam sometimes became an instrument of reaction and despotism, blindly opposing all change. As late as 1970, the elderly, fanatical Sultan of Oman, ruling in the name of Islam, prohibited the wearing of shoes in the vicinity of his palace and virtually prohibited education. There were only three or four schools in the entire country. But that is not Islam, it is only despotism and ignorance. A decade later, Oman had built roads, schools, and hospitals and had trained women to work in automated factories, but it was still an Islamic society. The women operating the date-packing machinery at the plant in Niswa can read now, and they have some money. That is more Islamic than the old way, not less.

Under pressure from reform thinkers within Islam and new ideas from outside, many of the reactionary attitudes associated with the self-serving *ulamas* have been overcome. But some of the archaic (and, arguably, un-Islamic) laws relegating women to inferior status, denying support payments after divorce, and stripping them of custody of their children remain in place, legitimized by Koranic passages assigning superior place to men. Traditions validated by religion die hard.

Muhammad Nowaihi of the American University in Cairo —a crusty soul who scorned the Egyptian *ulama* for calling themselves "men of religion" when in Islam "we are all men of religion"—was a leading exponent of the view that women's rights and progressive reforms of family law are consistent with, not antithetical to, the spirit of *sharia*.

In *Middle East Review* (Summer 1979), he explained once again that there is a difference between *sharia* and laws enacted on the basis of *sharia*. The first two sources of *sharia*, the Koran and the *hadith*, "contain the fundamental Islamic tenets on creed, ritual and ethics and are permanent and immutable," he wrote. But mundane provisions affecting daily life "are not immutable. They can be changed, indeed they must be changed if circumstances change, and must be modified or replaced by other provisions in the light of *al-maslaha,* the public good or common weal of the Muslim nation."

It was the erosion of the distinction between Koranic principle and flexible application after the "closing of the door of *ijtihad*" that led to "almost total decay, political, economic, cultural and social. Bigotry, intolerance and obscurantism became rampant," in the Muslim world, he wrote.

Of those unhappy centuries, Nowaihi wrote: "No scholar was allowed to form a new opinion; he was required to adopt the opinion of one or another of the ancient jurists. It is to this later period, the 'dark ages' as they are termed, that the present Egyptian laws on personal status belong . . . It is these fossil provisions, governing as they do the relationships of husbands and wives, parents and children, and affecting every man, woman and child in their daily life that cause the greatest amount of suffering and the brutalization of Egyptian society."

That was vintage Nowaihi, an iconoclast who awed his students by dismissing the doctors of al-Azhar as fossils and reactionaries. As an Egyptian, he believed that Egypt's culture is more advanced than that of other Arab countries. He found it insupportable that Egypt should continue to tolerate unrestricted divorce, polygamy, and even the notorious "house of obedience rule," by which a wife who leaves her husband can be brought back by the police, while countries Nowaihi regarded as less advanced, such as Iraq and Tunisia, have enacted far-reaching reforms that bring their laws closer to the true spirit of *sharia.* In Tunisia, polygamy not only is illegal but also is punishable by a prison term of up to five years. In Iraq, a man wishing to take a second wife must have the permission of a judge, who grants it only if he determines that the man is financially able to support another woman.

Laws and customs affecting the relationship between the sexes cannot be so easily altered with the stroke of a pen as those affecting taxation or military service or work permits. But a process is under way, a process that has encouraged reevaluation and reform while upholding the principles of the Koran. *Sharia* is still Islam, but it is no longer synonymous with rigidity and obscurantism.

The Caliph's Rule

A Muslim is duty-bound not just to profess belief, not just to perform the rituals of worship, but to lead a virtuous life out of his commitment to do as God wills. *Sharia* is the guide to the performance of that duty. The *qadi* (religious judge) deciding a case between two litigants today has before him a legal system that was codified a thousand years ago, but he must decide on the basis of contemporary realities. In his ruling, he should apply *sharia* in such a way as to uphold God's definition of virtue as recorded in the Koran: "Righteousness does not consist in whether you face towards the east or the west. The righteous man is he who believes in Allah and the last day, in the angels and the Scriptures and the prophets; who for the love of Allah gives his wealth to his kinsfolk, to the orphans, to the needy, to the wayfarers and to the beggars, and for the redemption of captives; who attends to his prayers and pays the alms-tax; who is true to his promises and steadfast in trial and adversity in times of war. Such are the true believers; they are the God-fearing." (2:177)

In the purely Islamic state, the *qadi* was part of a legal system that had at its pinnacle the Caliph, or successor to the temporal power of Muhammad. Nothing in the Koran suggests the existence of such a position as Caliph; the community had to create it, because someone had to take charge after Muhammad died.

It became the Caliph's duty to enforce *sharia,* not by presiding over litigation himself but by appointing the wisest and best religious judges. The caliphs were often corrupt, but that did not affect the validity of the law for the community as a whole.

Young men studied the law, as compiled in law books and collections of *fatwas,* under the guidance of masters at the *madrasas.* When they had mastered the law and the commentaries, they were certified as *qadis.* In litigation, they heard directly from participants and witnesses; there were no lawyers. In presiding over the functioning of the system, the Caliph (or any other ruler after the Caliphate began to break down) might be guided by a *mufti,* or jurisconsult, who was an authority on technical points of the law. The Grand *Mufti* of a country was the chief legal authority, but generally his opinions were advisory, not issued for specific cases.

The Caliphate has vanished into history, replaced by parliaments or royal courts or military juntas or political parties as nation-states supplanted the Islamic Nation; several countries have abolished religious courts, *muftis,* and *qadis* along with the Caliphate. But they have not abolished *sharia,* because *sharia* is Islam. Muslims live according to its principles, and if the new forms of government and legal authority violate it, they do so at their political peril. In a Muslim country, the balance of interests between ruler and ruled must take into account the requirements of religion, as embodied in *sharia.*

Chapter 5

The Advance of Islam

WITHIN a century of the death of Muhammad, Arab armies were masters of a vast, diverse territory that stretched from the south of France to the Indus River. Their domain embraced North Africa, the Arabian peninsula, the Fertile Crescent of the Levant and Mesopotamia, Persia, and much of Central Asia.

By the time of the Battle of Tours in 732, when the Franks under Charles Martel put an end to their advance into Western Europe, the Arabs were vastly outnumbered within their empire by peoples more culturally advanced than they. Then, as now, Arabs were a minority within this Arabian-born religion.

The Egyptians and the Mesopotamians (who now consider themselves Arabs but did not before Islam and the Arabic language came to them in the seventh century) and the Persians had their own religions and their own traditions of poetry, science, art, and public administration, which reached back thousands of years. Yet they all adopted the religion of the invaders. From the borders of Persia westward across the Levant and North Africa they adopted the language too, the language of the Koran. Except for the people of Spain, none of those who fell under the sway of Islam in its first hundred years have abandoned it since then.

The story of those early Arab conquests, one of the most dramatic chapters in history, has been fully told, but some events in the spread of the faith and the rise and fall of the caliphal empire are worth reexamining, because they contribute to an understanding of the contemporary Islamic world.

Muslim historians believe that the Prophet himself envisioned Islam as a universal religion, despite the emphasis in the Koran on the Arabness of his mission and his professed intention to bring holy scripture to the people who had no book—that is, to the Arabs.

Ahmad Galwash, in a book written specifically for non-Arab readers, says, "Islam claims to be a universal religion" (which is certainly true now, though it is not clear that it was true in the Prophet's lifetime) and, "It was not revealed to meet the requirements of a particular race or age." As evidence of this claim that the universality of Islam originated with Muhammad, Muslims cite the letters the Prophet is said to have sent to the Persian and Byzantine emperors, to the rulers of Egypt, Abyssinia, and Oman, and to some other regional potentates, urging them to accept Islam.

Gibbon, in *The Decline and Fall of the Roman Empire,* says of the Persian monarch Chosroes that while he "contemplated the wonders of his art and power, he received an epistle from an obscure citizen of Mecca, inviting him to acknowledge Mahomet as the apostle of God. He rejected the invitation and tore the epistle." Informed of the Persian's gesture of contempt, Muhammad is said to have exclaimed, "It is thus that God will tear the (Persian) kingdom, and reject the supplications of Chosroes."

Later Western historians reject the tale of the letters as spurious. But even if it was not the clear intention of the Prophet to carry the new faith beyond Arabia, there were enough passages in the Koran calling for a struggle with the infidels to encourage his successors to do what circumstances invited them to do anyway.

Muhammad certainly envisioned Islam as the religion of all the tribes of Arabia. Once he understood that the Jews were not going to accept him as a prophet, he concentrated on conversion of the Arabians, as demonstrated by the treaties and agreements he entered into with them after his conquest of Mecca. The weakness of these arrangements was that the tribes made the treaties with him personally, not with the *umma* (community of believers). According to Bernard Lewis in *The Arabs in History* (a widely respected classic, even though some Arabs reject it because they suspect Lewis of Zionist sympathies), it was traditional for such agreements to expire with the death of one of the parties. Released from their contract by the death of Muhammad, the tribes ceased to pay tribute, not because they were sliding back into paganism, but because they had no political obligation to the Muslim community when Muhammad died. The "brotherhood" of Islam that Muhammad preached was not yet self-sustaining.

The First Caliphs

Muhammad left no male offspring. He designated no successor to his temporal authority over the Muslim community (though Shiite Muslims believe that he did, as we shall see). And the Koran offered no guidance on the choice of a person to lead the community, aside from the general instruction that men should "conduct their affairs by mutual consent."

No one could claim succession to the Prophet's position as revelator or spiritual leader, but someone had to lead the community that he had created. Cities had to be governed, taxes collected, armies led, disputes judged, agreements enforced, Islam upheld. A leader had to be designated who would be acceptable to the community and be worthy of the Prophet's ideals.

A small group of the Prophet's companions in Medina designated Abu Bakr, Muhammad's father-in-law and one of his first converts, as Khalifa, or Caliph, successor to the temporal authority of the Prophet and defender of the faith. Abu Bakr was not exactly elected. He was chosen by a group of insiders and presented to the community as a *fait accompli.* The piety and courage of Abu Bakr were such that most Muslims accepted him, but some did not. The decision to award the Caliphate to Abu Bakr instead of to Ali, Muhammad's cousin and son-in-law, husband of his daughter Fatima, was soon to create a schism that endures to this day. Moreover, the informal method by which Abu Bakr was selected ensured that similar difficulties would arise in the choice of later caliphs, because a formal system of making the selection was never established.

The duties, authority, and method of selection of the Caliph changed many times, but the position was never analogous to that of the Catholic Pope; in fact it was the opposite. The Caliph's authority was temporal, not spiritual. But in a Muslim community that recognized no distinction between church and state, the source—and the purpose—of the Caliph's authority were religious. He ruled in the name of Islam, for the purpose of upholding Islamic teaching and law and defending the believers against infidels. The Caliph was Commander of the Faithful and servant of the Prophet; in theory, at least, he had no personal claim to or stake in the office.

As Caliph, Abu Bakr had to establish his authority over the community, preside over its day-to-day affairs, and ensure that the rules of the Koran were enforced. He also had the duty of compelling the recalcitrant tribes to submit to Islam and to the hegemony of Medina. Those who had repudiated the treaties were to be brought back; those in the more distant corners of the peninsula who had never accepted the authority of Islam were to be made to do so.

"Arab chroniclers," says Philip Hitti, "say that as soon as Muhammad died all Arabia outside Hijaz broke off from the newly organized state. The fact is that, with the lack of communication, the utter absence of organized methods of missionary activity, and the short time involved, not more than one-third of the peninsula could actually have professed Islam during the life of the prophet or recognized his rule. Even Hijaz, the immediate scene of his activity, was not Islamized until a year or two before his death."

That was to change swiftly. The banner of Islam was raised by a great general, Khalid ibn-Walid, "the sword of Allah," a Meccan who had accepted Islam only near the end of Muhammad's life. With the zeal of the new convert, he charged across the peninsula in a lightning campaign and in a few months had united the tribes under Medinese rule. That does not mean that all those who were compelled to acknowledge the primacy of Medina were also compelled to embrace Islam; there was a fundamental difference between military conquest and religious conversion. But the Arabians were probably inclined to accept Islam because the evidence showed that the Muslims had Allah on their side. Had they not taken Mecca and the Kaaba? Was not the inspiration of the Muslims a book in Arabic addressed to the Arabians? Following behind Khalid ibn-Walid, the Holy Book and the banner of Islam, the Muslims, militant in spirit and successful in battle, now began to look outside the frontiers of Arabia.

Abu Bakr was Caliph for only two years before he died,

to be succeeded by Umar. But even in his brief reign, when the campaign to Islamize the tribes was the most urgent consideration, raiding parties were sent into Iraq and Syria—some on the initiative of local commanders, some at the instigation of the Medinese authorities—in a quest for plunder, for territory, for power.

United for the first time under a central authority, the Arab armies were a cohesive and suddenly powerful force, which was encouraged by the feeble resistance offered by the Persian and Byzantine rulers who controlled the territories to the north, east, and west of the peninsula. Exhausted by their wars against each other, these superannuated powers were unable to command the loyalty of the peoples who lived under their dominion, such as the Egyptians, who actually welcomed the Arabs as liberators.

"Placed on the verge of the two great empires of the East," Gibbon commented, "Mahomet observed with secret joy the progress of their mutual destruction; and in the midst of the Persian triumphs, he ventured to foretell, that before many years should elapse, victory would again return to the banners of the Romans." By "Romans," Gibbon meant the Byzantines or Greeks, *al-Rum* in Arabic. Their defeat by the Persians in Syria in 615 is mentioned in Sura 30 of the Koran, which predicts that in a few years victory will again lie with the Byzantines, a reflection of Muhammad's preference for the Christian Byzantines over the idolatrous Persians.

So strong was the Persian ascendancy at that time that there seemed to be no basis for the prediction of their downfall. Still less did there seem any likelihood that both contestants would soon be swept away by a force of which they had not yet even heard. Their enlightenment was not long in coming.

No sooner had the Byzantine Emperor Heraclitus reversed the tide of the struggle with the Persians—as the Koran had predicted—than he was confronted with an Arab invasion of Syria. After a series of skirmishes, the Byzantines were taken by surprise. Khalid ibn-Walid led an Arab force in a camel-borne forced march across the desert from southern Iraq and laid siege to Damascus. The city fell after six months, and the Arabs were masters of a largely Christian town that was reputed to be the world's oldest continuously inhabited settlement.

Heraclitus sought to retaliate by sending an army of 50,000 men against the Muslims. On August 20, 636, only four years after the death of the Prophet, an Arab army half that size, led by Khalid, met the Byzantines on the banks of the Yarmouk River, a tributary of the Jordan. The Arabs crushed the enemy. The battle was a milestone in Islamic history, commemorated today in the name of the Yarmouk Brigade, one of the three units of the so-called Palestine Liberation Army. The victory allowed the Arabs to move unhindered into the rest of Syria and Palestine, which they promptly did.

Yarmouk's counterpart on the eastern front occurred only a year later, when the Arabs decisively defeated the Persians at Qadisiya and marched into the heartland of Mesopotamia (now called Iraq).

Then it was Egypt's turn. An army under the command of Amr ibn al-As, who had become a Muslim at the same time as Khalid ibn-Walid, stormed into Egypt in 639. Within a year, aided by the restive indigenous population of Coptic Christians, who were persecuted under Byzantine rule, they had seized the fortress of Babylon, near what is now Cairo. With that they established an Arab empire that comprised the entire heartland of what is today the Arab, Muslim Middle East: the Arabian peninsula, Iraq, Egypt, Syria, and Palestine. The Caliph Umar found himself almost by accident presiding over a community that had expanded so far beyond Medina and Mecca as to defy comprehension. The Muslims had every reason to believe that Allah was indeed on their side; but the conquests, while expanding the power of the Arabs, inevitably changed the nature of the religious community which provided its leadership. Overnight, the world of Islam was pluralistic and polyglot, incorporating whole nations, ancient languages, and traditions, and philosophical concepts that were beyond the scope of anything known in Arabia. The Arabs got a sudden crash course in philosophy, literature, architecture, science, and public administration.

There are several reasons why they were able to achieve these pellmell, unplanned conquests and still retain the cohesion of their own army and state. The weakness of Persia and Byzantium and the restlessness of their subject peoples contributed. So did the mobility and desert skill of the Arabs and their knowledge of how to use the camel in warfare. The Caliph, Umar, was adept at maintaining discipline among his commanders. He insisted that the Arab armies stay in garrison, rather than mingle with the captured peoples in their cities and perhaps succumb to their abundant temptations. But probably the most important reason is that the Arabs left in place the infrastructure and administrative systems of the communities they conquered, and they refrained from imposing their habits or their faith on reluctant subjects. They occupied, but did not destroy; they subdued, but did not crush. Their rule was therefore tolerated and even welcomed, not resisted.

Living in a cultural tradition that has been hostile to Islam since the Crusades, we are taught in school that these early Arab campaigns were wars of religious conquest, fought to spread Islam by the sword. In fact, while it was no doubt Islam that molded the Arabs into one force and motivated commanders and troops, the military campaigns were wars of Arab conquest, not of Muslim conversion. The conquered people were generally not forced to accept Islam; the grim choice of convert or die was seldom, if ever, offered. On the contrary, the Arabs set up a system of administration and taxation that assumed the right of the subject peoples to retain their own religions.

Jihad

The Koran and the Prophet taught that Muslims were required to fight for the faith and that those who died in its defense were assured a martyr's reward in Paradise. But the Koran also says, "There shall be no compulsion in religion." (2:256) The belief that the Arabs swept out of the peninsula on some fanatical religious mission, a mission embodied in the term *jihad*, has been substantially refuted by historians of the era.

The concept of *jihad*, which is customarily but erroneously translated "holy war," inspires a collective fear of Islam even today. Muslim leaders contribute to that fear with demagogic talk of *jihad* in freeing Jerusalem from Israeli occupation, punishing the United States for supporting the Shah of Iran, liberating oppressed Muslims in the Philippines, and other unlikely missions. But there has been no effective call to *jihad* for centuries, and even if there were such a call, it would not necessarily mean armed subjugation of non-Muslims. *Jihad* must be the most overused and ill-understood word in contemporary Islam.

Muhammad is recorded in the *hadith* as saying, "Shall I not tell you of the peak of the matter, its pillar and topmost part? The peak of the matter is Islam; the pillar is prayer; and its topmost part is jihad." The translators of the edition from which that quotation is taken, both Muslims, append this note: "Though the Arabic 'jihad' is generally rendered 'holy war,' its meaning is wider than this and includes any effort made in furtherance of the cause of Islam." Literally, the word means "utmost effort" in promotion and defense of Islam, which might or might not include armed conflict with unbelievers.

Early in 1981, the leaders of most Islamic nations met in conference in Taif, Saudi Arabia (the inhabitants of Taif drove Muhammad away with stones when he sought to convert them). The conference issued a predictable call for *jihad* against Israel, and Western newspapers just as predictably reported that the conferees had resolved to wage "holy war." Neither Egypt, which is at peace with Israel, nor Iran, which was at war with Iraq, participated in the conference, and without them any such appeal could be only rhetorical. Even those who took part recognized that their call to *jihad* was a political statement, not a military commitment: When speaking English, they did not translate *jihad* as "holy war." King Hussein of Jordan, for example, who lost much of his country when he went to war against Israel in 1967, said that the term *jihad* as used by the conference was a "very comprehensive term that is difficult to specify." In the true spirit of *jihad,* the conference reinforced Islamic opposition to the peace treaty between Egypt and Israel, but it did not result in any direct action against Israel. In the words of Khalil Abdel Alim, Washington leader of the American Muslim Mission, "*Jihad* does not mean fighting a war; it means to struggle for what is required of one in obedience to God." Getting out of bed for dawn prayer, he said, is *jihad.*

The Koran's promise that those who die in conflict with unbelievers will find Paradise, however, is not to be dismissed as a motivating force in political and military action by Muslims. It is important in understanding the willingness of religiously motivated revolutionaries, such as the Sudanese of the Mahdist revolt in the nineteenth century, the students in Iran and the anti-Soviet guerrillas in Afghanistan, to accept death. But the Koran does not unequivocally command believers to seek out conflict. When the faith is challenged, they are obliged to respond, but not all the Koran's commands are martial.

The Medinese *suras,* revealed during the years when the Muslims were skirmishing with the Quraish, stress that a higher place in God's favor is accorded to those who fight than to those who stay at home: "The believers who stay at home—apart from those that suffer from a grave impediment—are not equal to those who fight for the cause of Allah with their goods and their persons. Allah has given those that fight with their goods and their persons a higher rank than those who stay at home. He has promised all a good reward; but far richer is the recompense of those who fight for Him." (4:95)

Those who enter the fight are assured that God is with them: "Prophet, rouse the faithful to arms. If there are twenty steadfast men among you, they shall vanquish two hundred; and if there are a hundred, they shall rout a thousand unbelievers, for they are devoid of understanding" (8:65)—just as happened at Badr and in the Valley of the Yarmouk.

Jews and Christians who spurn God's message are mentioned specifically as a target of the struggle: "Fight against such of those to whom the Scriptures were given as believe neither in Allah nor the Last Day, who do not forbid what Allah and His apostle have forbidden, and do not embrace the true faith until they pay tribute out of hand and are utterly subdued." (9:29) The Jews and Christians knew the truth, but "they worship their rabbis and their monks, and the Messiah the son of Mary, as gods besides Allah; though they were ordered to serve one God only. There is no god but Him." (9:31)

These and a score of similar verses could hardly be clearer in the duty they imposed on the Prophet's followers to join the battle against the infidels who spurned Islam and persecuted the believers. That duty to defend the faith is embodied in the word *jihad,* translated by Yustaf Ali as "striving." The Koran is less clear on the circumstances in which believers are obliged to undertake the struggle and upon what provocation. The tone of the Koran is martial, but it is also flexible. It calls for war on the infidels and for courteous treatment of them; it calls for ruthlessness and for tolerance; it brands the unbelievers as doomed infidels, yet teaches that whoever believes in God and lives virtuously, whether Moslem or not, will be admitted to Paradise.

Contemporary Muslim writers often cite two verses of Sura 2 to argue that the command to fight and the call to crush the infidel were purely defensive. One is the verse already quoted, "There shall be no compulsion in religion." The other is this: "Fight for the sake of Allah those that fight against you, but do not attack them first. Allah does not love the aggressors." (2:190)

It is possible to use those admonitions to support the argument that the early wars were not wars of religious conversion, especially since the Arabs generally imposed their political rule but not their creed upon the peoples they conquered. But it is disingenuous to argue, as some apologists do, that the early campaigns of Muhammad against the Meccans and the wars of the Arabs against their neighbors were purely defensive. The Muslims in Medina raided caravans for booty; the Arabs attacked their neighbors because they were zealous and warlike and their neighbors were weak. Even if it is conceded that the community in Medina was on the defensive against the Quraish, it is not possible to argue that Amr ibn al-As was on the defensive when he invaded Egypt. The important point is not that the Muslims were unwarlike or that they did not march against their rivals; the point is that the Arabians, in marching against their neighbors, did not do so primarily to force conversion to Islam.

Fazlur Rahman dismisses as "unacceptable on historical grounds" the arguments of "modern Muslim apologists who have tried to explain the jihad of the early community in purely defensive terms." He notes that in the Medinese period, as the Koranic verses show, "there is hardly anything with the possible exception of prayer and zakat that receives greater emphasis than jihad. Among the later Muslim schools, however, it is only the fanatical Kharijites who have declared jihad to be one of the 'pillars of the faith.' "

The Kharijites were a fanatical and violent group of dissidents who struggled with the orthodox community in the first two centuries of Islam. Their name is derived from the

Arabic word meaning "to go out," and they are often referred to in English as "the seceders." Believing that the Caliph should be chosen in an open election among the faithful put the Kharijites in opposition to the central authorities who, from the time of the fifth Caliph, made the office hereditary.

The Kharijites also espoused an aggressive view of Islam in which the profession of faith was considered meaningless unless accompanied by visible good works and Islam was to be imposed by force. They sought in effect to make their vision of *jihad* a sixth pillar of the faith. If they had succeeded, they would have turned Islam into an intolerant creed which, by guaranteeing the rebellion of the conquered peoples, contained the seeds of its own destruction. As it turned out, the conquered peoples grew restive not because they were forced to accept Islam but because the Arab Muslims were slow to accept into the faith those who wanted to join and because when they had embraced Islam, the Arabs still looked down on them.

When the Kharijites were crushed by the ruling caliphs at the end of the seventh century, their belief that *jihad* as an aggressive principle should be elevated to the status of an Islamic obligation on a par with prayer went with them, never to be seriously revived. The call still goes out occasionally, but it usually does not refer to armed conflict and in any case it seldom produces any response. The last serious call for a universal Muslim rising against unbelievers was made by the Ottoman Sultan in 1914. Not only did it fail, but also the Arabs of the peninsula rebelled against the Turks and threw in their lot with the British. They put their aspirations for Arab political independence above the claims of Islamic unity.

The great century of Arab conquest after the death of Muhammad was also a century of turmoil and violence within the community of Islam. Peace, justice, and political consensus among Muslims were as elusive then as they are now. Umar reigned as Caliph for ten brilliant years, holding the community together with piety and managing the Empire with discipline, but he was assassinated by a discontented slave in 644. A period of intrigue, rivalry, and dissension ensued, and it is fair to say that no caliph ever again commanded the full support of Muslims that Umar did.

Umar's successor, the third Caliph, was Uthman (or Osman in another transliteration), one of Muhammad's early followers. He is remembered as a weakling. The epitaph of history on his reign, which lasted from 644 to 656, is this tribute to his predecessor: "The luck of Islam was shrouded in Umar's winding-sheet." Uthman served Islam well by ordering an official compilation of the Koran, which headed off a proliferation of texts and variations that would have fragmented the faith. But he was evidently a thoroughgoing failure as an emperor.

A gentle man, he lacked Umar's ability to impose discipline on the garrisons. Where Umar was ascetic, Uthman amassed riches. Seeking to consolidate his authority through family ties, he installed relatives in sensitive posts and picked the wrong ones. The ascension to power of his clan, the Umayyads, stirred resentment among the Hashemites, who were related to the Prophet.

Uthman's cousin, the Umayyad Muawiyah, was a successful and powerful governor of Syria (already the provinces of the instant empire were breeding local strongmen), but outside Syria, rebellion was brewing. In 656, rebels from Egypt attacked Uthman's house in Medina and killed him and his wife.

Now at last the elders of Medina bestowed the Caliphate on the man whose claim was among the strongest from the beginning: Ali, son of Abu Talib, cousin and son-in-law of Muhammad. This gesture came too late to placate the partisans of Ali, who thought his claim was stronger even than Abu Bakr's—and who remain dissidents within Islam to this day. (See Chapter 6.) Nor did the elevation of Ali to the Caliphate still the dissent in the provinces.

Ali was forced to defend his authority in a battle against malcontents from the ranks of Muhammad's companions, including the Prophet's widow, Aisha, who accused him of complicity in the murder of Uthman.

Ali's troops triumphed in 656 in a bloody engagement, known as the Battle of the Camel because Aisha's camel-borne litter was at the center of it. But the victory was hollow. It put upon Ali the stain of having been the first caliph to lead Muslims in battle against other Muslims. Less than thirty years after the death of Muhammad, the brotherhood of Islam that he preached was buried in the graveyard of political rivalry and caliphal intrigue. It has never been disinterred.

Muawiyah, the governor of Syria, challenged Ali for the Caliphate, ostensibly on the grounds that Ali and the other Hashemites of Medina had not protected Uthman from his assassins. Ali, in a gesture that historians have used to illustrate his lack of fitness for the Caliphate, agreed to submit the issue to arbitration.

This was a doubly fatal blunder. First it stirred a revolt among the Kharijites in Iraq, who said that Ali had no right to submit to arbitration an issue that had been decided by God. Second, the arbitrators awarded the decision to Muawiyah. Ali maintained his claim to the Caliphate, but his authority had been undermined and his support faded away. In 661 he was assassinated by a Kharijite, and the Caliphate passed forever out of the hands of the Prophet's Medinese companions. Ali's son Hasan had a claim to the Caliphate, but he was a notorious womanizer said by historians to be more interested in amour than administration. He allowed himself to be bought off by Muawiyah. Even Shiite Muslims, who insist upon a caliphal line of succession from Ali, make no credible claim of accomplishment for Hasan, though they consider him to have been the second Caliph.

The first four caliphs recognized by most Muslims—Abu Bakr, Umar, Uthman, and Ali—are known collectively as the *rashidun,* or rightly guided. They knew Muhammad personally and worked with him in building Islam. They based their rule in Medina and were selected by the elders of the Medinese community, who also had known the Prophet. Their credentials were unique, and the years of their rule, 632 to 661, were years of accomplishment. They presided over the transformation of the *umma* from an obscure sect into a vast, well-organized polyglot empire, and they set up rules for governance that lasted for centuries. But even in those idealistic decades, trouble was developing. Three of the rightly guided caliphs were assassinated, two of them by Muslims. The last two, Uthman and Ali, lacked Umar's capacity for statecraft and they were unable to preserve the cohesion and discipline upon which stability depended.

When Muawiyah succeeded to the Caliphate—or usurped it, as the Shiites believe—he transferred its seat to Damascus, where he was governor, and made it hereditary. It remained a hereditary office thenceforth; the line of succession changed with whatever dynasty was in power, and there were often rival caliphs in different capitals. Removed from Medina, severed from the Hashemite succession, and held by assorted soldiers, adventurers, and weaklings, the Caliphate ceased to carry any moral weight. The Caliph was the ruler of an Arab empire that was dominated by Muslims and ruled in the name of Islam but never again the purely religious society built on the principles of the faith that Muhammad had envisioned.

The Umayyad dynasty established by Muawiyah endured less than a century, from 661 to 750, but the events of those years shaped the destiny of Islam for all time.

Military expeditions carried the Empire to its farthest limits. A map reproduced in Langer's *Encyclopedia of World History* shows "territory overrun by Muhammadans" in the seventh and eighth centuries: from Aquitaine to the Punjab, from Armenia to the Indian Ocean. Repeated Muslim attempts to take Constantinople were rebuffed, and the plain of Anatolia remained a province of the Byzantine Empire, but all else was ruled from Damascus.

Within that vast territory, most people were neither Arabs nor Muslims. Christians in Egypt and Syria, Zoroastrians in Persia, Jews, Hindus, and pagans, once conquered, had to be ruled. In accordance with the precepts of the Koran and the practice of Muhammad, who had been magnanimous to the conquered Meccans, the Muslims generally tolerated diversity, winning converts more by example than by force.

The process by which Islam spread was almost opposite to that by which Christianity had been propagated. Islam was not carried to hostile shores by dedicated individuals such as Paul or Mark who made converts by oratory and dedication. Islam went with the armies of the Empire, so that those who embraced it were joining, not defying, the ruling authorities.

The Koran taught the Muslims to be resolute and ruthless in the struggle with the infidels, but it also taught them to avoid imposing their beliefs by force and to respond in kind to overtures toward peace. No prisoners of war were to be taken until the enemy had been totally vanquished, but once taken, prisoners of war were not to be treated brutally. Muhammad was instructed to say to prisoners of war, "If Allah finds goodness in your hearts, He will give you that which is better than what has been taken from you and He will forgive you. Allah is forgiving and merciful." (8:70) Prisoners are to be bound, not killed; they may be freed or held for ransom, but only so long as the war continues.

(The Americans who were held hostage in revolutionary Iran from November 1979 to January 1981 were evidently both the victims and the beneficiaries of these instructions. If, as the Iranian extremists believed, the Islamic revolution was engaged in a struggle with the "great Satan," the United States, then it was legitimate to take the hostages and bind them or hold them for ransom; but it would have been sinful to kill them.)

The preponderant tone of the Koranic passages dealing with unbelievers is aggressive. To Muslims, the Christian ideal of turning the other cheek represents tolerance of evil. Believers are instructed to put to the sword those who attack them, to fight unbelievers until they pay tribute, and even to execute the incorrigible. "Those that make war against Allah and His apostle and spread disorders in the land shall be put to death or crucified or have their hands and feet cut off on alternate sides or be banished from the country." (5:36) But the martial passages are balanced by instructions to live in peace with, and show mercy to, those who repent and who abandon their hostility to Islam. In practice, the Umayyads followed these instructions by imposing political and military dominance on the peoples of the Empire, forcing them to accept Islamic rule, but allowing individuals to worship as they pleased and leaving local administrative hierarchies intact.

Relations with Jews and Christians

Muhammad and the Koran differentiated between unbelievers. Pagans were idolaters fit only for slavery whose idols were to be smashed. But Jews and Christians, despite Muhammad's rage against the Jews of Medina, were accorded special status as "people of the book." They were to be respected, because they had received God's revelation, but they were to be condemned, because, having received it, they distorted and rejected it. "When the revelations of the Merciful were recited to them, they fell down on their knees in tears and adoration. But the generations who succeeded them neglected their prayers and succumbed to temptation. These shall assuredly be lost." (19:58)

Muslims believe the Hebrew patriarchs were servants of Allah, and there is light in the Torah, but the Jews, guardians of revelation, strayed from the true path by practicing usury and rejecting the new apostle. Christians, recipients of revelation through Jesus, erred in espousing the idolatrous doctrine of the Trinity, which Muslims believe falsely elevated the man Jesus to divinity. According to the Koran, Jesus was one of a long line of prophets, a man like Moses and Muhammad, who preached the truth and taught men to worship God. The Koran says Jesus was not crucified but was taken up into heaven by God after another who resembled him was killed in his place. (4:157) The tale of his crucifixion is only a slander against Mary, his mother. Christians erred and Jews erred more, the Koran says, but both groups are worthy of consideration as monotheists who strayed but may return. The God they worship is the same God who spoke to Muhammad.

The result of this melange of rewritten history, conflicting directives, and ambivalent feelings was the development of a hierarchical system within the caliphal Empire, with Arab Muslims at the top and pagan slaves at the bottom. Jews and Christians were designated "people of the book" *(ahl al-kitab)* or "people of the covenant" *(ahl adh-dhimma,* or *dhimmis),* and accorded a protected status under the law. They were exempt from military service but required to pay a special tax, the *jizya.* This tax was either tribute to the Muslims extracted from subjugated peoples or a voluntary payment to the Muslims in exchange for their protection, depending on which version of history one reads, but either way, it financed the Empire. Some historians say that the Muslims actually discouraged *dhimmis* from converting, because conversion absolved them from payment of the tax and thus reduced the income of the state, though of course as Muslims they would have been subject to the requirement of *zakat,* which as *dhimmis* they were not.

According to Philip Hitti, the hierarchical system originated under Umar, before the rise of the Umayyads: "Evidently the caliph proceeded on the political theory that in the Arabian peninsula none but Muslims should be tolerated, that the Arabians abroad should remain a distinct religio-military community, that the conquered peoples should be left undisturbed in their varied professions and land cultivation, and that the Christians and Jews should be subject to heavy tribute but not to military duty. This put Arabian Muslims on the top of the sociopolitical order, with the Neo-Muslims next, the dhimmis one rung below and the slaves and prisoners of war at the bottom."

In short, the wars of conquest were not wars of conversion, and the various peoples of the Empire were not forced to embrace Islam. The Umayyad caliphs imposed Arabic as the language of administration, but they allowed *dhimmis* to continue working as civil administrators within the Islamic state, a wise policy that enabled life in the main population centers to go on much as it had before and minimized resentment of the conquerors. In Egypt, more than two centuries elapsed before the majority of the populace converted to Islam.

It was this relatively benign policy toward the conquered peoples, rather than compulsion, that led to the large-scale, voluntary, and sincere conversion of non-Arab peoples. Resentful of the Byzantines and Persians, seeking a new cultural impetus to replace outworn Hellenism, and surrounded by practitioners of a new faith that offered simple belief in place of complex ritual, many people who had been brought under the flag of Islam by the power of Arab arms embraced the teachings of the Arab faith of their own volition. (Ironically, these new, non-Arab Muslims, especially those in Persia, were to become troublesome because of their resentment of the Arabs; treated as second-class citizens by the Arabs, they felt cheated of the equal status that Islam professed to offer them.)

Gibbon, who thought Muhammad was a faker, says it is easy to understand why Islam spread but not easy to understand why it endured. Perhaps what Gibbon failed to appreciate is that Islam offered a source of direction and comfort that appealed to ordinary folk. Islam is a straightforward and practical religion, unencumbered by priesthood or sacrament, in which a comprehensible God speaks directly to men and tells them how to live. In the words of Henry Treece, "The Mediterranean world had known 3,000 years of spiritual confusion: a multitude of gods, god-pharaohs, god-emperors, goddesses made flesh, priests who were God's mouthpiece, kings annointed by God and emperors who interpreted Holy Writ to suit their secular ends. There had been blood sacrifice, incomprehensible taboo and ritual, the chanting and dancing of temple servants, the dark pronouncements of oracles. Now for the first time in history God had made Himself clear through the mouth of a plain-speaking fellow, demanding no temples, no altars, no rich vessels and vestments, no blood."

Islam was later to fall victim to many of the very weaknesses enumerated in that passage: mystic rituals by secretive cults, political manipulation, and theological squabbling, all of which presented targets for the reformers who have in the past hundred and fifty years cleared away a lot of that underbrush. In the early years Islam had the appeal of its simple virtues; it was an inviting refuge for those in search of spiritual and social order. Even as the first cracks appeared in the facade of Islamic brotherhood, as Muslim began to battle Muslim and the piety of Muhammad's companions gave way to the corruption and opportunism of the caliphal court, Islam was attracting adherents who found it comforting and fulfilling, as well as convenient.

A massive cultural exchange developed within Islam. From the conquered territories of the Empire, Islam absorbed new ideas, new systems of philosophy, and new forms of literary and architectural expression. The religion acquired overlays of Persian, Egyptian, and Hellenic culture. From the Muslims, the people of the Empire acquired the social cohesion and sense of spiritual purpose that they had been seeking.

There was never again to be a time when united armies marching toward new horizons under the banner of Islam would expand the community of believers. The limits of armed expansion were reached in the first century of Islam, and the limits of Arabic linguistic expression were defined by geography—the Persian mountains, the plain of Anatolia, the Sahara. Since then, Arabs and other Muslims have fought each other as often as they fought infidels; periods of unity against crusader and colonialist have alternated with longer periods of strife within Islam (which must always be remembered when Muslim political gatherings call for *jihad)*. Despite the political differences, however, the religion of Islam has continued to expand from the time of the Umayyads to the present, because traders, mystics, scholars, and self-appointed missionaries carried it into China, sub-Saharan

Africa, southeast Asia, and North America long after the power of Arab arms had spent itself.

For all their military and administrative achievements, the Umuyyads were unable to prevent the development of factional disputes that were to bring about their own downfall and create permanent divisions in the Muslim community.

The Shiites, the partisans of Ali, took up arms in support of the claim to the Caliphate of Ali's second son, Hussein. The Umayyads killed Hussein in the battle of Karbala, in Iraq, in the year 680. The battle was militarily decisive, but it perpetuated the dispute. The Shiites elevated Hussein to martyrdom and persisted in their refusal to acknowledge the legitimacy of the Umayyads. Though Shiism was of Arab origin, the followers of Ali found their greatest support among the Persians, and so was created a Persian-Arab division within Islam that still exists, as reflected in the war between Arab Iraq and Persian Iran that broke out in 1980. (See Chapter 6.)

Within the Umayyad domain, the Caliphate was eroded by the very kinds of power-struggles that Muhammad had feared. In 743-744, the Caliphate changed hands four times. Revolts erupted in the provinces, not against Islam but against Umayyad rule. One of the uprisings, in which a faction from Medina claimed the Caliphate, even led to the burning of the Kaaba. Shiites, Kharijites, and Berbers took up arms against the Umayyads. As a religion, Islam was developing and expanding. *Sharia* was being codified, commentaries on the Koran were being written, churches were being converted into mosques, new believers were adopting Islam. But as a government, the Umayyad Caliphate was tottering.

The Islamic identification of the state with the community of believers, the equation of doctrine with law, and the belief in a religious brotherhood that would transcend ethnic and political rivalries in a unified community were tested during the Umayyad period and they broke down almost immediately. A thousand years later, the Muslims of the world still consider themselves brothers in faith, united in a spiritual fraternity that is renewed at each year's pilgrimage, but political cohesion is as elusive as it has been since the rightly guided caliphs.

The Rise of the Abbasids

The reign of Marwan II, the last Umayyad caliph, was brief and stormy. Insurrections broke out within Syria, in Palestine, in Arabia, and in Mesopotamia. The Shiites renewed their challenge in Mesopotamia and Persia. Non-Arab Muslims throughout the Empire were discontented and resentful over their second-class status in a religion that promised equality. The power of the Arabs was eroded by their own bickering and rivalry. Undermined by all these strains, the Umayyads were ready to be brought down by a determined rebellion, and in 747 that rising erupted.

Partisans of a Hashemite clan, known as the Abbasids for their descent from the Prophet's uncle Abbas, organized a challenge to the usurper Umayyads among the Arabs in Iraq and among the Persians. A Persian known as Abu Muslim unfurled the black banner of the Abbasids in Iraq and marched to confront the Umayyads. As he led the armies toward Syria, a Hashemite known as Abu al-Abbas, who was orchestrating the rebellion from Kufah in Iraq, claimed the Caliphate. Arab marched against Arab, Muslim against Muslim, in the beginning of a cycle that seems to have been perpetuating itself ever since.

In the year 750, the Abbasid armies of Abu Muslim gained a decisive victory. An Umayyad army of 12,000 men, led by Marwan II himself, was wiped out in a battle on a tributary of the Tigris. The Caliph escaped and fled to Egypt, but the Abbasids pursued him and killed him there. A rump of the Umayyads survived in Spain, but the Caliphate passed to the Abbasids, whose long reign brought the zenith of Islamic civilization.

The Abbasids moved the seat of the Caliphate to Iraq and built a new capital at Baghdad. The Abbasids were Arabs, but their move eastward, both geographic and political, led to a strong Persian influence on their society, an influence of poetry, science, art, and luxury that came to be associated with the Baghdad court. Abu Bakr and Umar would hardly have recognized the Caliphate in its Baghdad incarnation, the wine-women-magic-carpet world of *The Thousand and One Nights*. (Neither, for that matter, would today's visitor to the sprawling, dusty, and largely charmless contemporary capital of Iraq recognize it as a once-splendid capital of a great empire.)

The caliphs were no longer first among Muslim equals; they were oriental despots. Some of them were enlightened, many were not. They presided over a court renowned for pomp and luxury and over a society renowned in history for its achievements in science, mathematics, astronomy, poetry, and civil administration. While Europe was passing through the Dark Ages, the Abbasid Empire was establishing itself as the custodian of civilization, where ancient traditions of science and philosophy were preserved, works in Greek, Syriac, Sanskrit, and Persian were saved from oblivion by being translated into Arabic, and innovations such as the decimal system and the zero were developed.

If ever there was a time when the mythical Islamic Nation—a global, centralized, self-perpetuating empire ruled in the name and on the principles of Islam—could have been created, it was in the early years of the Abbasid Caliphate. The Abbasids had military power, vast wealth through control of the trade routes, cultural and scientific supremacy, and a claim to religious legitimacy through the Hashemites. People of every color in every climate paid at least nominal allegiance to the Caliph of Islam.

Under the great caliphs Harun al-Rashid (789–809), whose name means Aaron the Wise and whose exploits are recounted in *The Thousand and One Nights,* and al-Mamun (813–833), he who established Mutazilism as official doctrine, Abbasid power reached its apogee. The Muslim Arabs, who were untutored traders and nomads in the time of Muhammad, delved eagerly into the scientific and philosophical traditions of the Greeks, Hindus, Persians, and Chinese, just as their twentieth-century heirs would pursue the political and technological developments learned from the West while retaining their Islamic faith.

But under the Abbasids, as under the Umayyads before them and all dynasties after them, Islam failed to ensure political cohesion, just as it fails to do so among Muslims today. Even as the court in Baghdad became the world center of science and culture, the political fragmentation of the Empire was beginning. Blunders like the attempt to impose Mutazilite absolutism contributed to this.

The court was corrupted by wealth and luxury. The wine-drinking, brocade-clad caliphs abandoned their role of religious exemplars. Administrative power was delegated to bureaucrats and tax collectors. Decrees were written by scribes at the command of *viziers*, or prime ministers, for the Caliph's signature. Hired provincials replaced Arab troops in the army. Turkish mercenaries, imported to protect the caliphal court, gradually seized control of it, reducing the Caliph to a puppet under their tutelage.

With the weakening of the central power in Baghdad, the Empire inevitably began to break up. Islam was entering a chaotic period, which Arthur Goldschmidt in his history of the Middle East refers to as "one damn dynasty after another." While the Abbasid caliphs were using their administrative energies to impose Mutazilite beliefs about the eternality of the Koran, their subjects were breaking away from Baghdad's authority. Rival dynasties within Islam sprang up in Turkey, North Africa, Oman, and even inside Baghdad. A local Persian dynasty called the Buwaihids seized the capital in 945, retaining the enfeebled Abbasid caliphs as puppets for the next century.

If any of these upstart groups had rejected Islam, if they had apostasized, the eroding caliphal state might have been forced to rouse itself to action to reassert its primacy as defender of the faith. But none did; they were all Muslims too. Islam was demonstrating, as it was to do when the Ottoman Empire reached the same feeble state and as it does today, that the faith is more durable than political arrangements made in its name. There is no unified Islamic nation, but the faith of the masses survives every coup and dynasty.

The most important defection from Baghdad's rule was that of the Fatimids, an independent Shiite dynasty claiming descent from the Prophet's daughter Fatima and from Hussein the son of Ali. They swept out of Tunisia in the tenth century to seize all of North Africa, including Egypt. In the year 969, the Fatimid leader al-Muizz founded a new city near the site of the encampment of the first Arab conquerors of Egypt three centuries before. He named it al-Qahirah (the victorious, the ascendant), which is the name it still bears today: Cairo, in English. Cairo became the Fatimid capital and quickly supplanted Baghdad as the great center of Islamic culture and learning. The Fatimids established al-Azhar, still the greatest center of Muslim and Arab scholarship.

Like the Roman Empire before it, the caliphal empire in Baghdad became the creature of outsiders who ruled in its name: Turkish mercenaries, then Persian Shiites who legitimized themselves by ruling in the name of a caliph whose claim to the title they disputed, then the Seljuq Turks. The Abbasid Caliph reigned throughout, but did not rule.

The ascendancy of the Seljuqs and their raids into Armenia and Asia Minor provoked the first of the two great, sustained military conflicts that were to put an end to the Baghdad Caliphate and the Arab Empire—the Crusades.

Our textbooks and popular films have often portrayed the Crusades as an attempt by the forces of civilization to regain control of the Holy Places of Christianity from the heathens who had seized them—to oust the "wicked race," as Pope Urban said in the speech that launched the Crusades in 1095. In fact, the Crusaders represented a Europe that was then culturally far behind the Muslim world. The historical impact of the Crusades was greater on Europe than on the Middle East; it was the Europeans who burst out of the Dark Ages to have their minds opened and their horizons expanded by the arts and ideas of the Middle East and by the rediscovery of trade with the east. The behavior of the "heathen" Muslims toward their captives was hardly less civilized and magnanimous than that of the Crusaders, who were motivated as much by adventurism and greed as by piety.

The Crusades sputtered on for nearly two hundred years, and nothing could have better dramatized the weakness of the Caliphate and the fragmented condition of the Muslim state than its erratic response to the Christian invasion of the heartland of Islam. If ever there was an occasion when a vigorous call to *jihad* ought to have been issued and answered, it was the arrival on Muslim soil of infidels bent on wresting sacred sites from Islamic control. But no such call was issued.

The enfeebled Abbasids were in no position to do it, and the Seljuq Turks were by then ensconced so far eastward, at Isfahan, that the invasion was of no immediate concern to them. Some Muslim princes formed alliances with the Crusaders or entered into live-and-let-live arrangements with Christian settlements. The Levant and Palestine were split into rival petty Arab and Turkish principalities, incapable of offering a unified response to the Crusaders. In short, the

Crusades offered proof, if proof were still needed, that the Empire of Islam had ceased to exist. The likelihood of united, transnational Islamic political and military action in the modern world of nation-states pursuing the interests of nation-states should be gauged by the Muslim world's response to the direct religious challenge of the twelfth century: each prince, sultan, and crypto-caliph made his own decision.

The campaigns of the twelfth century confirmed the rise of Egypt and the decline of Iraq as the center of Islamic civilization (although the two nations are still waging the contest for supremacy among the Arabs if not among all Muslims). The rise of Egypt meant the ascendancy of non-Arab influence, for the Egyptian champion was the Kurd known as Saladin.

This famous figure, Salah al-Din al-Ayubbi, or Saladin, was *vizier* to the last Fatimid Caliph. He was personally committed to the elimination of Shiism from Egypt and he accomplished it by a swift political stroke that Egyptians still speak of with awe. As the Fatimid Caliph lay on his deathbed, Saladin arranged to have his name replaced during Friday prayers with that of the Abbasid Caliph in Baghdad, a transfer of caliphal allegiance that accomplished in a word what other leaders had fought long wars to determine. The elimination of Shiism from Egypt condemned that branch of Islam perpetually to the role of a discontented minority. (See Chapter 6.)

When the Fatimid Caliph died in 1171, Saladin proclaimed himself Sultan of Egypt. Declaring his independence of the Turks, who had sent him to Egypt in the first place, he seized control of Syria, and after overcoming the resistance of Shiites there, he turned his attention to the Crusaders. The soldiers of the Cross not only had occupied Jerusalem but also were threatening Mecca itself by way of the Red Sea.

His military exploits marked Saladin as the greatest Muslim general since Khalid ibn-Walid. He restored Jerusalem to Muslim control with a great victory over the Frankish Crusaders in 1187; the golden cross atop the Dome of the Rock was ripped down by his troops. By the end of that year, Saladin's armies had ousted the Crusaders from most of the strongholds that they had established in the Levant. Only Antioch, Tripoli, and Tyre (on the coast of what is now Lebanon), and a few small redoubts remained of the kingdom that the Christians had established.

These triumphs did not end the Crusades; they only provoked the princes of Europe to undertake a new campaign—the famous Third Crusade of romantic legend, which matched Saladin against Richard the Lion-heart. That conflict lasted three years and ended inconclusively in a truce, by which the access of pilgrims to Jerusalem was guaranteed. Saladin died a few months later, in February 1193, his great work incomplete. But as it turned out, his accomplishments saved Islam. The Crusades dragged on for another century, but the survival of Islam now depended more on how the Muslims weathered the greatest threat the faith had ever faced—the invasion of the Mongols, who swept out of Central Asia bent on destruction.

Under Saladin, the epicenter of Islam had been shifted from Baghdad to Cairo. In the Egyptian capital, a new golden age was beginning, an age of architectural splendors that still stand and of intellectual development that survived the bloody rivalries within the alien Mameluke dynasty that ruled Egypt after Saladin. The westward shift of the capital of the faith occurred not a moment too soon, for in the eastern provinces the caliphal state that represented the temporal authority of the faith was about to be annihilated.

The Mongol Invasion

Throughout the thirteenth century, first under the famous Genghis Khan, then under his grandson Hulegu, brother of Kublai Khan, the pagan hordes of the Mongols ravaged Asia Minor, burning cities, flooding fields by opening dams, murdering captives, and torturing religious leaders.

The Mongols seem to have been a particularly savage group of invaders, relishing destruction for its own sake and thoroughly hostile to the institutions of civilization, such as libraries and schools. Even household pets are said to have been wiped out as the Mongols advanced westward.

It is not clear what the long-range intentions of the Mongols were, if they had any. They destroyed and they pillaged, but their campaigns do not seem to have had any higher purpose. If their objectives were conquest, booty, and devastation, then they achieved them.

In 1258, driven by Hulegu's hatred of Islam (said to have been inspired by his wife, a Christian), the Mongols laid siege to Baghdad. They assaulted it with rocks flung from catapults and they inundated the defenders' camp by breaking a dam. The Abbasid Caliph was obliged to surrender. Arthur Goldschmidt gives this account of the consequences in his *Concise History of the Middle East:*

> The Mongols pillaged the city, burned its schools and libraries, destroyed its mosques and palaces, murdered possibly a million Muslims (the Christians and Jews were spared), and finally executed the whole Abbasid family by wrapping them in carpets and trampling them beneath their horses' hooves. Until the stench of the dead forced Hulegu and his men from Baghdad, they loaded their horses, packed the scabbards of their discarded swords, and even stuffed some gutted corpses with gold, pearls, and precious stones to be hauled back to the Mongol capital. It was a melancholy end to the independent Abbasid caliphate, to the prosperity and intellectual glory of Baghdad, and, for some histories, to Arabic civilization itself.

That long-ago disaster is, for the Muslims of today, more than just an episode of history. It had lasting significance in that it put an end to the primacy of the Arabs in Islam, the religion of the Arabians. The Arabs slipped into sad eclipse, not to rise again until the twentieth century. But the destruction of the orthodox Caliphate did not put an end to the Muslim religion, as it might have done four centuries earlier. By the time of Hulegu, Islam had become an international religion sustained by its own institutions and was no longer dependent on fragile links to its Medinese origins. By the time Hulegu destroyed the Abbasids in Baghdad, the seat of Islamic culture was Cairo under the rule of the Mamelukes.

The Mamelukes were neither Arabs nor Egyptians but an imported force of Turkish and Circassian slave-soldiers. They seized control of Egypt from Saladin's descendants, who had been their masters, in 1250. After the sack of Baghdad in 1258, Hulegu sent word to them that they were next on the Mongols' "hit list," but the Mamelukes, unimpressed, killed his envoys and marched into Palestine to confront him.

In September, 1260, they defeated the Mongols at Ain Jallout (the "Spring of Goliath"), another great Islamic victory that is commemorated, like Yarmouk, in the name of a brigade of the Palestine Liberation Army. The advance of the Mongols was halted; Islam was saved, its legal, cultural, and religious traditions uninterrupted, the mercy of God demonstrated anew.

The Islamic empire of the Arabs was consigned to history. Until the rise of the Ottoman Turks, petty dynasties continued to proliferate, and no one power could claim to rule the world of Islam. But Islam was by then independent of the comings and goings of those who ruled in its name. Mosques, religious schools, and *sharia* courts kept the community intact no matter who sat on the throne of political power, just as they do today. Islam continued to expand into new corners of the world, propagated not by marching armies or caliphal will but by osmosis—by human contact, commerce, and example. That process is a testament to Islam's appeal to people of many cultures. Even as the religion was entering a period of intellectual decline, even as those who claimed the Caliphate and ruled in the name of Islam betrayed its principles by violence and corruption, even as Muslim warred against Muslim, the world of Islam continued to grow. Propelled not by arms but by zeal and example, Islam advanced into Asian mountains, tropical paddies, and African bush. No central authority dispatched missionaries; men went where business and inclination took them, carrying their religion with them.

The Mongols themselves, descendants of Hulegu established in Persia, generally adopted Islam in the late thirteenth century. A new Muslim civilization arose on the ashes of the old one.

In China, also under Mongol rule at that time, a Muslim community that could be traced back to the eighth century was flourishing. Traders on the famous "silk road" across Central Asia through Samarkand, and on the Indian Ocean, established regular contact between China and the Muslim Middle East. Arab mercenaries who had fought in China stayed to marry Chinese women. Rewarded with gifts of land, they formed stable Muslim communities. When native Han Chinese once more regained control from the Mongols, the Muslims were isolated, but they retained their communal identity. They rose in rebellion against Han domination late in the eighteenth century, and their struggle continued for more than fifty years. In 1856, a Muslim named Tu Wehhsiu proclaimed himself sultan of a separate Muslim state in Yunnan province and held out through fierce fighting for almost twenty years. The Muslims of China were denounced as reactionaries during the Cultural Revolution, but the community survived that challenge too. Friends who traveled in Muslim regions of China in the late 1970s told me that they found the Muslims committed to their faith and increasingly active in it. Only about 3 percent of the people of China are Muslims, but that means 30 million people.

Traders carried Islam to the archipelago of Indonesia, which is now the biggest Muslim country of all in population; about 90 percent of the 160 million Indonesians profess Islam. Though mixed with non-Islamic practices of folk religion, Islam survived the efforts of Dutch missionaries to eliminate it, and it is prevalent everywhere except on the Hindu island of Bali.

In the fourteenth and fifteenth centuries, Sufi saints—mystical missionaries of Islam (see Chapter 6)—brought the faith to Kazakhstan in Central Asia and to the Bengali-speaking regions of the Indian subcontinent, carrying it into regions where Arab arms had never penetrated.

The Islamization of Africa is still in progress. The Berbers of the North African coast at first resisted the new religion of the Arab invaders, but when they accepted it, they initiated a long, subtle process of centuries in which Islam filtered down through the Sahara. In western Africa, merchants, scholars, and preachers found the impoverished tribes of the hinterland receptive to Islam. In East Africa, the first Muslims arrived in the time of Muhammad, and there is a long history of exchanges between Africa and Arabia across the Red Sea; people in Djibouti and Mogadishu, in decades of European colonial occupation, learned to drink white wine at lunch and to speak more French and Italian than Arabic, but their spiritual traffic is still with the Arabian peninsula, just across the Strait of Bab el-Mandeb, at the mouth of the Red Sea.

Some Black African resentment of Arab slave-trading lingers, but Islam continues to spread slowly southward from the Sudan and the Horn of Africa into the interior. On a religious map of Africa, a nearly straight line can be drawn from Liberia east-southeastward to coastal Kenya. Almost everyone north of the line, except in the mountains of Ethiopia, is Muslim. Most of the people south of it are not, except on the Tanzanian island of Zanzibar, which was once part of the Arab empire of Muscat. The line itself is moving southward.

The newest territory for the expansion of Islam is the United States, where it is one of the fastest-growing and most vigorous religions, claiming about six million adherents, thirty times the number of a decade ago. Some of these American Muslims are Arabs who brought their religion with them when they immigrated. Sizable colonies of these Arab Muslims—Lebanese, Palestinians, Yemenis, and Egyptians—can be found in Detroit, New York, and the Southwest (although a good many Arab immigrants have been Christians, not Muslims). In other communities, the Muslim Americans operating bookstores, schools, and information centers are Pakistanis and Bengalis.

Most of the Americans who profess Islam, however, are native-born blacks. They call themselves Bilalians, after an Ethiopian named Bilal who is said to have been the first *muezzin;* these converts have traced the origins of Islam among American blacks back to the slaves who were brought from Muslim communities in Africa.

Since the death of Black Muslim leader Elijah Muhammad in 1975 and the accession of his son, Warith Deen Muhammad, as *Imam*, or leader of the community, the American blacks who profess Islam have officially set aside the racial exclusivity and antiwhite hostility that characterized their movement in the heyday of "black power." Repudiating their acknowledged racism, they have begun to work with traditional Jewish and Christian organizations in local interfaith councils and community groups. Their official name now is the American Muslim Mission. The beliefs of Louis Farrakhan's Nation of Islam diverge from true Islam in so many ways that its members cannot truly be called Muslims.

The overriding reason for the appeal of Islam in Asia and Africa and among American blacks is hardly compulsion; nobody is offering American blacks or Africans a "convert or die" choice. Islam is attractive because it embraces and welcomes as equals those who accept it. Islam is the least racist of faiths. There are no segregated mosques (except where segregation was imposed by Christians, as in South

Africa) and no congregations where a beggar seeking to worship would be looked at askance. Islam is not a white man's religion preached by missionaries who represent colonial powers and who attempt to change the dress or table manners of those to whom they preach.

For all its complex theological history and rich cultural heritage, Islam remains a religion that appeals easily to simple folk. No long period of study and assimilation under the tutelage of emissaries from the privileged classes is required for membership. A man or woman who professes the faith before witnesses is at once a Muslim, welcomed as an equal into a world community of shared ideals.

Chapter 6

Schism and Mysticism

As we have seen, Islam is not absolute or monolithic. Under the umbrella of the unifying creed, there have been divisions in the community almost from the day Muhammad died in 632.

Probably the divisions were inevitable, given the absence of a central doctrinal authority and the absorption by Islam of non-Arab cultures steeped in different philosophical and social traditions. The divisions have not vitiated the vitality of the faith but they have affected the course of Islamic history and they continue to do so.

Within the Islamic community, different branches, groups, and political organizations have developed over such questions as these:

> Should the temporal leadership of the community be bestowed by consensus or should it be hereditary in the line of descent from the Prophet?
>
> Do the omniscience and omnipotence of God imply predestination for individuals? If so, how and why should the conduct of individuals be regulated by society?
>
> Can Allah be known and loved or only feared and obeyed?
>
> What system of law and regulation best guides the believers on the right path and enables the community or state to be pure in the faith?
>
> Is it really possible to eliminate the distinction between the secular and the religious in government? If not, what should be the relationship between them?

Differing answers to these questions account for the proliferation of sects, offshoots of sects, branches, schools of theology and jurisprudence, and secret brotherhoods—based on political as well as spiritual foundations—that have marked Islamic history. In the contemporary world, they combine with the residual effects of Turkish and Western European colonialism to account for the amazing variety of governmental systems in Muslim countries and the great differences in the extent to which governments operate according to religious considerations.

Many of the subgroups in Islam faded into history as quickly as they arose and are of interest only to specialists. For example, in all the time I traveled in Muslim countries I never heard a single reference to the Qarmatians, a fanatic terrorist group that originated in Iraq in the ninth century and was suppressed in the tenth.

But some of the historical divisions and groups are of direct relevance to current events. The most important is the difference between Sunni Islam, the mainstream faith of the majority, and Shia or Shiite Islam, that of the largest minority. The revolution in Iran and the war between Iran and Iraq can be understood only in the context of Shiism.

About 85 percent of all Muslims are Sunnites, or members of the Sunni branch of Islam. Sunnism is often referred to as orthodox Islam, but technically there is no orthodoxy in a religion that lacks a central doctrinal authority to determine what is orthodox and what is not.

Sunnites are usually defined as followers of the *sunna*, the "path" or "way" of the Prophet. In practice, they are those who historically accepted the authority of the Caliphate, whoever held it and however he attained it, as opposed to those who believed that the office should be hereditary in the Hashemite line.

Most Muslims in North Africa, Egypt, Palestine, Syria, and Pakistan are Sunni. Shiism is the religion of Iran (where its primacy was confirmed by imperial decree in the sixteenth century). Shiites make up a third of the population of Lebanon, about half the Iraqis, and one-sixth of Pakistanis. There are an estimated 135,000 Shiites in Saudi Arabia, mostly in the Eastern Province, where the oil installations are.

Shiism derives its name from the words *Shiat Ali*, or partisans of Ali, Muhammad's cousin and son-in-law, who was the last of the "rightly guided" caliphs and the last caliph based in Medina. When the Umayyads seized the Caliphate and moved its seat to Damascus, the Shiites rejected the Caliph's authority. They believed, and still fervently believe, that Ali was designated by Muhammad as his successor, that he was endowed by divine will with spiritual as well as temporal authority, and that the correct line of succession was through the descendants of Ali and the Prophet's daughter Fatima.

Other distinctions between Shiism and Sunnism are more profound than a dispute over the caliphal succession. The Shiite rituals of prayer and pilgrimage differ little from those of the Sunnites; Shiites believe in Muhammad, the Koran, the *hadith*, and the authority of *sharia.* They participate with Sunnites in international Islamic conferences and organizations. But Shiism has unique characteristics that affect the political as well as the religious behavior of its adherents (though its devout practitioners would deny that there is any distinction between political and religious behavior).

The violent deaths of Ali and his son Hussein (or Husayn), whom the partisans of Ali regarded as Ali's rightful successor, instilled in the Shiites an admiration and even a desire for martyrdom, a trait they still exhibit. In Iran during the revolution, there appeared to be no doubt that many of those dark-bearded, field-jacketed young men challenging the Shah's troops in the streets of Qasvin and Meshed and Tehran would have accepted death under the imperial guns as martyrdom in the cause of Allah. Scornful of the armchair leftists and political moderates who were seeking secular reforms, they were fighting to establish the primacy of Islam and they believed that death in that cause would earn them a place in Paradise and the veneration of their companions.

In contrast to Sunni Islam, which in its conventional form is marked by emotional detachment and a certain arid legalism, Shiite Islam is characterized by what Fazlur Rahman calls "the centrality of the passion motive." Devotion to martyrdom, rejection of formalism, belief in saints and worship at the tombs of holy men, and a mystical faith in the eventual return of the vanished *Imam*, or spiritual leader designated by God to guide them, combine to instill in the Shiites a demonstrativeness, a tendency to physical exhibitions of spiritual devotion, that sets them apart. Shiites perform passion plays, and during holy seasons they partake in mass processions and demonstrations of penitence and mourning that are unknown to Sunnites. These events are sometimes marked by rites of self-flagellation. Young men rake their backs with hooks, especially on Ashura, the tenth day of the month of Muharram, the anniversary of Hussein's death.

It is a volatile faith, one that requires outlets for the passion it encourages. These outlets may be devotional, such as pilgrimages to the tombs of Shiite saints, or they may be political, as in revolutionary Iran. Sometimes, as in the desperate defense of Khorramshahr during the Iran-Iraq war, they seem to be both.

Shiites argue that their interpretation is not heretical or a deviation from orthodoxy but a natural development that was inherent in the Koranic revelation. It was, they argue, natural for man to seek a middle path between the formal, legalistic faith of the Sunnites, based on submission to an impersonal God, and the outright mysticism and love-cultism that later became widespread. But non-Shiite historians, both Muslim and Western, trace the development of Shiism to political, not spiritual, considerations.

As one of the earliest converts, and as the Prophet's cousin and the husband of Muhammad's daughter, Ali had as good a claim to the Caliphate as anyone. He was passed over three times, but finally chosen upon the death of Uthman in 655. Most historical accounts uphold the judgment of the Medinese elders who decided against him. He is said to have been a weak, indecisive ruler, whose personal piety did not give him the moral stature of his predecessors, and his reign was brief. Outmaneuvered by Muawiyah, he was living as a powerless pretender when he was assassinated in 661. (See Chapter 5.)

The Shiites have never accepted the outcome of that struggle. They believe that Muhammad himself designated Ali as his successor in the leadership of the community and that even the three caliphs who preceded him were usurpers.

Western historians say there is no evidence to support the Shiite claim that Muhammad selected Ali. (Bernard Lewis says it is "certainly a forgery.") They argue that if Muhammad had designated anyone, his choice would have been accepted by the community, and the difficulties that arose in choosing a leader after Muhammad's death demonstrate that no such choice had been made. Since Muhammad left no male heir, and in any case measured virtue and righteousness by faith and steadfastness, not by birth, Ali was no more than first among equals in his claim. But to the Shiites, it is not only logical but required to reject all other lines of authority and cling to that of Ali and his descendants, as they believe the Prophet commanded.

The first of those descendants was Hasan, he of the voluptuary's reputation, who did not press his claim. He retired to Medina, leaving the field to Hussein. Hussein, second son of Ali and Fatima, raised an army to challenge the Umayyads. On the tenth day of Muharram in 680, the year 61 on the Islamic calendar, Hussein and his forces, accompanied by members of his Hashemite family, faced the troops of the Umayyad Caliph Yazid at Karbala, in Iraq. The following account of what ensued is from *Shiite Islam,* by M. Husayn Tabatabai:

> That day they fought from morning until their final breath, and the Imam, the young Hashemites and the companions were all martyred. Among those killed were two children of Imam Hasan, who were only thirteen and eleven years old; and a five-year-old child, and a suckling baby of Imam Husayn. The Army of the enemy, after ending the war, plundered the "haram" of the Imam and burned his tents. They decapitated the bodies of the martyrs, denuded them, and threw them to the ground without burial.

This was the second great martyrdom (after that of Ali himself) still mourned by Shiites in pilgrimages to the mirror-tiled mosque in Karbala and to Hussein's tomb. It confirmed the split between the Shiites and the Umayyads and drove thousands of Muslims to transfer their allegiance to the Shiite faction.

Believing in the divinely inspired selection of Ali as the successor to the Prophet the Shiites have attributed to him virtues and accomplishments surpassed only by those of Muhammad.

In their accounts of his life, Ali was one of Muhammad's favored, constant companions who, distinguished by devotion and courage, risked his life by volunteering to sleep in the Prophet's bed to fool the Quraish when Muhammad slipped away to Medina.

The Shiites believe that it was Ali who compiled the

Koran, codified Arabic grammar, and introduced metaphysics to Islam. They believe that Ali exhibited such courage in Islam's early battles and such integrity in his personal life that the Prophet chose him as executor of his personal estate. And they believe Ali was the true custodian of the Prophet's words as recorded in the *hadith.* To the Shiites, Ali was not the fourth in a long line of caliphs but the first in a line of divinely guided *imams.* The Imamate is a fundamental precept of Shiism and the one that most distinguishes it from Sunni Islam.

To the Shiites, the *Imam* is a divinely inspired, infallible spiritual leader. While the Caliph's functions were temporal and his religious authority limited to defending the faithful against unbelievers and ensuring the enforcement of *sharia*, the *Imam* possesses doctrinal authority and the divinely inspired right to guide the believers in matters of faith. In place of *ijma*, the consensus of the community in Sunni Islam, the Shiites accept the authority of the *Imam.*

To the Shiites, the five principles of the religion are divine oneness, the prophecy of Muhammad, resurrection, the Imamate, and divine justice. In the words of Fazlur Rahman, the *Imam* is "both sinless and absolutely infallible in his supposed pronouncements on the dogma and indeed in all matters. In fact whereas in classical and medieval Sunni Islam the office of the caliph is recognized as only a practical necessity, belief in the Imam and submission to him is, according to the Shia, the third cardinal article of faith, after a belief in God and His apostle."

Shiism rejects the Sunnite belief that the divine law bestows upon the people themselves the authority to select the ruler of an Islamic society. That belief, the Shiites argue, is inconsistent with Muhammad's practice; Shiites say that a prophet who was so meticulous in laying down instructions for such mundane acts as eating and washing could not have left up in the air the question of who was to preside over the community.

The Koran stresses that Muhammad was a mortal man who would die like all others, and conventional history does not record any suggestion that he viewed his divine mission as transferable or as something that could be bestowed upon future generations. But Shiites trace the authority of the *Imam* not just to their belief that Muhammad designated Ali as his successor but also to the Koran itself. They find authentication of the Imamate in verses such as this: "Apostle, proclaim what is revealed to you from your Lord; if you do not, you will surely fail to convey His message." (5:70) That is said to show that Muhammad felt both the urgency and the fragility of his mission and was moved to designate a successor in case he himself died with the divine commands unfulfilled.

As explained by Tabataba'i, in *Shiite Islam*, "It is not necessary for a prophet always to be present among mankind, but the existence of the Imam, who is the guardian of divine religion, is on the contrary a continuous necessity for human society. Human society can never be without the figure whom Shiism calls the Imam whether or not he is recognized and known." Citing a passage in the Koran in which Allah says that if this generation rejects wisdom and prophethood, "We will entrust them to others who truly believe in them," (6:89) Tabataba'i says that the "others" to whom it refers are the *Imams*.

No person alive today is recognized as the *Imam*. Shiites believe that an *Imam* always exists, but they also believe that the last recognized one has been living for a thousand years in a state of "occultation," or hidden from human perception, and will return as the *Mahdi* to preside over a perfected society.

In the absence of a physical person whom the Shiite community accepts as the rightful continuation of the line of Ali, however, individual religious leaders arise periodically who are accorded some of the spiritual and temporal authority of the Imamate. The latest of them was the Ayatollah Ruhollah Khomeini, the Iranian revolutionary leader, who was referred to by his followers as "Imam." Khomeini did not actually proclaim himself to be the living *Imam* or the *Mahdi*, but he wore the title *Imam* comfortably; his position as spiritual leader and *de facto* ruler of revolutionary Iran could only have developed in a Shiite society conditioned to the acceptance of ecclesiastical authority.

Ali was the first *Imam*, Hasan the second (briefly), Hussein the third. Most Shiites recognize a line of successors down to the twelfth *Imam*, Muhammad al-Muntazar, "the awaited one." He disappeared—in the year 872, according to Tabataba'i, in 878 according to other accounts—and his "occultation" will continue as long as God wills it. Shiites who recognize him, known as Twelvers, believe that he continues to live in some form and will eventually return as *mahdi*. To skeptics who point out that if he were still and continuously alive since his disappearance he would be twelve hundred years old, Tabataba'i replies, "The protest is based only on the unlikelihood of such an occurrence, not an impossibility." The history of monotheistic religions is replete with miraculous and wondrous occurrences, he says, so there is no inherent reason not to believe in another one. "Miracles are not impossible," he says, "nor can they be negated through scientific arguments."

The Shiites argue that it is not necessary for the Hidden Imam to be physically visible to men in order to fulfill his function as spiritual guide and interpreter of divine commands. That function is exercised by spiritual communion with the believers, which continues uninterrupted even while the *Imam* is in "occultation."

A smaller group within Shiism is known as the Seveners because they accept the line of succession only down to the seventh *Imam*. They maintain that when the sixth *Imam* died, in about the year 757, his son Ismail was wrongly passed over for the succession in favor of another son, Musa. The Seveners, otherwise known as Ismailis, a heterodox group infused with crypto-Platonic notions such as the triad of the One, the Intellect and the Soul, which then translated into esoteric attributes of Muhammad, Ali, and the *Imam* flourished in the tenth century and spread their influence from North Africa to India.

The Ismailis are remembered as violent and heretical fanatics who waged a ruthless struggle against all non-Ismailis. It can be said in their favor that they gave rise to the Fatimid dynasty of North Africa, which made constructive contributions to the cultural development of Egypt. (See Chapter 5.) But they are better remembered for the savagery and destructiveness of the offshoot groups that espoused their beliefs. The worst of these were the Assassins, a terrorist group based in Syria whose objective was murder, ostensibly as part of a campaign against the Abbasid Caliph and his Seljuq Turkish allies. In the late eleventh and early twelfth centuries, they murdered with their knives one prominent political figure after another. Their leaders were said to have endowed them with courage in the form of hashish—hence the name *hashishiyun*, "assassins."

Ismailism survives today in the form of a small, peaceful

sect found mostly in Pakistan, venerating as *Imam* the Aga Khan.

A third Shiite sect, the Zaydis, split off even before the Ismailis. Recognizing as their *Imam* Zayd, who rebelled against the Umayyad Caliph in the eighth century, they set up independent states and continued to rule in Yemen until the civil war that began in 1962.

The belief in the Imamate and the ideal of martyrdom find their contemporary expression among Shiites in the emotional periods of mourning and ritual processions that were televised to the world during the Iranian revolution, in passion plays and religious dramas depicting the tragedies of Hussein and other *Imams*, and in devotional pilgrimages to the holy cities of Karbala and Najaf, in Iraq. The tomb of Hussein is in Karbala, that of Ali in Najaf, the city where Khomeini lived and preached for nearly fifteen years after he was expelled from Iran by the Shah. Iraq, which is dominated by nonreligious Baath Socialist party officials of mostly Sunni origin, expelled Khomeini in 1978. His subsequent denunciations of Iraq's rulers and his attempts to foment restiveness among Iraq's Shiites contributed to the outbreak of war between Iraq and Iran in 1980.

Khomeini was the leader of a group of religious leaders in Shiite Islam who do approximate a clergy. As agents or servants of the *Imam*, they have an elevated spiritual status that is not claimed by Sunni *ulama*; in Sunni societies all believers are equal before Allah.

Even before the revolution, the network of *ayatollahs* and *mullahs* in Iran not only conducted the country's religious affairs but also controlled great wealth, owned estates and developed a countrywide political organization, independently financed, that has no parallel in Sunni countries.

When the clerics of Iran threw their resources behind the revolution in 1978, they demonstrated a power that could not be matched by the sheiks or learned doctors of such countries as Egypt where the religious authorities are appointed and paid by the state, or Saudi Arabia, where the leader of the religious community is the King and the national wealth is controlled by the royal family, or Iraq, where religious activity is under the thumb of the Baathists. The power and the prestige of the clergy in Iran were strengthened at the time of the revolution precisely because they were largely independent of the Shah's government, both economically and politically, and were not creatures of the government, as in most Sunni countries.

Certain legal practices within Shiism also distinguish it from Sunnism. The most notable is the tolerance for "temporary marriage." This is a union of man and woman that is neither permanent and legal nor adulterous but in between. It is justified by the Shiites as having been tolerated by the Prophet and as occasionally necessary to give mankind a way of satisfying sexual appetites without committing one of the sins condemned in the Koran.

From the point of view of Western policy-makers and strategic planners and geopoliticians, the most important distinction between Sunnism and Shiism today is not religious but political. Shiism has established its credentials as a revolutionary and anti-Western, culturally indigenous force, which gives it a broad appeal that cuts across the borders of state and language. The power of that appeal was immediately recognized by the fragile states along the Arab side of the Persian Gulf, which sought accommodations with it, and by Iraq, which felt obliged to confront it. It helps to explain why no Arab country except Jordan gave its unequivocal support to Arab Iraq in its war with non-Arab Iran. The puritanism and anti-Westernism of the Iranian revolution attracted the sympathy even of many who, as Sunnis and Arabs, might otherwise have entered the fray on the Iraqi side. The Shiites of Khomeini, both anti-communist and anti-Western, had the allure of being closer to the ideals espoused by Muhammad than were other Muslims who were in the camp of Washington or Moscow. The full impact of the triumph of Iran's Shiite revolution will not be known until the revolution runs its course and Iran's new political configuration is determined, but whatever the outcome, it will be difficult for any new leader to return to the old ways of overriding religion in setting national policy.

Though Shiism is the only numerically significant schismatic group in contemporary Islam, other schools of thought, minor sects, politico-religious organizations, brotherhoods, and dynasties exist within the framework of the religion, which continue to influence events. They differ in origin, purpose, and size but are listed together here for the sake of convenience.

Sufism

Sufis are Muslim mystics, espousing a personal relationship with God based on love, in contrast to the submission based on fear and prohibition that characterizes the official religion.

The word Sufi is derived from the Arabic *suf*, meaning wool, because the first practitioners of mysticism and its accompanying asceticism in the ninth century wore a coarse woolen garment similar to that worn by Christian monks.

George Kirk, in his *Short History of the Middle East,* gives this lucid summary of the origins of Sufism: "The mystics were impelled by the insistent desire to find a more intimate and personal approach to, and union with, God than was provided by Sunni formalism and detachment, which placed Man at an almost infinite distance from his Creator and provided the prophet as merely an interpreter of God's word, but not as a mediator between God and Man. Though the Sufis sought justification for their ritual practices in some few and exceptional passages of the Qur'an, their main inspiration was in fact drawn from other religions, in particular from Christian mysticism, the Zoroastrians of Persia and the mystery-religions of the pre-Christian Middle East."

The influence of Sufi mysticism on the people and events of the Muslim world is difficult to gauge, because in daily life and commerce one is hardly aware of its existence. Islam itself is a palpable force, from the call to prayer to the invocations of Allah in the most routine transactions; but the practitioners of Sufism are secretive, and the official religious authorities treat the subject with a conspiracy of silence. Guidebooks for newcomers and orientation tours by Ministry of Information officials give copious details about mosques and historic sites, but they do not give the names and addresses of the Sufi brotherhoods.

In the idea of mystical communion with God, as in the veneration of saints, there is a longstanding difference between the teachings of Islam embodied in the Koran and *sharia* and what the faithful actually do. There is an Islamic folk-religion, analogous to the Catholicism tinged with local custom that is practiced in parts of Africa and the Caribbean. Sufism evidently satisfied the natural craving of the soul for warmth, for love, and for knowledge of the worshiped being. Sufis would understand the formula from the old Baltimore Catechism of the Catholics: "God made me to know, love and serve him in this world and to be happy with Him forever in the next." The key words are "know" and especially "love."

First as individuals, then organized into groups or brotherhoods, the Sufis turned away from what Hitti calls "the wranglings of the ulama, the arguments of the canonists and the hair-splitting discussions of the philosophers" to seek a personal and loving relationship with the Almighty.

The Sufis were not eccentrics or misfits. Fazlur Rahman notes that in the tenth and eleventh centuries, Sufism attracted the ablest thinkers in Islam: "The systems of the ulama had become rigid and their legal casuistry and empty theological pedantry drove the more serious-minded men of religion and originality into the Sufi fold."

The Sufis found encouragement and justification in the story of Muhammad's "night journey" to Jerusalem, which was evidently a mystical experience that brought Muhammad into personal contact with God, and in Koranic verses such as this: "Whether you hide what is in your hearts or reveal it, it is known to Allah." (3:29) They also cited scattered passages that emphasize love rather than fear as the determinant of man's relationship with God. While the Sufis sought legitimacy in those verses, however, their ritual practices were in fact outside the mainstream of Islam, and the brotherhoods have always been semi-clandestine.

Yet they have made unquestionable contributions to the history of Islam. They provided the religion with a sense of compassion and personal commitment that prevented it from lapsing altogether into arid formalism. The Sufis and their African counterparts the *marabouts* spread the faith into new parts of the world long after the power of Arab arms had spent itself. They carried out charitable and educational programs. They participated in military campaigns against the enemies of Islam. And they contributed some of the most influential works of philosophy and theology. The most notable was the work of Abu-Hamid al-Ghazzali, an eleventh-century scholar who turned from orthodox Islam to spiritualism and succeeded in arranging, if not a merger of the two approaches, at least a mutual tolerance that gave

Sufism a cover of acceptability while humanizing the orthodox faith.

The Sufis were viewed with suspicion and hostility by conventional religious authorities. The *ulama* feared that the gathering-places of the brotherhoods would supplant the mosque, that miracles (of which Muhammad disapproved) would be claimed as a corollary of spiritualism, and that Sufism would challenge the supremacy of *sharia* as the key to carrying out God's will on earth. The brotherhoods, formed around holy places and the tombs of "saints," resorted to elliptical phrasings and poetic expressions that avoided direct challenges to orthodoxy, and they flourished because they filled a spiritual need among the faithful.

The first brotherhood, the Qadiri, was founded in Baghdad in the twelfth century, well after the rise of the phenomenon of mysticism itself. Many others were established later; some initiates belonged to more than one. Some, like the Nakshabandi, are world-wide, others obscure and regional. One order, the Senussi, once ruled an entire country—Libya. The king who was overthrown in Qaddafi's coup of 1969 bore the name of the order: Idris al-Senussi.

(The Sufis left traces in our own language. A member was called a fakir or a dervish—*darwish* in Arabic; the term "whirling dervish" is derived from the pirouetting of the initiates of one of the Turkish orders.)

Practices such as those of the "whirling dervishes," the introduction of music and dancing into the rituals of the orders, and the use of prayer-beads that look like rosaries—all inappropriate in orthodox Islam—account for the embarrassed silence with which Sufism has been treated in public commentaries and ceremonies. Only recently have the history and viewpoint of the brotherhoods begun to be explored in depth. The literature of Islam has usually meant the literature of orthodox or conventional Islam; as recently as 1978, *Meccan Conquests*, the great work of Mohieddin ibn-Arabi, a Spanish Muslim mystic of the thirteenth century, was banned as heretical by the Egyptian parliament even though Sufism found new popularity among the Egyptian people in the 1970s. Despite the hostility of the religious establishment however, the practices of the Sufis and their appeal to love as the way to knowledge of God have often been closer to the religion of the common people than has the formal, legally oriented Islam of the orthodox leadership.

Wahhabism

It was partly as a reaction to the saint-worship, ritual excesses, and doctrinal heterodoxy of the Sufis that the Wahhabist reform movement arose in the eighteenth century. Wahhabism in Islam is roughly analogous to Puritanism in Christianity.

The history of Wahhabism is virtually coterminous with the history of modern Saudi Arabia, where it is the dominant religious interpretation today. In the West, we may think of Saudi Arabia as a country where reactionary attitudes and obscurantism still prevail while other Muslim societies are modernizing, but the Saudis would hardly agree. They see Wahhabism as the movement that freed Islam from the superstition and worship of holy men and holy places, which infiltrated Islam in the medieval era and which the Wahhabis view as tantamount to idolatry, and from the morass of legalistic hairsplitting that passed for theology and resulted only in stultifying Islamic thought.

The movement is named for Muhammad ibn Abd al-Wahhab, a well-traveled legal scholar and jurist of the Najd, in central Arabia, who was born into a religious family in 1703.

Abd al-Wahhab was trained as a jurist in the Hanbali school of law, the most rigorous of the Sunni schools, but he also had early experience as a Sufi, which introduced him to the practices he was to reject and condemn. Under the influence of reformist scholars whose works he studied, he began a public campaign against the rites of the mystics and of the folk-religionists—against worship at tombs, prayer to holy men, minor pilgrimages, belief in Muhammad's intercession with God, initiation rituals.

Seeking to strip Islam of these beliefs and practices that had been hung upon it in ossifying layers over the course of a thousand years, he preached what might be called a back to basics form of Islam: man, God, Muhammad, and the Koran, and nothing else. He called for more rigorous and literal application of *sharia* and Koranic penalties for infractions, and he preached against such social innovations as smoking tobacco.

As a corollary of his fundamentalist or puritan interpretation of Islam, Abd al-Wahhab also rebelled against the automatic acceptance of the doctrinal views of the learned scholars who had arrogated unto themselves the sole right to expound upon faith and law. This challenge was to have an impact far beyond the borders of Arabia, for it inspired the reform movements that swept through Islam and freed it from rigidity and reaction in the late nineteenth and early twentieth centuries.

Rejecting all that had been built onto Islam since the Koran and the Sunna, Abd al-Wahhab leaped backward across the medieval theologians and legists, who had not only stifled intellectual inquiry but also accepted the questionable compromise with Sufism. Abd al-Wahhab returned to what he saw as the pure religion of Islam's first century.

Literalists in interpretation of the Koran, the Wahhabis paradoxically liberated the individual believer from the grip of the obscurantists who wrote endless commentaries upon the previous generation's commentaries on obscure points in *sharia* or the Koran. The Wahhabis sliced through the underbrush to the original sources, enabling believers to think for themselves.

Fazlur Rahman says of Wahhabism, "On the one hand by emphasizing the text of the Qur'an and the Hadith, it inevitably resulted in ultra-conservatism and almost absolute literalism. On the other hand, however, by encouraging the exercise of independent reasoning (ijtihad) rather than merely analogical reasoning with regard to those problems which were not directly covered by the text, the door was opened for more liberal forces to interpret the text more freely than the principle of analogical reasoning as developed by the medieval legists would allow."

Abd al-Wahhab might have remained an obscure voice in the wilderness if he had not in the mid-1740s formed an alliance with Muhammad ibn Saud, a scion of the House of Saud, a prominent clan of the Najd, and begun to impose his views by military action. When Muhammad died, he was succeeded by an inventive and courageous warrior named Abdul-Aziz ibn Saud, the ancestor and namesake of the first king of modern Saudi Arabia.

Under Abdul-Ariz, the Wahhabis marched into western

Arabia and Iraq. They seized Mecca and Medina and sacked the tomb of Hussein at Karbala. By the end of the eighteenth century, they had reached the gates of Baghdad, where they forced the Turkish governor to sign an armistice, and invaded Syria.

These forays inevitably attracted the attention of the Ottoman Sultan. Since the Sultan claimed also to be Caliph and bore the title Protector of the Holy Places, and since the lands the Wahhabis were raiding were nominally under Turkish rule, the Sultan was obliged to reassert his authority.

In 1811 the Sultan persuaded Muhammad Ali, his viceroy in Egypt, the "great modernizer" who built the modern Egyptian state, to undertake an expedition against the upstart Wahhabis. The campaign lasted seven years and ended with a nearly total victory for Muhammad Ali's forces. The Sultan's rule over the holy places was restored, the Wahhabi ruler sent in captivity to the Ottoman capital of Constantinople and executed, and the sect confined to its place of origin, the oasis towns of the Najd.

The spirit of Wahhabism, however, remained alive, as did its alliance with the House of Saud. From their desert capital, Riyadh, the Wahhabis carried on a sputtering struggle against the rulers of western Arabia, the area known as the Hijaz, which was the homeland of Muhammad; the rulers of the Hijaz were nominally aligned with the Sultan of Turkey and controlled Mecca and Medina in his name. After a series of defeats, the low point for the Wahhabis came with the expulsion of the Saudi princes to Kuwait by a rival clan in 1891. Wahhabism appeared destined to retreat into the history books, as other sects and movements had done for a thousand years.

But once again the history of Arabia was transformed by the genius and determination of a single inspired individual. In 1902, a young prince of the exiled Saudi family returned from Kuwait and with a raiding party of only forty men retook Riyadh in a daring attack. That exploit is still talked of with wonderment and admiration in Saudi Arabia, as is the man who engineered it: Abdul-Aziz ibn Abd ar-Rahman ibn Saud, the first king of unified, independent Saudi Arabia, known to the West as King Ibn Saud but to the Arabs by his given name, Abdul-Aziz.

Restored to power in the Najd by the young prince's exploits, the Wahhabis resumed the struggle for control of

Arabia against Hussein, the Hashemite ruler of Mecca.

Hussein has a unique and honorable place in Arab history. It was he who authorized the revolt against the Turks during World War I and cast the Arab lot with the British and French, not in the service of colonialism but in the expectation that his action would be rewarded with independence for the Arabs after the war. Ignoring the Ottoman Sultan's call for *jihad* against France and Britain, Hussein gambled that he could help all the Arabs gain their political freedom by rising against the Caliph. This was the rebellion in which British officers, including T.E. Lawrence (the famed Lawrence of Arabia), fought with Arab raiders in their celebrated desert campaign, a guerrilla war that featured such now-familiar tactics as the blowing up of a railroad—the Hijaz railway, which linked Medina with Damascus.

But Hussein was unable to convert his nationalist credentials into durable power after the war. First the British and French betrayed him by substituting their own colonial rule for that of the defeated Turks in Syria, Palestine, and Iraq, instead of granting independence. Then, a band of young Turkish officers under Mustafa Kemal Atatürk overthrew the Sultan and converted Ottoman Turkey into a secular republic. When they also abolished the Caliphate, Hussein made an ill-advised attempt to claim the long-dormant office for himself. His effort met a nearly total rebuff among the Arabs and left him a figure of ridicule.

The erosion of Hussein's power and influence provided the opportunity for Abdul-Aziz to lead his Wahhabi forces westward from the Najd against the Hijazis, and the outcome appears never to have been seriously in doubt. The Wahhabis were dedicated, disciplined, and ascetic warriors from a harsh environment organized into armed brotherhoods imbued with puritanical zeal, more than a match for the relatively indolent and sedentary Hijazis, who had bowed under Turkish rule for four hundred years. The Wahhabis did to the Hijazis what the Hijazis had done to the other Arabians in the days of the Caliph Abu Bakr thirteen hundred years before.

Hussein abdicated in favor of his son Ali, but Abdul-Aziz was not to be deterred. He took Mecca, then Jeddah. Ali fled to Baghdad. In January, 1926, Abdul-Aziz was proclaimed King of the Hijaz. It required less than ten years to eliminate all remaining resistance in the peninsula, unify the tribes into the Kingdom of Saudi Arabia, and impose on them the puritanical, austere principles of Wahhabism, to which they still officially adhere.

Abdul-Aziz exhibited from the beginning the ability to reconcile puritanical personal conduct and rigid application of *sharia* with technological advancement that still characterizes Saudi Arabia. He forced the reactionary elders of the Hijaz to accept such satanic innovations as the telephone and the wireless, just as his son later forced them to accept television and the education of women.

In a larger sense, the triumph of Wahhabism in Saudi Arabia had a therapeutic and invigorating impact upon all of Islam, similar to that of the Reformation on Christianity.

Freeing Islam from its association with "Turkish vanities," as the excesses of the Ottoman court were described in Western Europe, and from the Turks' reputation for corruption and cruelty, it enhanced the world's image of Islam as a serious and dignified religion. It "re-Arabized" Islam, restoring Arabian practices as the standard by which other Muslims were measured. And, just in time for the surge of oil wealth in Muslim countries and the revolution in communications that brought even the most remote village into contact with the world, it demonstrated that Koranic literalism, the *sharia*, and Islam itself were not incompatible with technology and science.

One of Abdul-Aziz's first acts as King was to call an international Islamic conference aimed at narrowing the gap between Wahhabism and conventional Islam. The process begun at that meeting of bringing the two camps closer together has continued to the point where the Wahhabis are no longer thought of as being outside the mainstream of religion. In many ways they are the mainstream.

In *The Arab Awakening,* his classic study of the rise of Arab nationalism, George Antonius paid tribute to Abdul-Aziz, whose triumph, he said, "introduced a system of government and a conception of civic duties which, in a few years, were to supersede practices in vogue for centuries. It re-established the ascendancy of Muslim ethics and Arab traditions, in the conduct of public affairs as well as in the code of collective and individual behavior. It is probably the most profound, and may yet prove to be the most beneficial, change that has supervened in Arabia since the preaching of Islam; and, as in the seventh century, the new order thus brought into being, while fashioned to some extent by the social and economic forces of the day, owed its existence in the first place to one man of genius."

Wahhabism was a reform movement within, not a deviation from, orthodox Sunni Islam. The same can hardly be said for the Druze and the Alawites, small offshoot sects found in Syria, Lebanon, and Palestine.

The Druze

A reclusive people who live in the hills of Lebanon, Syria, and Israel, the Druze are not regarded as Muslims at all by orthodox believers. They are monotheists, and their religion is an offshoot of Shiism, but they trace their origins to a *sheikh*, or elder, named Darazi, who was a devotee of Hakim, the Fatimid Caliph of Egypt from 996 to 1021.

Darazi preached that Hakim was the last incarnation of the Deity. He did not persuade the Egyptians and was forced to flee to Syria. There he attracted adherents among Ismaili Shiites. Collectively, his followers are known as the *duruz*, or Druze.

The faith of the Druze is a closed religion; they seek no converts and they preserve a distinction between initiates and "the ignorant." It is said that few even among the initiates know all the beliefs and practices. The Druze believe that Hakim was the last and most exalted in a series of ten divine manifestations on earth and that he, like the *Imam* of the Shiites, will return.

In their closely knit community, the Druze, who number about 200,000, adhere to a rigorous moral code; their society is characterized by cohesion and loyalty. Though they live in the most volatile corner of the Arab world, at the center of the conflict between Israel and the Palestinians, they are generally apolitical. They have survived by adopting the old Shiite practice of dissimulation, disguising their beliefs and adapting themselves to the society around them so as not to call attention to their differences.

In Israel, Druze are generally law-abiding citizens. Unlike orthodox Muslims, they serve in the Israeli army, and they stayed out of the antigovernment demonstrations organized by Israeli Arab Muslims beginning in 1976. In Lebanon, the

Druze were dragged into the civil war of 1975-76 by the alliance of their most prominent leader, Kemal Jumblatt, with the Palestinian and leftist forces. They retreated from the political front line after he was assassinated in 1977, but resumed their position in the alliance under Jumblatt's son, Walid, during the Israeli invasion of 1982.

The Alawites

The Alawaites are an even more obscure sect than the Druze, but they rule Syria. President Hafez el-Assad is an Alawite, as is his brother, Rifaat, ruthless commander of the internal security forces until he was exiled after a power struggle. Under Assad, Alawites have dominated Syria's important political and military offices, although they constitute only about 11 percent of the country's 11 million people.

Historically, the Alawites have been a scorned and impoverished minority, concentrated in agrarian villages above the port of Latakia, oppressed by the Ottoman Turks, manipulated by the French, reviled by their Sunni compatriots. After Syria became independent in 1946, young Alawites found that membership in the armed forces conferred the social and economic status of which they had long been deprived, and they began to join the officer corps in numbers disproportionate to their numbers in the country. They now control the armed forces (Assad was an air force officer) as well as the security forces and, consequently, the country.

Little is known to outsiders about the beliefs and rituals of the secretive Alawites. Their creed is an outgrowth of Shiism but far removed from it. The Sunnis do not consider them Muslims at all, with good reason. As described by Albert Hourani in *Minorities in the Arab World,* their creed originated as an early variant of Shiism, in about the ninth century. They expanded the cult of Ali, whom they regarded as an incarnation of God, into a "divine triad" successively incarnated in seven cycles of world history. The triad, similar to that found in Ismaili Shiism, consists of Ali, "The Meaning," Muhammad, "The Name," and Salman the Persian, "The Gate." Salman was an early convert to Islam and a companion of the Prophet. He is revered by

Shiites, who credit him with devising the strategy of the Battle of the Trench, in which Muhammad and his followers foiled an attack by the Quraish by digging a trench around their camp near Medina.

The Alawites believe that men were originally stars in a world of light but fell from the firmament through disobedience. Men must be reincarnated and transformed seven times, once in each of the seven cycles of history, before they can return to a place among the stars. Infidels will be reincarnated not as men but as animals, although it is not clear whether the Alawites regard non-Alawite Muslims as unbelievers.

Like the Druze, the Alawites hold to esoteric teachings known only to initiates. Theirs is a secret faith which they generally refuse to explain to outsiders. They do not worship in mosques, except when forced to do so (although President Assad has, for political reasons, frequently joined Sunni Moslems at prayer), and their rites are secret. Their rituals are said to include elements adapted from Christianity, including the use of wine.

In 1973, a group of Alawite elders proclaimed that the Alawites are Twelver Shiites and their only Holy Book is the Koran, but they did not produce any supporting documents.

Alawite dominance is a sensitive issue in Syria, a country plagued by political and religious violence and notoriously difficult to govern. Assad's opponents, both within the country and outside, play upon his membership in the cult to stir up animosity among the Sunnis. (During a period of great tension between Egypt and Syria after Sadat's peace initiative, for example, the Egyptian press regularly referred to Assad's government as the Alawite Baathist regime, thus in a single phrase branding it heretical, leftist, and illegitimate.)

Throughout the late 1970s and into the 1980s, Assad's government was challenged by assassinations, bombings, and terrorist attacks aimed at prominent citizens, most of them Alawites, including the head of the army missile corps, the rector of Damascus University, and the head of the Dentists' Federation. At first Assad blamed agents of the government in Iraq, which is run by a rival wing of the Arab Baath Socialist party; but when the violence continued even during the brief Syrian-Iraqi rapprochement that was inspired by their common opposition to Egyptian peace policy, Assad shifted the blame to a shadowy band of religious terrorists known as the Muslim Brotherhood.

The Muslim Brotherhood

By Western standards, the Muslim Brotherhood is more a political organization than a religious one. Fusing religion and nationalism in a volatile blend, it was, until the Iranian revolution, the most significant modern attempt to establish a purely Islamic society through mass popular action. In its uncompromising adherence to the objective of a totally Islamic state, the Brotherhood aims at imposing its concept of law and its standards of behavior on the whole community, by persuasion and example if possible, by force if not. To the Brothers, religion and politics are inseparable, and any Muslim society failing to live by the Koran and *sharia* is impious. That leads to the conclusion that the ends justify the means. When preaching, good works, education, and exhortation failed to cleanse society to their satisfaction, the Brothers resorted to terrorism and assassination. In fact, nothing in Islam teaches that murder of government officials or bombing of cafes is the proper way to propagate the faith, and when in 1954 the Brotherhood confronted the Egyptian revolutionary government, the *ulama* of al-Azhar took the government's side, rebuking the Brotherhood for its terrorist tactics.

The Muslim Brotherhood was founded in Egypt in 1928 and its program was rooted in conditions that prevailed in Egypt at the time: flourishing nationalism challenged by Western encroachment and a conspicuous foreign presence. But the Brotherhood's principles transcended local issues and cells soon appeared throughout the Arab world.

The largest foreign branch was the one in Syria, established in 1937. The Syrian organization was abolished by government decree in 1952, but it survived underground to harass the Assad regime. Whether the Brotherhood was truly responsible for all the terrorist acts that plagued Syria in that period cannot be known with certainty, but the organization was a convenient scapegoat for the Alawite regime. Membership in the Brotherhood was made a capital crime in Syria in 1982, after government troops slaughtered an estimated 20,000 residents of the city of Hamah, mostly Sunnis, to quash religious dissent.

In Egypt, Nasser crushed the Brotherhood, but the embers of its zeal flared back to life when Sadat encouraged religious conservatism as a counterweight to leftism and secularism in the early 1970s. No longer clandestine and now well-financed through its control of several prosperous businesses, the Brotherhood in Egypt has foresworn terrorism, but its objectives are unaltered: Islamization of the state and purification of the religion itself according to principles summarized by Ishak Musa Husaini, biographer of Hassan al-Banna, the Brotherhood's founder: "Belief in the unity and perfection of the Muslim system, the identification of the state with religion, the execution of the Muslim law, the return to the Koran and the Hadith and to no other sources, the refrain from scholastic theology, opposition to mystic innovations, and the imitation of the early righteous ancestors."

Though its history is one of failure, the Brotherhood cannot be disregarded, because its ideas are incendiary and in hard times they have a seductive appeal. In Egypt, by renouncing violence in favor of mainstream organizing and proselytizing among politicians, military officers, and students, members of the Brotherhood have achieved a new respectability and gained seats in parliament, where they are noisy and sometimes effective advocates of religious conservatism. While its tactics have changed, however, the Brotherhood's program still frightens those who believe that a militant, transnational Islamic movement could drag Egypt into religious reaction and threaten stability in the Middle East. The organization was built on a foundation of puritanism and xenophobia and stresses its opposition to Western cultural influence, a program that inevitably leads to conflict with Egypt's cosmopolitan middle class. It was not surprising that the Brotherhood welcomed the Iranian revolution.

The Muslim Brotherhood—known as the Ikhwan, from its Arabic name *al-Ikhwan al-Muslimun*—was founded by Hassan al-Banna, a charismatic schoolteacher. Horrified by what he saw as Egypt's social corruption and the erosion of Islamic traditions, he preached piety and virtue to bands of zealous young followers. He saw himself as a religious reformer in the style of Muhammad ibn Abd al-Wahhab and such influential teachers of the modernist school as Jamal al-Din al-Afghani and Muhammad Abdouh. But whereas Afghani and Abdouh are studied and admired as thinkers who contributed to the liberation of Islam from its long stagnation, al-Banna is remembered mostly as an extremist who believed in promulgating his version of an absolute Islamic truth through bombings and assassinations. This is probably unfair because the Brothers' terrorist phase developed only late in his life and some of their worst excesses were committed after his death, but the Brothers were so much his personal organization that their reputation was his.

He taught that it was the Muslim reformer's duty to act, as well as to preach, in the service of Islam as "a total order that encompasses all aspects of life." He said, "Islam is a system of laws and execution, as it is legislation and teaching, law and judicature, one inseperable from the other. If the Islamic reformer satisfies himself with being a jurist-guide, taking decisions, chanting instructions, and quoting the principles and consequences of actions, and leaves to the executives the making of national laws—which are not permitted by God—and is led to the breaking of His commandments by the force of imposition of these laws, then the natural consequence is that the reformer's voice will be a cry in the wilderness." That is, secular legislation is prohibited by God. If the laws made by the state violate the principles of Islam, it is the duty of the devout to break them. This ensures that relations between the Brotherhood and a modern government can never be better than an uneasy truce.

In Banna's opinion, virtually everything that was being done by the government and the ruling classes of Egypt was irreligious and sinful. The Brothers' absolute commitment to the Islamization of Egyptian life meant that conflict was inevitable between the Brothers and the leaders of a society that mimicked European culture and allowed the British to keep troops in the country and the French to live like colonial occupiers at Suez Canal headquarters in Ismailia.

The Brotherhood's program included restoration of the Caliphate and enforcement of *sharia*, but the purely religious activities were subordinated to the campaign to rid Egypt of secularization, corruption, and foreign influence. Preaching in cafes gave way to terrorist attacks on foreigners and government officials.

The Brotherhood numbered perhaps half a million active members in Egypt during the 1940s, the period of its greatest power, in addition to unknown numbers of members abroad and symphathizers. Most of them were from the poorer classes—workers, peasants, and impoverished students, then as now the very people least tainted by Western influence and most resentful of exploitation by Egypt's haute bourgeosie and their European friends.

After World War II, as the monarchy tottered and the fractious politicians and sterile ideologues of Egypt's many political parties demonstrated their increasing inability to run the country, the Brotherhood flourished as a ruthless, well-organized movement, the members of which saw themselves as the vanguard of an Islamic revolution. By sending volunteers to fight on the Arab side against the new state of Israel, the Brothers demonstrated that their objectives were pan-Islamic, not just Egyptian.

The Ikhwan had cells everywhere. They had representatives in factories, schools, and trade unions. They ran a publishing house and papered the country with tracts and pamphlets. They owned a textile company, an engineering firm, and an insurance company—using the profits to finance their activities, much as their successors do today—and they had camps where members underwent paramilitary training.

Through a network of schools, labor organizations, and clubs, the Ikhwan performed prodigious feats of charity and social welfare, which were undoubtedly beneficial to Egypt. But their political program clearly threatened the government. In December 1948, Prime Minister Mahmoud Nuqrashi ordered the dissolution of the Brotherhood and a ban on its activities. Three weeks later, one of the Brothers murdered Nuqrashi. Then, on February 12, 1949, Hassan al-Banna was assassinated, probably by government agents.

Revolution was brewing in Egypt, but it was not the Muslim Brothers who were to bring it off. Years before his death, Hassan al-Banna had sought a political alliance with the Free Officers, the cabal of young nationalists organized by Nasser within the officer corps. But Nasser, Sadat, and their companions were neither terrorists nor religious zealots. Their motivations were nationalism and patriotism, not religion, and they were sufficiently shrewd to recognize that their interests were essentially incompatible with those of the Brotherhood, which wanted a religious state.

Some of the Free Officers—including Sadat, who was their liaison with the Ikhwan—were devout Muslims, but others were irreligious leftists. They had no program other than the ouster of the monarchy and the political liberation of Egypt from British domination. They understood that a return to *sharia* and Koranic literalism would mean a retreat from the social liberation and political modernization that Egypt, almost alone in the Muslim world, had achieved since the time of Muhammad Ali.

Therefore the Free Officers and the Ikhwan, while equally opposed to the government and united in their determination to rid Egypt of the British, were inevitably opposed to each other. The showdown between them occurred after the Free Officers' revolution of 1952, which overthrew the monarchy.

Preoccupied with land reform, economic development, foreign relations, and the establishment of a new political system, Nasser and his companions established a regime that was neither religious nor xenophobic, and made no attempt to impose puritanism on Egypt's easygoing society. In 1954, the Ikhwan attempted to assassinate Nasser, and he responded with swift, sure retaliation that cut off the Brotherhood's challenge before it coalesced. Six leaders of the Ikhwan were hanged and about a thousand imprisoned, some to remain locked up until after Nassser's death sixteen years later. When the Brotherhood attempted to regroup as an underground movement in the mid-1960s, Nasser, who by then was running an efficient police state that permitted no opposition, rounded up thousands more suspected members and imprisoned them too.

After Sadat became president in 1970, he gradually released almost all Nasser's political prisoners of both the left and the right, including the surviving Ikhwan. Though the organization is technically illegal, he permitted it for several years to function in a limited, nonviolent way, apparently in the hope that its conservative religious influence would counter leftist activism among university students, which it did. Religious activists dominate campus politics in Egypt, and throughout the 1970s and 1980s there was a trend among students toward Islamic traditionalism. Young men began to grow beards, a symbol of piety and conservatism—the Prophet was bearded—and young women to wear monochromatic, full-length dresses that covered everything except their hands and faces. The clothes symbolized their espousal of Islamic values and their repudiation of Western cultural influence.

At first discreetly, then more and more openly, the Brothers surfaced, publishing a magazine, organizing prayer rallies that were advertised in public places, and sponsoring candidates in student elections. Sadat and the Brotherhood struck a tenuous and informal balance. He permitted the Brothers to organize, preach, and even express opposition to some of his policies, such as the peace treaty with Israel and his grant of refuge to the deposed Shah of Iran, but he did not permit them to form a political party or enter a slate in parliamentary elections. The Brotherhood generally refrained from violence and from incitement to violence.

This arrangement broke down in the summer of 1981, when Sadat ascribed to the Brotherhood a large share of the blame for Muslim-Christian rioting in Cairo. Declaring that "the Brotherhood as an association does not exist officially and is illegal" and therefore had no right to publish a journal, Sadat ordered the arrest of its leaders and suppression of its magazine.

Sadat himself was assassinated on October 6, 1981, as he reviewed troops in a military parade, by members of a small fanatic group, an offshoot of the Brotherhood, who at their trial brandished Korans and said their deed was Allah's work. They were hanged, but the Brotherhood lives on, tolerated by Sadat's successor, Hosni Mubarak, and forming alliances with legal political parties to gain seats in Parliament.

The organization is no longer clandestine, though there probably are underground cells. It operates out of a shabby office above a vegetable market in central Cairo. The office is clearly marked with a seal bearing the name *al-Ikhwan al-Muslimun*, along with a representation of the Koran and crossed swords like those on the Saudi flag—the same emblem as used under al-Banna. Next to the seal hang photographs taken at the trial of an earlier generation of Brothers, under Nasser.

No individual claimed to be the leader or guide of the revived Brotherhood. Its spokesman in the 1970s was a mild-mannered septuagenarian lawyer, Omar Tel-Massani, who talked like a zealot but not like a revolutionary or terrorist. His official title was that of editor of the Brotherhood's magazine, *al-Dawaa* (*The Call*). When I asked him who was actually presiding over the Muslim Brotherhood and making its decisions, he replied with a smile, "Hassan al-Banna."

Tel-Massani, who has since died, argued that "the Muslim Brothers were never terrorists or fanatics." He said that "foreign hands, aimed at destroying the Islamic Nation," were behind such accusations. The Brotherhood at that time, he said, was "just a group of friends," who were "puritans, but not fanatics."

He said the Ikhwan believe that Islam is "a comprehensive system, which regulates human life in all its aspects. A Muslim can find his political, social, economic and even family laws in our religion. Nobody can be a good Muslim who adopts some principles of Islam and not others," which is of course not a radical viewpoint but a restatement of the classical Islamic ideal. In practice, he said, "Islamic laws must be applied in Egypt. We want it all Islamic."

Under Sadat, the Ikhwan were prohibited from pressing their demands through overt political campaigns, though conservative, religious members of parliament, who sympathized with the Brotherhood's ideals, agitated for legislation along lines conforming to *sharia* that the Brotherhood advocated. Under Mubarak, the Muslim Brotherhood is still prohibited from organizing as a political party—as are all other religious groups—but they have a *de facto* political organization that arranged for known members to gain seats in Parliament through marriages of convenience with legal organizations.

At the same time, the Brothers spread their message through sermons, articles in their magazine (legal once again under Mubarak), speeches, and literature addressed to student groups, charitable organizations that work among the poor, and argument by analogy. This last technique allows the Brotherhood to challenge the Egyptian system of law and government without calling directly for its overthrow. Its magazine, for example, printed an article about a conference of Arab ministers of justice. At the conference, statistics were presented purporting to show that France has 32,000 serious crimes per million residents per year, Finland 63,000, and Canada 75,000, but Saudi Arabia only 22. Whether the figures were valid or not, readers could not miss the message: The Islamic way, especially as practiced in theocratic Saudi Arabia, is more beneficial to society than secularism.

Tel-Massani's references to the "Islamic Nation" and "foreign hands" were illustrative of the Brotherhood's suspicion and xenophobia. A decade later, successors such as Hamid abu al-Nasr, a well-known official of the Ikhwan, were denouncing peace with the "Zionist entity" (Israel) as a result of the "exploitation" of Egypt by foreigners. The Brothers remain pan-Islamists, and they envision a "nation" not in the English sense of the word but in the Arabic sense of *watan*, "homeland," encompassing all the believers in one fraternity, as Muhammad envisioned. This nation would transcend geographic boundaries and secular politics, those satanic tools by which anti-Muslim colonialist powers manipulate the Islamic world, just as Muhammad called on the Arabians to rise above tribe and clan in one community of believers. In that spirit, the Brotherhood supported the Iranian revolution and opposed the treaty with Israel, but it also condemned the Soviet invasion of Afghanistan as an attack against the "Muslim Nation."

Increasingly, in the months before Sadat cracked down on it, the Brotherhood aligned itself with other fundamentalist groups in espousing extremist religious positions. Not only did the Brothers and their allies support Iran and denounce the United States, but also they stridently demanded domestic policy changes that would have turned Egypt into a fundamentalist Islamic state: abolition of secular and scientific education, elimination of television and movies, a return to religious law courts, and a ban on state-funded pensions as a violation of Koranic property laws.

Clandestine extremists have challenged the secular government with a long-running campaign of assassinations and attacks on tourists. The government has responded with a relentless security crackdown. The Ikhwan no longer represent the strongest force advocating an Islamic state.

Eventually the Ikhwan may disappear into Islamic history, as did the Qarmatians and the Assassins, but it is more likely to endure in some form because its ideals and objectives will continue to attract some segments of society in most Muslim countries. Muslim Brothers and their allies captured a quarter of the seats in Jordan's 1989 legislative election, to the shock of the secularized elite.

The organization's appeal—austere, puritanical, culturally untainted by the West, activist, dedicated—provides useful coloration for any revolutionary network in the Muslim world, where politics often takes on a religious guise. The Brotherhood's ideals and objectives, in outline if not in specific policies, can be held up as a model in almost any

Muslim society, whether the predominant power is Sunni, Shiite, Alawite, or avowedly secular because, like Islam itself, they transcend political boundaries and reach beyond local variations in religious law and practice.

Chapter 7

The Islamic Community Today

The years since the Iranian revolution of 1978–79 have not been kind to the Muslim peoples nor to the reputation of Islam. War, fanaticism, and political violence have afflicted the Muslim world from the Western Sahara to Bangladesh. One disaster after another contributed to the dark view of the Muslim world held by many outside it: the carnage of the eight-year war between Iran and Iraq, the disintegration of Lebanon, internecine feuding among rebel leaders that destroyed Afghanistan, the Palestinian uprising in the Israeli-occupied territories, Iraq's 1990 invasion of Kuwait, the international peacekeeping debacle in Somalia.

The death sentence against the author Salman Rushdie, proclaimed by Iranian theocrats who found his novel blasphemous, seemed to be an outlandish symptom of some chronic disease afflicting the Muslim body politic. Years of appalling atrocities in Algeria, committed by extremist rebels claiming to act in the name of Islam and by government security forces, further sullied the image of the Islamic world.

Many Americans regarded those events as distant conflicts among unknowns whose outcomes mattered little, but two headline-making incidents showed that the turmoil of the Islamic world could affect citizens of this country as well. The bombing of a Pan American World Airways jetliner over Scotland in 1988, a tragedy that killed 270 people, including scores of American college students returning home for Christmas, was almost certainly the work of Muslim terrorists, whether they were Syrians, Iranians, Palestinians, or—as Washington charged after a long investigation—Libyans. Then the 1993 bombing of the World Trade Center in New York filled newspapers and television screens with images of bearded exotics who seemed to embody Islam as an alien force.

In one sense, these events were unrelated to each other and not necessarily associated with religion, but it cannot be denied that recent Muslim history demonstrates a collective political immaturity. Material progress, which in some countries has been immense, has not brought stability or peace to the Muslims, and as the end of the twentieth century approaches, it is no longer realistic to depict this unhappy reality as a legacy of colonialism or Zionism or Ottoman rule.

It may be that a religion that challenges innovation and encourages individuals to put their religious commitment ahead of any commitments to government or nation is doomed to perpetual instability, especially in the absence of the Caliphate or any central doctrinal authority to tell Muslims what forms of political behavior and societal organization are acceptable.

When I met King Hassan of Morocco in 1995, he told me that his traditional role as "Commander of the Faithful" made him the repository of Islamic orthodoxy. But although he was the current leader of the international Islamic Conference Organization and claimed direct descent from the Prophet, he had little influence over the political and social behavior of any Muslims outside Morocco and especially not over any Shiites, whom Hassan dismissed curtly as "heretics." Morocco has been relatively stable, but its stability is not portable.

For individual Muslims, the challenge of contemporary life has been to balance the demands of their faith—the sole source of certainty in a tumultuous world—with the inevitability of material and social change. Governed mostly by petty despots, tribal chieftains, and fuzzy thinkers, Muslims cling to their religion as a source of solace and self-respect in a world that accords them little of either and as a source of political legitimacy in societies where Islam alone represents "the consent of the governed." The faith is the only constant. The more unsettling or dangerous day-to-day life becomes, the more the faithful cling to the one unchanging point on their moral and social compass.

In this sense, Islam thrives on the turmoil of which it is alternately the cause and the remedy. Among urbane and outward-looking Algerians, beset by cultural nihilists who claim to be defending Islam when they behead children, the response is not to turn away from Islam but to embrace it and try to reassert it as a wellspring of justice and order.

Anyone who has lived in the contemporary Muslim world can cite some scene or incident that symbolizes the spectacular social and cultural transformations that are taking place, from the election of a woman as prime minister of Pakistan to the replacement of the camel by the pickup truck among the nomads of Arabia. These are, of course, exactly the changes that the reactionaries and extremists oppose, as shown by the Iranian parliament's 1995 decision to make satellite television dishes illegal.

The physical surroundings and human conditions in which Islam exists have changed as stunningly in this century as those of Christianity did in the previous century. But in adjusting itself to a new world of airborne, televised pilgrimages, air-conditioned mosques, mass education, social mobility, and political independence, Islam as a creed has been spared many of the challenges that confronted Christianity, especially Roman Catholicism. In the informality of its organization and the universality and immutability of its message, Islam is able to modify itself gradually, community by community, taking a step here and a step there, without the need to mobilize the assent of all one billion adherents. There is no Islamic equivalent of the Catholics' debate on clerical celibacy or the admission of women to the clergy, for example. Islam has never had to decide whether to adopt new versions of Scripture because the Arabness of the Koran is absolute. In most Muslim countries, where the state supports religious organizations, individual congregations have not had to struggle to support themselves on recruit members. Neighborhood mosques conduct no bingo games or potluck suppers.

Muhammad said, "Beware of newly invented matters, for every invented matter is an innovation and every innovation is a going astray and every going astray is in Hellfire." By applying that injunction to doctrine and not to technology, Islam has been able to provide the moral guidance and stability that appeal to its adherents without obstructing material progress. The conflict lies in applying the Prophet's warning to social behavior.

Muhammad's vision of a united, polytribal community fused into one brotherhood by Islam has long since proved to be unattainable. But Islam thrives as a religion, if not as a polity, providing guidance for people walking unfamiliar paths.

The billion Muslims are so diverse in history, ethnic background, and political experience as to defy generalization. But most of them live in communities that emerged from European colonialism into independence just at the time when the transistor radio and motorized travel were bringing new ideas and experiences within reach even of the peasantry.

Overnight the most remote backwater was transformed into a member of the world community at the United Nations. Dots on the map—Djibouti, the Comoros, Bahrain—were independent countries whose leaders could use the radio to tell farmers how to improve their yields or, if they chose, to educate women about how to have fewer babies. Vast countries such as Algeria and Indonesia, under colonial control one day, were free the next to make their own decisions about the kind of society they wanted to be and the type of government they wished to have. In that environment, Islam demonstrated both its strength (in providing the rules and guidelines that helped shape those societies) and its weakness (in lacking a definitive political and social formula, leading to conflicts such as the one in Algeria).

Living in a society such as that of the United States, which emphasizes individual freedom and no longer makes political decisions on the basis of religion, we often assume that a similar evolution will take place in Islamic societies as they modernize. Americans tend to think of the religious impulse of Muslims as an outdated instinct that will be overcome by our idea of progress.

But the Iranian revolution belied that assumption. Cultural confrontation with the West and the politics of postcolonial independence have tended to strengthen Islam among the masses, not erode it. New generations are clinging to the faith, if not the ways, of their ancestors. It provides them with identity, a means of cultural self-defense against the inroads of materialism and secularism, and a channel of political expression in communities where dissent is limited.

Westernization and Materialism

For a century and a half, most Muslim communities that were not under Turkish dominion were controlled by or under the tutelage of European colonial powers: France, Britain, Russia, Holland, Spain, Italy. Even where nominal independence was maintained, as in Iran, European forms of law and commerce and European standards of culture were adopted by the elite, that small percentage who had education and money.

So impoverished and backward had the Muslim world become in its centuries of decline that it hardly had the strength to resist the political and cultural inroads of the West. Egypt fancied itself an advanced country, the citadel of Islamic learning; but when Napoleon invaded in 1798, he brought with him the first Arabic printing press ever seen in that country.

Europeans brought books and ideas, parliaments and railroads, mechanized armies, and long-distance telephones. For the Muslims, submission, and later imitation, were inevitable, just as they had been for the people of the Near East and North Africa who submitted to the superior power of the Muslim Arabs in the seventh century.

In its most advanced forms, cultural mimicry of Europe reached embarrassing extremes, as in the Khedive of Egypt's embrace of grand opera, a wholly alien art form. Innovation in Arabic literature often consisted of the adaptation of well-developed forms of Western writing, such as novels and dramas, which the authors learned in European universities. The Museum of Modern Art in Baghdad houses a large display of paintings by contemporary Iraqi artists. Since Muslims have traditionally shunned representational art in favor of calligraphy and idealized design, these paintings pass for innovation, but their style is entirely derivative: art-school copies of European impressionism and abstraction. In architecture, the ideal in boom towns such as Jeddah, Jakarta, and Abu Dhabi appears to be the Manhattan cereal box. Buildings attempting to adapt to the traditional style and environment, such as the Riyadh airport and the Sheraton Hotel in Damascus, are notable for their rarity.

In Saudi Arabia during the buildup to the 1991 Persian Gulf war, a friendly official of the Petroleum Ministry took me to his home village, an hour north of Riyadh, to show me the scope of the transformation of life. On one side of the road is the cluster of mud huts in which he grew up, still standing just as the residents left it. Even the mosque was a crude structure of dried mud. On the other side of the road is the new community of modern electrified houses with air-conditioning and off-street parking built by government oil wealth in the 1960s. No one would prefer the old dwellings, my guide said. But with the transformation, something had been lost, too—the communal sense of mutual responsibility and the shared code of behavior that glued Saudi society together. All the more reason to cherish the rituals of Islam.

On a superficial level, many Muslims, especially in wealthy countries, appear to be abandoning their traditions in an unseemly rush to urbanization, rock music, and fast food. Perhaps the extreme example of this is Dubai, the old gold-smuggling and trading port in the United Arab Emirates. The dhows still ply the waters of the Gulf, but the streets could hardly be taken for the traditional bazaar. Trade made Dubai prosperous long before oil. By the mid-1970s, as garish new hotels were springing up on both sides of Dubai Creek, the symbols of progress were for sale at Harvard Men's Wear, Wally's Jeans, the Playboy store, the Popeye Snack Bar, and a hundred other trendy shops, offering everything from watches to pizza to bourbon. At the bookstore, *Ebony* and *Rolling Stone, Claw* comics, and Nancy Drew mysteries offered their own versions of progress, Western style.

It was only natural that impoverished people leading lives restricted by ignorance and bigotry would aspire to the material achievements of the West. On the Omani side of the Buraimi oasis, in a mud-walled village where chickens scratched aimlessly in the dirt and a few crude shops peddled essentials, who would not have envied the opulence of oil-rich Abu Dhabi, with its newly built hotels and sparkling university just across the border? It was inevitable that young intellectuals who had served in the French parliament or taught at the London School of Economics would incorporate European political ideas into their postcolonial systems of government. And it was natural that societies seeking material development should turn to technological imitation of the West.

One result of this change is that doors are being pried open by ideas. Iran and Saudi Arabia may ban satellite dishes in an effort to keep alien culture at bay, but they cannot seal off the Internet. Yet it would be a mistake to assume that the influence of the West and the impact of materialism and technology on Islamic societies will inevitably diminish the influence of the faith on their peoples' lives and thought.

On the contrary, it is Islam that provides the rules by which innovations are judged. Though each country makes different decisions about what forms of development and social change are acceptable, the decisions must be seen as justifiable in Islam if they are to win popular acceptance. A decision to force farmers into agricultural cooperatives, for example, might be criticized as violating the Islamic guarantees of private property, but a government determined to enforce such a policy might seek to justify it as necessary for social justice and the overall welfare of the community and thus compatible with Islam.

It was profoundly upsetting to Saudi Arabian custom, anchored in Islam, to allow tens of thousands of non-Muslim foreign soldiers—including women—to enter the country in preparation for the 1991 war against Iraq. When the foreigners were no longer needed and left the country, the Saudis did their best to behave as if their guests had never been there. If contact with all those foreigners had any liberalizing effect on Saudi society, it was not visible when I returned there four months after the war.

Even in countries that are avowedly secular, governments that make decisions clearly in conflict with Islamic faith or custom do so at their peril. The Shah of Iran learned this the hard way, as did the short-lived leftist government of Afghanistan that preceded the Soviet invasion, which infuriated a conservative populace by tampering with social customs in the name of secular development. An attempt by the Indonesian government to have mystical beliefs recognized as a religion was beaten back by the concerted opposition of conventional Muslims.

Muslims from West Africa to East Bengal—a group that embraces people of every race, occupation, and social condition—are seeking to balance innovation, material improvement, and intellectual inquiry with traditions and rules inherited from the past to which they cling, not out of sentiment, but out of the conviction that these rules were ordained by God.

The popular will and the influence of religion can be overridden by force, as it was for years in South Yemen, then the only Arab Communist country. But the fact that Islam survived seven decades of Soviet atheism to emerge strong in the newly independent republics of post-Soviet Asia shows how difficult it is to snuff out. Even Turkey, which has declared itself secular and European for seventy years and banned religion in politics, is witnessing a religious revival.

In most Muslim countries there are powerful forces—student organizations, scholars, essayists, cleric-politicians, cultural societies—that function as custodians of the indigenous culture, protecting its religious and social traditions against the inroads of materialism and permissiveness. They urge their compatriots to be not second-class or ersatz Europeans but first-class Muslims, not dark-skinned mimics of alien culture but proud standard-bearers of their traditions and of their God-given faith.

Fazlur Rahman refers to "the development in the so-called Westernized classes of a naked and frightening form of materialism which recognizes hardly any moral demands whatsoever." That materialism, he wrote, stimulated the growth of two countervailing forces: Communism, which "develops as a form of attractive, tantalizing idealism," and entrenched conservatism, rejecting as immoral all that is new or forcign. With the appeal of Communism now vaporized, the challenge of contemporary Islam is to find some alternative to reaction, a course that will preserve the spiritual heritage while allowing material and social progress for the entire society, not just for privileged or corrupt individuals.

In the search for a balance between development and tradition, between the new reality and the old faith, the easiest choices have been those involving technology. Though the most wilfully backward countries, such as Oman and Yemen, resisted long beyond reason, Muslims generally had no difficulty in recognizing that nothing in *sharia* banned petrochemical plants or jet aircraft or air-conditioning.

Egypt embraced technology more than a century ago, building railroads and factories when other Arab countries were still almost primitive. (This was a strong element in President Sadat's contempt for the parvenu Arabs who criticized him for making peace with Israel.) Elsewhere the acceptance of innovation was neither immediate nor total. The *ulama* of Saudi Arabia resisted the introduction of television until King Faisal imposed it on them by the force of his personality. In Oman, the brutal Sultan Said bin Taimur banned education, banks, public health programs, and foreign travel, until he was deposed in 1970. As late as 1979, Qaddafi of Libya was lecturing a recalcitrant *ulama* about the compatibility of Islam and scientific progress. There is still scattered resistance to the dissection of cadavers in medical schools. But these are essentially rear-guard actions, understandable after nearly a thousand years of scientific inertia. In general, Muslims have embraced technology and scientific inquiry as easily in the twentieth century as they did in the tenth. The remaining arguments are about how to administer technological progress in ways compatible with Islamic customs. Should Malaysia's tin mines stay open on Friday? What kind of programs should be on television? May female doctors, of whom there are growing numbers, treat male patients?

Politics and Dissent

More difficult than the question of whether or not to modernize in a material sense are the social and political issues that must be faced by Muslims now free from colonial domination. If women are to be educated, what is to be their role in life after they finish their schooling? If our country is poor and crowded, can we and should we persuade our people to accept the need to limit their families? If we are a small country endowed by Allah with vast wealth, how should we spend it? If we are independent and running our own country at last, what form of government should we adopt?

The last question is the source of more or less continuous debate, much of it irrelevant to the realities of power in parts of the world where governments are established by coup and violence.

Since the abolition of the Caliphate, the other traditional sources of authority in Islam—the *ulama*, *sharia* courts, religious colleges, and the *Awqaf,* or religious foundations—have also declined in influence. New sources of temporal authority, mostly adopted from the West, have to a great extent supplanted them: trade unions, elected assemblies, political parties, codes of secular law, professional associations, military juntas. The interplay of these nonreligious forces, the traditional Islamic authorities, the profound devotion of the masses, and the activities of extremist groups such as Algeria's Islamic Salvation Front helps to account for the political turmoil that has afflicted many Muslim countries since they gained independence.

Even now, after a generation of freedom from colonial power and foreign tutelage, there is hardly a Muslim country, from Mauritania to Bangladesh, where one can say with certainty who will be in power and what form of government will be in place a year after the present leader dies or is ousted. Saudi Arabia is probably an exception, but even there, in the most theocratic of states, there are increasing signs of political dissent, disguised as agitation for more religious orthodoxy.

One reason for this instability is that Islam offers little support to any particular form of government, leaving advocates of almost every form free to claim legitimacy, and it virtually invites political dissent. Professing to eliminate the distinction between state and religion, Islam endorses no particular form of human government, teaching only that people should conduct their affairs by mutual consent. Ideally, the secular and religious leaders of the community are one, ruling on the basis of social justice as defined by *sharia*; but the form of government is never specified in the Koran or the law, so that no political system can say persuasively that it is the one sanctioned by Islam.

At the same time, the individual Muslim is instructed to dissent if he believes that the principles of the faith are being violated. According to *hadith*, Muhammad said, "Whosoever of you sees an evil action, let him change it with his hand; and if he is not able to do so, then with his tongue; and if he is not able to do so, then with his heart—and that is the weakest of the faith."

When dissent is identified with the faith, as it often is, it is difficult to suppress. The Iranian revolution was a political and economic event, but it was Ayatollah Khomeini's stature as a religious leader that enabled him to swoop into Tehran as the hero of the masses. Political parties and unruly newspapers can be banned, but sermons and prayer meetings cannot. Individuals can be thrown out of the country, as Khomeini was, and the printed word can be controlled, as it is by the Iraqis, who require special permits for the import of printing and duplicating equipment; but the unlabeled cassette tape, burning with the fiery words of some religious malcontent, cannot be prevented from circulating.

It is easy for governments in Muslim countries to claim to be ruling in accordance with Islam and to make symbolic gestures to support that claim. It was easy, for example, for the government of Algeria to change the weekly holiday from Sunday, as it was under the French, to Friday. It was easy for the military government of Zia ul-Haq in Pakistan to mandate the payment of *zakat* and to order that Arabic replace English as the first foreign language taught in the schools. It was easy for President Saddam Hussein of Iraq, a lifelong secularist, to pose as a defender of Islam against the heathen Americans and their allies during the 1991 Persian Gulf War. What is not easy is for any particular regime or form of government to demonstrate that it is inherently compatible with Islam and acceptable to the faithful. The quest for political legitimacy, and for a framework for development consistent with Islam, consumes much of the creative energy of the regimes in power.

No government is inherently invulnerable to the claims of dissidents that it is insufficiently Islamic. For every argument of legitimacy as a political system, there is a countervailing argument, both sides claiming to be rooted in Islam.

According to the Shiite scholar Tabataba'i, writing when the Shah of Iran was at the zenith of his power, "A government which is really Islamic cannot under any pretext refuse completely to carry out the *sharia*'s injunctions. The only duty of an Islamic government is to make decisions by consultation within the limits set by the *sharia* and in accordance with the demands of the moment." But even if a society is to accept that dictum, as Iran has since done, what is to be the form of consultation? A parliament? The traditional Arabian *majlis* (royal audience)? A consultative assembly appointed by the ruler? "Popular committees," as in Libya?

G. H. Jansen says in *Militant Islam* that an Islamic government "must be a republic, and it cannot be a dictatorship, for the head of state is removable by the people." Some legal experts who have attempted to draft a universal Islamic constitution have reached the same conclusion, based on the mutual-consent rule. But other Muslims argue that a republican form of government is un-Islamic because it implies legislation, for which there is no need since all law emanates from the Koran. The king of Saudi Arabia, who claims the title Custodian of the Two Holy Mosques, can hardly be expected to accept the argument that Islam prohibits monarchy. The Saudis argue that their system, based on an unwritten but well-understood balance of consent among the people, the *ulama* and the ruling family, is closest to an ideal Islamic state.

Kamil Avdich, a Muslim scholar of Yugoslav background, says in his *Survey of Islamic Doctrine* that, "as far as political theory is concerned, there is no clear indication in the main sources of Islamic doctrine as to the form of the state and the manner of setting up a ruling body. There are only broad outlines as to how Muslims should behave." The Koran and the *sunna* "lay down general rules for the conduct of a ruling body and set the goal for government. If a government observes those rules, it seems irrelevant what kind of government it is."

That being the case, almost any form of government can claim legitimacy within Islam, provided only that its actions conform, or are made to appear to conform, with the principles of the faith, at least in spirit. But by the same standard, any form of government is open to challenge, based on the claim that it is un-Islamic in composition or conduct.

Those challenges have been frequent, caused by and

contributing to the political instability that has characterized the Islamic world for the past several decades. The religiously based challenges (as opposed to the straightforward political coups and palace intrigues, which are just as frequent) take various forms—some merely symbolic, some verbal, some at gunpoint—but all claim to be rooted in Islam.

In an essay, "Islam and Political Development," the prominent scholar Michael C. Hudson wrote: "The Iranian revolution, of course, is the preeminent recent example of a successful Islamic opposition movement. It is also the only example." But that was published in 1980 and is no longer accurate. There was a second example in Afghanistan, and there could be a third in Algeria.

The guerrilla insurgency in Afghanistan originated in the late 1970s as an effort to protect local religious and social traditions against a leftist government in Kabul. The Soviet Union sent troops to Afghanistan to forestall an imminent triumph by the rebels, but after a decade of a war that came to be known as "the Soviet Union's Vietnam" and contributed to the fall of Communism, the rebels beat the Soviets, too. That the Afghan rebels then went to war against one another and the country descended into chaos does not diminish the scale of the *mujahideen* achievement as warriors of Islam against the infidels. They had a great deal of help from the United States, of course, but their motivation was faith and tradition, not geopolitics.

In Egypt, Sadat faced constant low-level agitation by the devout Muslims who in the 1970s became dominant in university student associations. They pamphleteered against the peace treaty with Israel, demonstrated against rock concerts and alcohol, and fomented attacks against Christians. Before Sadat's assassination, the boldest organized challenge to his rule was mounted in 1977, by a group of religious extremists known as the Society for Atonement and Flight from Sin (*Takfeer W'al-Hijra*), who tried to unleash a campaign of terror to force the country out of its tolerant attitudes about personal behavior and to impose *sharia*. Sadat's successor, Hosni Mubarak, struggled for years against terrorists who in the name of Islam assassinated government officials and attacked tourists.

The governments of Nigeria, Pakistan, Malaysia, Indonesia, and even Saudi Arabia have engaged in intermittent skirmishes with dissidents who acted, or claimed to act, in the name of Islam. In Syria, agitation by the Muslim Brotherhood provoked the Hamah massacre of 1982, in which government security forces attacked the city and killed an estimated 10,000 civilians. The longest-running and most brutal conflict has been the one in Algeria, where Islamic militants, denied a probable victory at the polls in 1992, took up armed rebellion against the secular military government, launching a bloody campaign of murder against foreigners, intellectuals, and journalists. More than 30,000 people perished in the first two years of what became a virtual civil war, which by mid-1995 showed no sign of ending.

Because Islam teaches believers to take action when they feel the faith is threatened, religious dissent is as difficult to appease as it is to suppress. In Pakistan, for example, General Zia's military regime in the 1970s and 1980s imposed *sharia* and proclaimed an Islamic state, which meant banning liquor, scrapping Western-style school uniforms, teaching Arabic in the schools, and enforcing the collection of *zakat*, but his opponents were not satisfied. They argued that Zia was only manipulating Islam to shore up his shaky grip on the country. At the other end of the spectrum is Turkey, the only non-Communist Muslim country officially to eliminate religion from government and public life, going so far as to prohibit the wearing of beards by civil servants. Seven decades of secular policy have, perhaps inevitably, stimulated the rise of a religious opposition that demands a return to *sharia* and the creation of an Islamic state. A religious rally at which men violated the law by wearing turbans and waving signs in the banned Arabic script, demanding an end to secularism, prompted the Turkish army to seize power in 1980.

The chronic instability of Muslim countries has many causes other than religion: ethnic rivalries, artificial national boundaries drawn by colonial powers, leftist agitation, the spectacularly unequal distribution of wealth. But there is no doubt that activist Islam provokes disorder, and the Muslims respond to disorder by embracing their religion all the more fervently. Islam offers solace in a world of injustice, continuity in a world of upheaval, brotherhood in a world of strife, and free expression in a world of oppression. Political dissent expressed in religious terms acquires almost automatic legitimacy.

An incident that occurred during the war between Iran and Iraq in 1980 illustrates the dedication with which Muslims cherish their faith and the lengths to which they will go in the most trying circumstances to fulfill their religious duties. As the time of the pilgrimage to Mecca approached, a convoy of empty buses assembled in Iran. Bypassing Iraq, the vehicles crossed from Iran into Turkey, then on to Syria and Jordan, where they rolled down to the Allenby Bridge. This bridge over the Jordan River is the crossing point between Jordan and the West Bank, which has been occupied by Israel since 1967. There the buses picked up a group of Muslim Arab citizens of Israel, who for the first time since the creation of the Jewish state were being allowed to go to Saudia Arabia to fulfill the duties of their faith. This exercise required cooperation among Iran (which sent the buses because it would have been politically embarrassing to use Israeli buses), Turkey, Syria, Jordan, and especially Saudi Arabia, which was breaking precedent by allowing citizens of Israel onto Saudi territory. It is probable that no mission other than fulfillment of an Islamic duty could have brought about that collective effort.

The religious impulse that sustains Islam as a community of believers superior to national borders, symbolized by the pilgrimage, is manifested in other communal endeavors aimed at promoting the faith and enhancing the well-being of Muslims. Wealthy countries provide funds for schools, books, and mosque construction in poorer states, even if the recipients are politically at odds with the donors. Special funds contribute to the health and nourishment of impoverished Muslims in Asia and Africa. An Islamic development bank provides capital to Muslim countries.

Occasionally this communal loyalty reaches into the political arena, when Muslims unite in support of other Muslims in a struggle against non-Muslims. Several Muslim countries that were quarreling with each other, for example, supported Muslim Somalia in its long conflict with non-Muslim Ethiopia. The presence of copies of Qaddafi's *Green Book* in the Peshawar offices of Afghan guerrilla groups suggested that they were being helped by Libya in their fight against Soviet troops, even though Qaddafi was on good terms with Moscow. Muslims are substantially united in their opposition to Israeli control of East Jerusalem and the West Bank, and in their sympathy for the Muslims of Bosnia struggling against Serb "ethnic cleansing."

Yet it can never be assumed that Muslims collectively will take a particular position on any issue. Political unity in Islam is chimerical. In the name of the faith, conferences are held, declarations are issued, attitudes are struck, envoys are dispatched, and proclamations of solidarity are read, but other interests often prevail. Muslims take up arms against each other at least as often as they take up arms against unbelievers. The vision of a global Islamic community, unified in a faith that overrides ethnic, economic, and linguistic differences, is as illusory now as it has been since Uthman was Caliph.

Fazlur Rahman, referring to such gestures as the establishment of a permanent Islamic secretariat at Jeddah and talk of a Muslim news agency, says, "These developments are undoubtedly born of the intense emotional attachment the average Muslim feels toward Islam and Islamic unity. Generally speaking, however, for the ruling elites it is more a matter of nostalgia for the shared historic past, heightened by bitterness against Western hegemony, than a conscious vision of an Islamic sociopolitical order." In fact, despite collective reverence for the *sunna*, and for *sharia*, there is no generally accepted "vision of an Islamic sociopolitical order."

Such an order might be definable in a laboratory setting, though even that is unlikely, given the divergence of strongly held views about what Islam really requires of state and citizen; in practice, it is illusory. Neighboring Muslim countries such as Tunisia and Libya, Iraq and Saudi Arabia, Oman and Yemen, Turkey and Iran have developed economic and political systems so divergent as to ensure rivalry rather than unity. Sincc 1970 these rivalries have repeatedly erupted into armed conflicts pitting Muslim against Muslim. Jordan fought the Palestinians. Urdu-speaking Pakistanis fought the Bengali-speaking Pakistanis of their own country. In the hinterlands of Oman, rebels sponsored by then-Marxist South Yemen battled the Sultan's troops and their allies from imperial Iran. Algeria and Morocco clashed over the future of the Western Sahara. Egypt fought a border war with Libya. Kurdish nationalists fought the Iraqis, the Iranians, the Turks, and one another. Iran and Iraq fought a devastating war for eight years.

And in 1990 Iraq invaded Kuwait and claimed to annex it, setting off a conflict that not only pitted Muslim against Muslim but also put an ignominious end to the myth of Arab solidarity. President George Bush, perceiving a threat to the United States in Iraqi expansionism and in potential Iraqi control of essential Persian Gulf oil supplies, organized an international coalition that went to war in 1991 to expel Iraqi forces from Kuwait. Saudi Arabia, which might have been Iraq's next victim, and Egypt, always a claimant to Arab leadership, sided with the U.S.–led coalition. The Palestine Liberation Organization and, to a lesser extent, Jordan aligned themselves with Iraq.

The roots of that conflict were geopolitical, not religious. But Iraqi President Saddam Hussein sought to portray it as a struggle of Islam against infidels, claiming to represent the cause of Arabism and Islam against the Americans and their allies. Few were fooled, because Saddam Hussein had long been known as perhaps the Arab world's leading secularist and his political organization, the Baath or Renaissance party, had been founded by a Christian. Saddam Hessein's invasion of Kuwait was naked aggression by one Arab, Muslim state against another, the antithesis of Islam.

These are the political realities against which reports of an Islamic resurgence must be measured. The Iranian revolution of 1979 and the successful Afghan resistance against Soviet troops inspired Islamic pride and stirred young people to a new activism all across the Muslim world. But there is no Islamic resurgence if the term is taken to mean a new effort by all Muslims to unite under the banner of Islam and strike the infidels, as they did in the seventh century. The term has meaning only as describes the new fervor of individuals and nongovernmental groups to reassert and promote Islam as an alternative to materialism, petty politics, corruption, secularism, and permissiveness. Many, perhaps most, Muslims approve of religious activism in that cultural and social sense; few approve of violence and murder carried out in the name of

Islam by such groups as Hamas among the Palestinians and Algeria's Armed Islamic Group.

There is a basic difference between Islamic nations and our own in that Muslims debate social questions on the basis of Islam, whereas we, by law and practice, generally exclude religion from our analysis. But it is necessary to distinguish between international and internal issues when calculating how Muslims will respond to any particular situation. Religious considerations are much more likely to affect domestic social policies, such as whether to promote birth control or have the state collect *zakat*, introduce coeducation, or change divorce law, than they are international issues.

Religion as such had nothing to do, for example, with Somalia's decision to end its partnership with the Soviet Union or with Sadat's determination to make peace with Israel or Indonesia's annexation of East Timor or Saudi Arabia's oil-pricing policy.

Between the end of World War II and Sadat's journey to Jerusalem in 1977, the most important inter-Arab political conflict was that between Iraq and Egypt over Iraq's participation in the Baghdad Pact of 1955. The Baghdad Pact was an anti-Communist defense alliance of Britain and Iraq, Turkey, Pakistan, and Iran, four Muslim countries. But the participation of those Muslims did not placate Egypt's Nasser; he saw the pact as a masterstroke of imperialism and set out to undermine it. The resulting struggle split the Arab world into pro-Western and pro-Soviet camps, touched off years of turmoil in Egypt, Iraq, Jordan, and Lebanon, provoked Nasser into nationalizing the Suez Canal—thus igniting the Suez war of 1956—and eventually led to the bloody overthrow of the Hashemite monarchy in Iraq. The reverberation of those events is still felt in the Middle East. But Islam as religion played no part in them. The principal actors, Nasser, Nuri as-Said of Iraq, Adnan Menderes of Turkey, and King Hussein of Jordan, were all Muslims, but their decisions were based on pragmatic, political considerations, such as Soviet intentions, arms supplies, regional influence, and oil markets.

The same could be said of most other international political decisions made by Muslim states. Generally they do not allow religion to intrude on practical considerations. Even the antipathy of most Muslims to Communism, which by its espousal of atheism was the antithesis of Islam, was tempered by pragmatism. Ever since Nasser signed the famous Czech arms deal and obtained aid from the Soviet Union to build the Aswan Dam, Muslim leaders have shown they will cooperate with the Devil if it means grain in the silos. When Sadat expelled Egypt's Soviet advisers after Nasser's death, he did it for strategic—not religious—reasons.

Yet the ideal of an international fraternity of Islam still exists and unites the believers. It is reinforced every year by the pilgrimage. Its unattainability has not diminished its appeal. Just as individual believers continue to espouse Islam and revere its traditions even if they themselves stray from the true path, so the Islamic nations, feuding to the point of war, uphold the Prophet's vision of a united community as their common goal.

They recommitted themselves to it at a summit conference of Islamic nations in January 1981. These are the words of that meeting's final communiqué: "Out of our belief that Muslims, despite the differences in language, color, countries, and situation, are one nation, holding on to the bond of Islam and inspired in their life by a course on which they do not differ, and derive their ideological source from a common heritage of civilization, and shoulder one mission in the world and are thus a nation which rejects bias toward any bloc or any ideological tendency and which refuses to be divided by whims and interests, we are determined to move forward in order to strengthen the ties of solidarity between our peoples and states, to transcend all that is likely to lead to division and dissension, and to amicably settle any conflict that might arise among us, seeking the arbitration of documents and the principles of fraternity, community, and linkage, and the standards of justice and tolerance in which we all believe, and which we get from the Book of God and the tradition set by His prophet, regarding them as a permanent resort in any arbitration."

With the breakup of the Soviet Union, there are now more than eighty countries where Muslims make up more than 2 percent of the population and at least forty-four where Muslims make up more than half, not counting the Western Sahara territory or the Palestinian autonomous zone. Most of those countries were independent in 1981 and sent representatives who signed that conference document. The absence of Egypt and Iran, for political reasons, mocked the declaration even as it was issued, and it is safe to say that most of the participants knew perfectly well that they could not "transcend all that is likely to lead to division and dissension." But that did not diminish the enduring strength and appeal of the Islamic ideal that they all espoused.

A fun-loving, wine-drinking Egyptian diplomat once told me that he had never made the pilgrimage to Mecca because "all that business is nonsense." But, he said, "I am a Muslim. I am always a Muslim." He meant Muslim, not in the ritual, but in the fraternal and communal sense; even in scorning the supernatural articles of the Islamic faith, he felt a common bond with other heirs of the Islamic heritage.

That heritage is traceable to the Prophet, who in the *hadith* left instructions on Muslims' duty to honor the ideal of the fraternity: "Do not envy one another, do not inflate prices to one another; do not turn away from one another but be you, O servants of Allah, brothers. A Muslim is the brother of a Muslim; he neither oppresses him nor does he fail him, he neither lies to him nor does he hold him in contempt. Piety is right here (as he pointed to his breast). It is evil enough for a man to hold his brother Muslim in contempt. The whole of a Muslim for another Muslim is inviolable: his blood, his property, and his honor."

Glossary

Allah. The Arabic word for God, used by Christian Arabs as well as Muslims.

ansar. Helpers; the residents of Medina who supported Muhammad.

Ashura. The tenth day of the month of Muharram in the Islamic lunar calendar; a day of mourning, especially among Shiite Muslims, commemorating the death of the Prophet's grandson, the Imam Hussein.

Caliph. Successor to Muhammad's temporal, but not spiritual, authority over the Muslim community. The Caliphate no longer exists.

darwish. An initiate in a Muslim mystic brotherhood; in English, *dervish.*

dhimmis. People of the covenant, Jews and Christians who as members of revealed religions had a special status in the Islamic empire.

eid. Feast or festival. Eid al-adha, festival of the sacrifice, at the end of the annual pilgrimage, commemorating Abraham's willingness to sacrifice his son; eid al-fitr, festival of breaking the fast at the end of the month of Ramadan.

fatwa. A pronouncement or ruling issued by the Muslim authorities of a country or institution.

hadith. The sayings of the Prophet, consulted as a source of doctrine on matters not made clear by the Koran.

hajj. The pilgrimage to Mecca, which all Muslims are obliged to make once in their lives, if they are able.

hijra. The migration of Muhammad and his followers from Mecca to Medina in A.D. 622; usually rendered as *hegira* in English.

iftar. Breakfast; the meal taken in the evening during the month of fasting.

ijma. Consensus; in Islamic law, the agreement of the Muslim community as a basis for legal interpretation.

ijtihad. Individual reasoning. In Islamic law, synonymous with freedom of interpretation and intellectual liberty.

ikhwan al-Muslimun. Muslim Brotherhood, semi-clandestine fundamentalist group, based in Egypt.

imam. The leader of group prayer; also, in Shiite Islam, the divinely inspired successor to the Prophet or, in general, the spiritual leader of the community.

jihad. Utmost effort or struggle, not necessarily physical, in support or defense of Islam.

jinn. Spirit-creatures, created by God along with men and angels.

jizya. A tax levied on *dhimmis* in the Muslim empire; it exempted them from military service.

Kaaba. The most sacred shrine of Islam, believed to have been erected originally by the patriarch Abraham. It stands in the courtyard of the Great Mosque at Mecca. The Kaaba is a boxlike structure of no obvious devotional significance; it is revered for its history.

Koran. The Holy Book of Islam, a transcript of God's word as revealed in Arabic to Muhammad.

madrasa. Religious school, where boys of high-school age study the Koran, Islamic law, and related subjects.

mahdi. In Shiite Islam, the awaited one, the Imam who will return to be the spiritual guide of the community.

Mecca. City in Saudi Arabia, Muhammad's birthplace and site of the Kaaba.

Medina. The city to which Muhammad and his followers migrated in A.D. 622, when the message of Islam was rejected by the people of Mecca; Muhammad died and was buried at Medina.

minaret. The tower of a mosque, from which the call to prayer is issued five times daily.

mosque. A building or enclosed courtyard where Muslims gather for prayer. Architectural styles vary, but almost every mosque contains a fountain for ablutions, a pulpit, and a niche in the wall indicating the direction of Mecca, which Muslims face as they pray.

muezzin. A corruption of *mu'adhdhin*; he who calls the faithful to prayer.

mufti. Islamic legal officer or legal adviser to the ruler.

Muhammad. The last prophet in a line that included Noah, Abraham, Moses, and Jesus. Muhammad (ca. A.D. 570–A.D. 632) brought monotheism and God's message as revealed in the Koran to the pagan people of the Arabian peninsula.

mujahideen or *mujahedin*. Those who wage *jihad*. Widely used term for guerillas or opposition groups claiming to be warriors of Islam.

qadi. Judge of a religious or *sharia* court.

qadr. Usually translated as "power," sometimes as "glory"; Night of Qadr, the night in the month of Ramadan on which the first verses of the Koran were revealed to Muhammad.

qiyas. In Islamic jurisprudence, reasoning by analogy.

rakah (plural *rakatin*). Bending. A collection of prayers at congregational service, so called because the prayers are accompanied by bending of the body, bowing and prostration. A service consists of several *rakatin.*

Ramadan. The ninth month of the Islamic lunar calendar. It is the month of fasting; no food or drink may be taken from first light to last light.

shahada. The profession of faith, a statement of the fundamental belief of Islam, "there is no god but God and Muhammad is the messenger of God."

sharia. The code of laws and rules governing the life and behavior of Muslims; comprises not a single book but various compilations of precedents.

Shiite. A member of the Shia branch of Islam, the official creed of Iran. Shiites accept the spiritual authority of a divinely inspired Imam descended directly from Ali, cousin and son-in-law of the Prophet Muhammad.

sufism. Islamic mysticism. Brotherhoods of Sufis, or mystics, exist throughout the Muslim world.

sunna. The "path" or "way" of the Prophet, the body of traditions recording the deeds, pronouncements, examples, and silent approvals of Muhammad, cited by Muslims as a guide to personal and communal behavior.

Sunnite. A Muslim of the majority Sunni grouping, comprising about 85 percent of all Muslims. Sunnites, unlike Shiites, recognize no divinely guided heir to Muhammad's spiritual authority; they are followers of the Sunna. Historically, the Sunnites have been those who, unlike Shiites, accepted the temporal authority of the caliphs.

sura. One of the 114 chapters or sections of the Koran.

ulama. Learned elders; the senior religious officials of a Muslim community.

umma. The community of Muslims, worldwide.

umrah. Lesser pilgrimage, an abbreviated form of the pilgrimage to Mecca, undertaken at any time of the year.

Wahhabism. A back-to-basics reform movement within Sunni Islam, named for its originator, Muhammad ibn Abd al-Wahhab, a legal scholar of eighteenth-century Arabia. Wahhabism, which is characterized by strict application of Koranic rules, is the prevalent form of Islam in Saudi Arabia.

waqf (plural *awqaf*). Religious charitable foundation; operated by the state or by private associations, the foundations often control vast wealth and large expanses of real estate, used to support various charitable and social-welfare activities.

zakat. The "alms-tax," a mandatory donation to charity, one of the essential duties of all Muslims.

Bibliography

A comprehensive bibliography for Islam would, of course, make a thick volume by itself. This list includes only works in English which are cited in the text or which I think would be useful to the reader seeking more detailed information.

Anderson, Sir Norman, Armitage, H. St. John, et al., *The Kingdom of Saudi Arabia.* London, Stacey International, 1977.

Andrae, Tor, *Mohammed: The Man and His Faith.* New York, Scribners, 1936.

Antonius, George, *The Arab Awakening.* New York, G. P. Putnam's Sons, 1946.

Avdich, Kamil Y., *Survey of Islamic Doctrine.* Cedar Rapids, Iowa, privately printed, 1979. (Available through Islamic book distributors.)

Badawi, Gamal A., *The Status of Woman in Islam.* Plainfield, N.J., The Muslim Students' Association of the United States and Canada, 1972.

Dibble, R. F., *Mohammed.* New York, Viking, 1921.

Esposito, John, ed., *Islam and Development.* Syracuse, N.Y., Syracuse University Press, 1980.

Farah, Cesar, *Islam, Beliefs and Observances.* Woodbury, N.Y., Barrons Educational Series, 1968.

Galwash, Ahmad, *The Religion of Islam.* Cairo, Dar al-Shaab, 1952. (Distributed by The Supreme Council on Islamic Affairs.)

Gibbon, Edward, *The Decline and Fall of the Roman Empire.* (Published in many editions. Quotations used here are from that of John W. Lovell Co., New York, undated.)

Goldschmidt, Arthur, Jr., *A Concise History of the Middle East.* Boulder, Colo., Westview Press, 1979.

Guillaume, Alfred, trans. and ed., *The Life of Muhammad* (an edited translation of *Sirat Rasul Allah,* a very early Arabic biography). New York, Oxford University Press, 1955.

Hitti, Philip K., *Islam: A Way of Life*. Minneapolis, University of Minnesota Press, 1970.

——— *The Arabs, A Short History*. Princeton, Princeton University Press, 1943.

Hourani, Albert, *Minorities in the Arab World*. New York, Oxford University Press, 1947.

——— *A History of the Arab Peoples*. Cambridge, Harvard University Press, 1991.

Husain, Ibrahim, *Handbook of Hajj*. Indianapolis, Islamic Teaching Center, 1977.

Husaini, Ishak Musa, *The Moslem Brethren*. Beirut, Khayat's Book Cooperative, 1956.

Hussein, Taha, *The Stream of Days: A Student at the Azhar*. London and New York, Longmans, Green and Co., 1943.

Ibrahim, Ezzedin, and Johnson-Davies, Denys, trans., *Forty Hadith*. Beirut, Holy Koran Publishing House, 1976.

Jansen, G. H., *Militant Islam*. New York, Harper & Row, 1979.

Kirk, George E. *A Short History of the Middle East,* 6th ed. New York, Praeger, 1960.

Kritzeck, James, and Lewis, William H., ed., *Islam in Africa*. New York, Van Nostrand-Reinhold, 1969.

Lane, Edward W., *Manners and Customs of the Modern Egyptians* (first published 1836). London, East-West Publications, 1978.

Lapidus, Ira M., *A History of Islamic Societies*. Cambridge, Cambridge University Press, 1988.

Lewis, Bernard, *The Arabs in History*. London, Hutchinson, 1950.

Pipes, Daniel, *In the Path of God: Islam and Political Power*. New York, Basic Books, 1983.

Rahman, Fazlur, *Islam,* 2nd ed. Chicago, University of Chicago Press, 1979.

Ramadan, Said, *Islamic Law,* 2nd ed. Privately printed, 1970.

Rauf, Mohammed Abdul, *The Life and Teachings of the Prophet Mohammed*. Washington, The Islamic Center, 1964.

———*Islam: Creed and Worship*. Washington. The Islamic Center, 1974.

Tabataba'i, Allamah Sayyid Muhammad Husayn, *Shiite Islam*. Albany, N.Y., State University of New York Press, 1975.

Treece, Henry, *The Crusades*. New York, Random House, 1962.

Index

Abbas, 125
Abbassid dynasty, 125–130, 143
Abdul Aziz, *see* Ibn Saud
Abdel Muttalib, 37
Abdouh, Muhammad, 158
Abdullah (Muhammad's father), 37
Abdullah (Muhammad's son), 38
Abraha, 38, 56
Abraham (*Ibrahim*), 5–7, 22, 24, 27, 28, 56, 64
Abu al-Abbas, 125
Abu Bakr, 41, 54, 61, 108–110, 117, 118, 125, 152
Abu Lahab, 42, 63
Abu Muslim, 125
Abu Sufyan, 52
Abu Talib, 37, 42, 117
Afgani, Jamal al-Din, al-, 158
Aga Khan, 144
Aisha, 53, 54, 63, 117
Ajami, Fouad, 49
Alawites, 154, 155–157
al-Azhar, 69
al-Bukhari, 79
Ali (Muhammad's cousin), 41, 108, 117–118, 124
  Shiat Ali and, 137–138
  and Shiites, 139–144, 155–156
Ali (son of Hussein), 152
Ali, A. Yusuf, 58–59
Alim, Khalil Abdel, 113
Allah
  instructions from, to Muhammad, 66; *see also* Koran; Muhammad
  nature of, 1–3, 6–9
  and profession of faith, 6–11; *see also* Faith
al-Mamun, 75, 126
Alms-tax, 18–19
al-Muizz, 127
al-Qasim (Muhammad's son), 38
Amina (Muhammad's mother), 37
Amr ibn al-As, 52, 111, 115
Andrae, Tor, 35–36, 43
Antonius, George, 153–154
Arabi, Mohieddin ibn-, 148
Ashura, 139
Assad, Hafez al-, 155–157
Assad, Rifaat, 155
Assassins, 143

Atatürk, Mustafa Kemal, 152
Avdich, Kamil, 79–80, 177

Badawi, Gamal, 96
Badr, Battle of (624), 48–50
Bahz, Abu, 88
Banna, Hassan al-, 158–160, 162
Bhutto, Zulfikar Ali, 93
Bilal, 134
Black Stone, 24, 26–27
Brohi, A. K., 74
Buwaihids, 127
Bush, George, 182

Calendar, 21
Caliphates, 4, 104–105, 108–112, 116–120, 167, 175
Camel, Battle of the (656), 117–118
Carter, Jimmy, 12, 95
Carter, Rosalynn, 95
Chosroes, 107
Christ, *see* Jesus
Clergy, 2, 3
  imams as, 14, 141–145
Criminal law, 91–94
Crusades (Christian), 128–130

Dante, 35
Darazi, 154
David, 6
Dawood translation of Koran, 42, 100
Dead, the, 17
Dibble, R. F., 53–54
Dissent, 174–85
Druzes, 154–155

Elijah Muhammad, 134

Fahd, 95
Faisal, 85, 174
Faith
  alms-tax as pillar of, 18–19
  fasting as pillar of, 19–21
  "five pillars" of, 6
  pilgrimage as pillar of, 22–30
  prayer as pillar of, 11–18
  shahada as pillar of, 6–11; *see also* Allah
Farah, Cesar, 6
Fasting, 19–21
Fate, 75–78
Fatima, 38, 108, 127, 138, 140
Fatimid dynasty, 127, 143
Fatwa, 85–86, 104

Galwash, Ahmad, 43, 76, 77–78, 98, 100, 107
Genghis Khan, 130
Ghazzali, Abu-Hamid al-, 147–148
Gibbon, Edward, 36, 59, 107, 110, 122
God, *see* Allah
Goldschmidt, Arthur, 127, 131
Government
  caliphates as, 4, 104–105, 108–112, 116–120
  law and, 85–91; *see also* Law

Hadith, 45, 71, 73, 175
  authentication of, 79–80
  defined, 4–5
  and school of law, 83
  Sunni and, 79
  and women, 97
Hafsa, 63
Hajj, 22–30
Hakim, 154
Hamid abu al-Nasr, 163

Hanafi, 82–83
Hanbal, Ahmad Ibn-, 34, 83
Hanbali, 83
Hanifa, Abu, 82
Harun al-Rashid, 126
Hasan, 118, 140, 142
Heraclitus, 110–111
Hijra (hegera), 21, 44–48
Hitti, Philip, 14, 16, 56, 57, 83, 109, 121–122, 147
Hourani, Albert, 155
Hudaibiya, Treaty of, 51
Hudson, Michael C., 178
Hulegu, 130–132
Husaini, Ishak Musa, 158
Hussein (Husayn; son of Ali), 124, 127, 138–144
Hussein (King of Jordan), 36, 113, 182, 183
Hussein (Meccan ruler), 152
Hussein, Taha, 69
Hypocrites, 47, 48

Ibn Saud, Abdul-Aziz ibn Abd ar-Rahman, 87–88, 150–154
Iftar, 20
Ijma, 83
Ijtihad, 81–82, 103
Imam, 14, 141–145
Islam
  advance of, 106–120
  in Asia, Africa, and U.S., 132–135
  defined, 1
  relation of, to Jews and Christians, 120–124
Ismail, 143
Ismailis, 143–144

Jansen, G. H., 177
Jesus, 6, 7, 8, 40, 64, 70, 120–121
Jihad, 112–120, 123
Jinn, 7–8
John Paul II, 3–4
Judeo-Christian tradition, 5
Judgment, Day of, 9–10, 65–66
Jumblatt, Kemal, 155
Justinian, 35

Kaaba, 5, 11, 42, 43, 62
  burning of, 124
  incorporated into Islam, 46
  as pagan shrine, 34
  and pilgrimage, 23–27
Karbala, battle of (680), 124, 140
Khadija, 38, 39, 41, 54
Khalid, 95
Khalid ibn-Walid, 109–111, 129
Kharijites, 115–116, 118
Khomeini, Ayatollah Ruhollah, 101, 142, 144, 176
Kirk, George, 146
Kissinger, Henry, 95
Koran (*Qur-an*), 1–6, 56–69
  commentaries on, 68–69
  compilation of text of, 61–68
  fate as viewed in, 75–78
  and *jihad,* 112–115
  language of, 56–58
  Mutazilites view of, 75
  polygamy and, 99–100
  and punishment, 91–94
  recitation of, 59, 60
  on the righteous, 104
  translations of, 58–59
  and unbelievers, 120–121
  and women, 96–100
Kublai Khan, 130

Lane, Edward W., 33–34
Last Judgment, 9–10, 65–66
Law, 70–105
  criminal, 91–94
  and government, 85–91
  ijma and *giyas* as sources of, 81–82
  and predestination, 75–78
  schools of, 82–86
  sharia as, 71–73, 77–78; *see also: Sharia*
Lawrence, T. E., 152
Legal duties, 30–33
Lewis, Bernard, 41, 52, 70, 107, 139

Madrasa, 15, 80, 104
Mahdi, 142, 143
Malik, Abu Hanza Anas Ibn, 79
Malik ibn Anas (of Medina), 83
Maliki, 83
Mameluke dynasty, 130, 131–132
Marabouts, 147
Maracci, 59
Martel, Charles, 106
Marwan II, 125
Masjid, 14
Materialism, 170–74
Menderes, Adnan, 183
Mihrab, 15
Minarets, 15
Mongol invasion, 130–133
Monotheism
  Muhammad and, 7
  See also Allah
Moses, 6, 7, 64
Mosque, 14–15
Muawiyah, Umayyad, 117–119, 139
Mubarak, Hosni, 162, 163, 178
Muezzin, 12
Mufti, 104–105
Muhammad (the Prophet), 33–55, 61, 113, 168
  Alawites and, 155–156
  and Ali, 117–118
  and Battle of Badr, 48–50
  biography of, 35–38
  birth of, 34, 35
  calendar and, 21
  character of, 53–55
  as example, 32, 78–81
  on fate, 76
  final message of, 53
  and first caliphs, 116–117, 118
  and first mosque, 14–15
  and Friday worship, 16–17
  general principles laid down by, 70–73
  and ideal of fraternity, 184–85
  Jews and, 50–51
  on *jihad,* 112
  and Kaaba, 24
  marriage of, 98, 100
  migration of, to Medina, 44–49
  mission of, 9
  and monotheism, 7
  and month of fasting, 19
  on newly invented matters, 168–69
  and occupation of Mecca, 51–52
  pilgrimage and, 25, 26–27
  and prisoners of war, 119–120
  as prophet, 1–4, 38–44, 60–61, 68; *see also* Koran

Muhammad (*cont.*)
Shiites and, 137–142, 145
and spread of Islam, 106–108, 110
and succession, 108, 116–118
Sufism and, 147, 148
and unbelievers, 120
victories of, 48–52
Wahhabism and, 149
Muhammad Ali, 151
Muhammad, Warith Deen, 134
Mujahideen, 178
Mullah, 16, 144
Muntazar, Muhammad al-, 142–143
Musa, 143
Muslim
defined, 1
See also Allah
Muslim Brotherhood, 157–165
Muslim, ibn al-Hajjaj, 79
Mutazilites, 75, 126, 127
Mysticism, 146–150

Nasser, Gamal Abdel, 72, 87, 91, 157, 160–162, 183, 184
Nowaihi, Muhammad, 82, 102–103
Nuqrashi, Mahmoud, 160

Paradise, 9, 10, 60
Pilgrimage, 22–30
Piscatori, James P., 88
Politics, 174–185
See also Government
Prayer, 11–18
Prayer rug, 12
Predestination, 75–78

Qaddafi, Muammar, 67–68, 148, 174, 180
Qadi, 87, 104–105
Qadiris, 148
Qadr, Night of, 38–39, 64
Qarmatians, 137
Qibla, 46, 47, 62
Qiyas, 81
Quiraish tribe, 36–37, 40–42, 46, 48–52

Rahman, Fazlur, 8, 39, 43, 69, 71, 74, 82, 115, 138, 141, 147, 150, 173, 181
Rakatin, 13
Ramadan, 19–21
Ramadan, Said, 72, 74
Rauf, Muhammad Abdul, 41, 47, 77, 83
Richard I, 130
Richardson, S. S., 89, 90
Rodwell, 36
Ruqayah, 38
Rushdie, Salman, ix, 62, 101, 166

Sadat, Anwar, 67–68, 85–86, 156, 157–158, 160–164, 174, 178, 184
Said, Nuri as-, 174, 183
Saints, 3
Salah al-Din al-Ayubbi (Saladin), 129–130, 131
Sale, George, 59
Salman the Persian, 155–156
Saud, 85
Saud, Muhammad ibn, 150
Schism, 136–145
Shiites as part of, 124, 125, 127–129, 137–145, 154–156
Sufism and, 146–150

Schism (*cont.*)
Sunnism as part of, 137–145
See also Government
Senussi, Idris al-, 148
Shafi, Muhammad Ibn Idris al-, 83
Shafi'i, 83–84
Shahada, 6–11, 13
Sharia, 32, 71–74, 77–78, 81–82, 163, 179, 181
and contemporary society, 100–105
and government, 85, 87–91
hadith and, 80–81; *see also: Hadith*
as moral basis of society, 86–87
and Sufism, 148
women and, 91, 98
Shiism (Shiite; Shia; Shiat Ali), 124, 125, 127–129, 137–145, 154–156
Social duties, 30–32
Sufism, 146–150
Sunna, 4, 32, 70–71, 74, 78, 86, 177, 181
Sunnism, 137–145
Sura
defined, 62
See also Koran

Tabari, ibn-Jarir al-, 69
Tabataba'i, Husayn, 140, 142, 143, 176
Taimur, Said bin, 174
Tel-Massani, Omar, 162–163
Tours, Battle of (732), 106
Treece, Henry, 35, 122–123
Trench, Battle of the (627), 50, 51, 156
Tu Weh-hsiu, 133

Ulama, 81–85, 87–88, 102, 148
Umar (Omar), 42, 110, 111, 112, 116–117, 118, 121, 125
Umayyad dynasty, 119, 122, 123–124, 137–138, 144
Umm Kulthum, 38
Umma, 46
Umrah, 25
Uthman (Osman), 61, 117, 118, 139, 181

Wahhab, Muhammad ibn Abd al-, 149–150, 158
Wahhabism, 149–154
Walters, Barbara, 95
Watan, 164
Westernization, 170–174
Women, 54–55, 90–100, 168, 169

Yazid, 140
Yusuf Ali, 42, 100

Zaid ibn Harithah, 41, 54–55
Zaid ibn Thabit, 61–62
Zainab (Muhammad's daughter), 38
Zainab (Muhammad's wife), 54–55, 63
Zakat, 18–19, 176, 179
Zayd, 144
Zaydis, 144
Zia ul-Haq, 176, 179